Out of
the Pocket

Out of the Pocket

Football, Fatherhood, and *College GameDay* Saturdays

KIRK HERBSTREIT

With Gene Wojciechowski

ATRIA BOOKS

New York London Toronto Sydney New Delhi

ATRIA
BOOKS

An Imprint of Simon & Schuster, Inc.
1230 Avenue of the Americas
New York, NY 10020

First Atria Books hardcover edition August 2021

ATRIA BOOKS and colophon are trademarks of Simon & Schuster, Inc.

For information about special discounts for bulk purchases, please contact
Simon & Schuster Special Sales at 1-866-506-1949 or business@simonandschuster.com.

The Simon & Schuster Speakers Bureau can bring authors to your live event.
For more information or to book an event, contact the Simon & Schuster Speakers
Bureau at 1-866-248-3049 or visit our website at www.simonspeakers.com.

Interior design by Silverglass

Manufactured in the United States of America

1 3 5 7 9 10 8 6 4 2

Library of Congress Cataloging-in-Publication Data has been applied for.

ISBN 978-1-9821-7101-8
ISBN 978-1-9821-7103-2 (ebook)

To all the football dads and moms, sons and daughters—
and to all the journeys you'll go on together. May the spirals be tight,
the hugs be long, and the highs outnumber the lows.

Contents

Prologue

How do you explain a miracle? Two of them, to be exact.

How do you not want to call the doctor who caused your wife to burst into tears years earlier when he said with clinical coldness, "You know, your twins are never going to play football."

How do you keep your composure on national television when all you really want to do is hug your firstborns?

January 13, 2020 . . . Mercedes Benz Superdome, New Orleans . . . Undefeated and No. 1–ranked LSU versus undefeated and No. 3–ranked Clemson in the College Football Playoff National Championship. And there on the field, with their last name stitched on the backs of their No. 86 and No. 37 jerseys, were Tye and Jake Herbstreit—the twins who, according to that doctor, were never going to play football.

How do you explain a miracle? You can't. One day my twin sons were clinging to life as preemies, born nearly three months before their due date. Their hearts would stop. Their tiny lungs couldn't provide enough oxygen. They each weighed slightly more than a quart of milk.

Not a day—not one single day—passes without my thinking about when they were born in the summer of 2000. We were thankful and fearful at the same time. If you could have seen us all at Riverside Methodist Hospital in Columbus, Ohio, that day: me; my wife, Allison; my mom; my dad; my sister; Allison's mom; a few of our closest friends—all there praying, hoping, wishing that the twins would make it to the next day, and the day after that, and the days after that. We thought in twenty-four-hour segments. *Just get through these twenty-four hours and we'll worry about the next twenty-four later.*

Had you been there in 2000, you'd know why I lingered on the Superdome field a few minutes longer than usual before heading up to the broadcast booth for the national championship game in 2020. I had some mother hen in me, and always will. I'm the guy who always knew that they had an algebra test on Tuesday, that their science project was due on Thursday. I was the guy at their high school games, and if I couldn't be there, I was the guy livestreaming on my phone or getting the play-by-play from Alli. I was seated in the front row for their entire lives. I had held them as newborns literally in the palm of my hand, and now they were dressed for a national championship game as college freshmen. It didn't seem possible. Where did those nineteen years go?

So, yes, I looked for my twins that night at the Superdome. I always went down to the field during pregame warm-ups. It was a chance to see the field conditions, to gather a few last bits of information for the broadcast, to wish the coaches well, to watch the kickers, to gauge the confidence level of each team as kickoff neared.

But this time I also searched out Tye, a reserve wide receiver, and Jake, a reserve defensive back, on the field during drills. I saw

Tye first and we hugged. As we did, Clemson head coach Dabo
Swinney walked over.

"Give me your phone, Kirk," he said.

I tried to politely resist—I mean, Dabo was about to face the
No. 1–ranked team in the country and its Heisman Trophy–winning
quarterback, Joe Burrow. Not much was at stake—only a national
championship. He had more important things to do.

"Nah, give me your phone," he said. "Now get in there—get in
there nice and close."

Dabo aimed the phone camera and clicked away like a wedding photographer.

"Okay, that's a good one," he said. "C'mon, one more. Tye, let's
see you smile."

Only Dabo, man . . .

I smile at those memories. I let my mind wander back to those
harrowing days at the hospital, and then to the aftermath of that
national championship game between Clemson and LSU. During
the three-plus hours of the broadcast, I was all business in the
ABC booth with Chris Fowler. That's my job. I owed it to the
viewers of the game, to the fans of both teams to provide analysis
and opinion that was the result of my video study, my interviews,
my phone calls, my research help from Chris Fallica, my years of
experience, my own instincts.

But after the game was done, after LSU had beaten Clemson,
42–25, after I was off the air, *then* it was about family. My family.

If you think about where they started and where they are now,
my twins are miracles. I carry with me a gratitude toward all those
who helped make that moment on the field possible: doctors, nurses,
Allison, my family, her family, friends, colleagues, coaches—but
most of all, two tough dudes named Tye and Jake.

They each reached a national championship game. They each have ACC championship rings. Imagine that. I'm proud of their accomplishments, but mostly I'm just a proud father. Of them. Of their younger brothers, Zak and Chase. And I'm in awe of Alli, who was an absolute rock during each of those difficult, sometimes dangerous pregnancies and deliveries.

Nothing matters to me more than trying to be a good father. That isn't by accident. Instead, it's by practice. It was almost self-taught, because my own father couldn't or wouldn't completely commit to being a full-time dad. He was just enough of a dad that I always wanted more of him. I vowed that would never be the case with my own kids. Not only would my support and love be unconditional, but it would be constant and dependable.

I have been described as a pretty boy. The Ken Doll. The former quarterback with the perfect TV job, the perfect smile, and the perfect life. As always, there is more to it than that.

My life is filled with imperfection and trauma. I was raised in an imperfect and broken family that tried—and often failed—to glue the pieces of their lives back together. I had an imperfect mom and dad who loved us—and whom we loved back—but there were limits to what they could provide. I had an imperfect college football playing career. I had an imperfect plan for how to start my working career. And I had—and have—my own failures and shortcomings. I definitely don't have all the answers. In fact, I'm still learning them.

I think constantly of my own dad and his struggles and journey. I think of our similarities and our differences.

Ken Doll? Ken Dolls don't pray that their newborn twins survive the night. Ken Dolls aren't raised at times by an older sister still in high school. Ken Dolls don't wish their dad could have a do-over.

We are all a product of our imperfections. In my case, fatherhood and football remain at the core of who I am, and who I strive to be. My story is about overcoming what people saw in my life, and what they didn't. It's about perseverance.

Maybe that's why I never felt closer to my twins and my family than that night of the national championship in January 2020. That night we shared more than football. We shared a history of overcoming life's obstacles.

I just wish my dad had been there to see it.

Out of
the Pocket

Chapter 1

My Dad, the Superhero

Imagine that your dad had the secret entry code to the Hall of Justice, which was built by Superman, designed partly by Wonder Woman, and bankrolled by Batman. Your dad would take you inside a place that few kids—or just about *any* outsider—ever saw in person. Then he would introduce you to the rest of his friends in the Justice League of America.

It would be the best day—made possible by the best dad—a kid could have.

Thing is, I didn't have to imagine it. It was my life when I was a kid. The only differences were that the Hall of Justice was the Ohio State football facility, and the Justice League of America was actually the Buckeyes of Columbus, Ohio.

Superman was legendary Ohio State head coach Woody Hayes. Batman was running back Archie Griffin, the only two-time Heisman Trophy winner in the history of the award. Big Ten MVP and Rose Bowl–winning quarterback Cornelius Greene was the Flash *and* a wonder.

My dad, though, was my superhero. He had a lifelong crush on Ohio State; I have a lifelong crush on Ohio State. He taught me the game; I teach my kids the game. That was my common denominator with my dad, the string that stretched across our lives: college football . . . *Ohio State* football.

Jim Herbstreit's first love was Buckeyes football. As a grade schooler, he wrote a detailed essay about Ohio State's 1949 Rose Bowl victory against Cal. He came to Columbus from Reading High School (just north of Cincinnati) as an undersized and underdog 5-foot-8, 150-pound running back and defensive back, small even by 1957 standards. When he was a freshman, he would sit by himself in a deserted Ohio Stadium, close his eyes, and imagine the Horseshoe filled to the brim, all 78,677 fans watching him making his way to midfield as a Buckeyes captain for the pregame coin toss.

It was a crazy, preposterous dream. But the dream didn't know the willpower of my father.

By his senior season in 1960, my dad was voted by his Ohio State teammates as a co-captain, the highest honor you can receive from your football peers. Of course, you'd know none of this had you walked into our house.

There was no man cave, no trophy room dedicated to his football career. The walls featured no framed photos of him in his No. 45 Buckeyes jersey, no evidence of his later becoming one of the youngest major college assistant coaches in the country, no sign of his lifelong friendship with two giants of the game: Woody Hayes and Bo Schembechler. His letterman jacket was in hiding. It was a modest house owned by a modest man. He had taken down all the newspaper clippings, all the pictures before his two sons were born. "I didn't want either one of my boys to feel intimidated," he would later tell a *Columbus Dispatch* sports columnist.

Only one memento was displayed in public. It sat atop the fireplace mantel for all to see: his Ohio State Captain's Mug.

You can buy a lot of things in this world, but you can't buy one of those. You can't buy the trust and respect of your teammates. You have to earn it.

The rest of his football artifacts were stored in cardboard boxes in the basement. As a little kid I would rummage through those boxes, fascinated by all things Ohio State football. Nothing captured my attention more than the black-and-white newspaper photos of him that my mom, Judy, had collected. I'd concentrate on his determined face as he was running the ball. I'd stare so long that I could separate the pixels on the newsprint. *That's him! That's No. 45, Jim Herbstreit. That's my dad.* He was sort of a football Zeus to me.

My mom and dad first met in high school. She was from Fort Worth, Texas, and had moved to the Cincinnati area after her father, an engineer, transferred to a job at the General Electric headquarters. My dad was a year older than my mom, and he used to carry her books as he walked her home from school. He grew up poor. My grandfather delivered Lance crackers, and they lived paycheck to paycheck in an eight-hundred-square-foot house. My uncle Rick, my dad's younger brother, told me it was not a house filled with hugs and warmth. My grandfather was a tough German immigrant who had survived the Great Depression. Self-reliance mattered more than warm and fuzzy.

The romance between my mom and dad almost ended a year later, when my mom's family moved to the San Fernando Valley, just a little north and east of Los Angeles. They wrote letters to each other every day. My mom saved each one of them.

They got engaged during my dad's sophomore year at Ohio State. My mom came back to Ohio and lived with my dad's aunt and grandmother in Cincinnati until the wedding in December 1959. There was no living together, no wink-wink arrangements. This was the 1950s.

During the 1958 season, when my mom was living with Dad's aunt and grandmother and my dad was playing ball at Ohio State, there was an incident—and it was my mom's fault.

According to my mom, Woody Hayes had a rule for the night before a home game: the players weren't allowed any contact with their girlfriends or, in my mom's case, fiancées. There were no exceptions.

My mom decided she would become the first.

She missed my dad so much that on a football Friday she borrowed a car and made the nearly two-hour drive from Cincinnati to Ohio Stadium, where the team was going through a late-afternoon practice. She saw my dad come out of the stadium, honked the horn, and stole a few minutes—and a kiss—through the car window before the Ohio State coaches shooed her away.

As she made the long drive back to Cincinnati on Highway 3, her car ran out of gas. By then it was dark, and she realized she had no money, except for a single dime in her purse. She walked to a pay phone at a gas station and, out of desperation, called the Ohio State football office. Of all people, Woody Hayes answered the phone.

Between sobs, she told Woody, "Oh, Coach, I know I wasn't supposed to see Jim, but I only saw him for a few minutes. Now my car has run out of gas. It's so dark. I'm so scared."

Woody's voice grew soft.

"Judy, calm down, calm down," he said. "It's going to be okay. Where are you?"

My mom gave him the gas station address.

"You stay right there," Woody said. "Keep your car locked and roll down the window just a little bit."

An hour or so later, a car pulled up behind hers, the headlights filling her rearview mirror. It was my dad, in Woody's car. Woody had given him twenty dollars to give to my mom for the drive home.

And just in case, he sent along a five-gallon can of gasoline. From that moment on, nobody could criticize Woody Hayes in her presence.

My dad was one of the smallest players on the team. In those days, Ohio State's roster had only four players who weighed more than 225 pounds. The school would do publicity photos of my red-headed dad being held up by some of the bigger guys on the team. That didn't stop him from playing both ways, as well as returning kickoffs and punts. He was fast, and he was fearless.

It was interesting to go back and look at the team's 1960 media guide, which was edited by Wilbur E. Snypp, the athletic department's director of publicity. It was only 56 pages. The 2020 OSU football media guide was 293 pages, thick enough to stop a bullet.

My dad's player bio was concise: "HERBSTREIT, James, 21, 5-8, 164, senior . . . from Reading, OH . . . was a regular right halfback last season, playing a total of 269 minutes . . . one of the fastest backs on the squad . . . will concentrate chiefly on defense this year . . . is an excellent defensive back, with quick reactions and a good sense of timing . . . majoring in history . . . hobbies are fishing and photography . . . was a regular shortstop on the Ohio State baseball team last year . . . won 13 high school letters . . . was an All-Ohio halfback . . . caught six passes last year, tops among the backs . . . carried the ball 14 times in 1959 . . . wants to teach or work in personnel after graduation . . . wears glasses off the field . . . led Ohio State in punt returns and kickoff returns last season . . . will start in the deep defense this year."

And just to give you an idea of where college football was sixty-plus years ago, how about this:

"The 1960 season might be described as a year of 'transition' at Ohio State as the Buckeyes plan to employ platoon football. This marks a radical departure from the 'iron man' tactics used so successfully the past seven years."

This was a different era. The heaviest player on the 1960 Buck-eyes' roster weighed 248 pounds. Compare that to OSU's 2020 roster, which had 44 players who weighed more than that, including 17 players who were 300 pounds or heavier. And until 1960, Ohio State's starters almost always played offense *and* defense.

My dad's 1960 Ohio State team scored 209 points. Ryan Day's 2019 team, the one that reached the College Football Playoff National Championship game, scored 656 points.

Sure, the 1960 team played only nine games compared to the 14 games the 2019 team played. But you get the idea. Even the 2020 Ohio State team, which played a COVID-19-reduced schedule of only eight games while reaching the CFP Championship, scored one and a half times as many points as my dad's team during his senior season.

College football in my dad's era was almost prehistoric compared to today's game. Even the road hotels sounded old (the 1960 OSU media guide had detailed team travel itineraries—can you imagine Alabama's Nick Saban allowing *that* to be made public? Never happen): the Lincoln Lodge Hotel at Illinois, the Albert Pick Motor Lodge at Michigan State, the University Union at Purdue, the Cedar Rapids Montrose Hotel at Iowa.

College football wasn't a 24-hour/7-day-a-week/365-day-a-year obsession like it is today. My dad and his teammates had full-time jobs during the summer. They had other aspirations. The NFL was an afterthought. James Lindner, a center, worked for a brick company. Offensive guard Charles Foreman and halfback Robert Klein worked for a construction company. Backup quarterback Bill Mrukowski worked for a lumber company. Guard Rodney Foster repaired bicycles. Star defensive end Thomas Perdue wanted to play pro baseball. Paul Martin, who played guard, end, and halfback in 1959, wanted to be a social worker. Guard Oscar Hauer, whose family escaped

Hungary just before communist Soviet troops invaded the country in 1956, listed his ambition as "to graduate from college." Guard Aaron Swartz said the same thing. Linebacker Gary Moeller wanted to coach football after he graduated—and he did, for forty years, including as a head coach at Illinois, Michigan, and the Detroit Lions. He coached the Wolverines to a Rose Bowl, and his 1991 team featured a wide receiver who would win the Heisman Trophy: Desmond Howard.

During my dad's era, college football still had a certain innocence to it. But don't kid yourself—Woody was a demanding coach (as were his assistant coaches, including an offensive line coach named Schembechler), and his teams bent to his will. He liked to say, "You win with people," and he was right. But Woody also believed that you won by wearing down an opponent. He was proud of his "three-yards-and-a-cloud-of-dust" offense. He once said, "Three things can happen when you pass, and two of them are bad." His players played physical, and if they didn't, they didn't play at all. They loved Woody, but they also feared him.

My mom often tells a story about a defining moment in the 1960 season—and, she says, in her life, and eventually in the life of our family. During a game that season, Woody got mad at my dad and questioned my dad's toughness. A few plays later, my dad came up on run support as a defensive back and hurled himself at the blocker and the running back right behind the blocker. He knocked both of them down. My mom, who was several months pregnant at the time, cheered like everyone else in the Shoe. It was a spectacular play.

Except that my dad didn't get up after the hit. He tried, but he couldn't regain his balance. Instead, he staggered, fell back to the ground, and then crawled helplessly in a circle.

My mom raced down from her seat to the field, the whole time thinking, "I've lost the father of my child. I've lost him." She was in a panic.

The team trainers took my dad to the locker room, but they wouldn't let my mom in to see him. To this day, my mom says that tackle affected him, changed him, damaged him. His smile was never the same. It was something only a wife would notice, but she is convinced the head injury changed who he was for the rest of his life.

My dad didn't return to the game, but he did return to the lineup the following game. I never asked him about the tackle or the effects it might have had on him. But in those days there was no concussion protocol, and the helmet equipment wasn't remotely comparable to the state-of-the-art headgear that players wear now. If anything, it was a sign of weakness if you didn't shake off a hit like the one my dad had sustained.

Meanwhile, the 1960 media guide was right about one thing: Ohio State wasn't a national championship team, but the Buckeyes did finish 7-2, including a season-ending 7-0 win against Michigan. Back then, either you won the Big Ten championship and represented the conference in the Rose Bowl, or you stayed home. Ohio State, which finished third in the standings, stayed home. Minnesota played Washington in Pasadena.

Running back Bob Ferguson was a consensus All-America pick. Quarterback Tom Matte, a converted running back who completed a grand total of 50 passes that year, finished seventh in the Heisman voting, just behind a Pittsburgh tight end named Mike Ditka.

My dad didn't earn any national or conference awards, but he did have that Captain's Mug, which meant everything to him. Think about it: My dad grew up in the Cincinnati area without much attention paid to him by college recruiters. He was small, sort of an afterthought kind of athlete. They'd say, "That Jim Herbstreit plays his heart out, but he'll never get a scholarship from Woody Hayes." And then he did get a scholarship. Not only that, but he started on both sides of the ball, became a team captain, and led the Buckeyes in interceptions as a senior. To Woody—and to my dad—being an Ohio State captain was the highest football honor you could receive. It was the greatest thing you could ever do in a Buckeyes uniform.

My dad had that mug, and he also had a wife, a tiny apartment in Columbus, and, on March 24, 1961, he had his first child, a daughter, Teri. What he needed was a job. His initial plan was to get a graduate degree and then a teaching job in California.

Once again, Woody came to the rescue. This time he didn't send his car, twenty dollars, and a gas can. Instead, he convinced my dad to delay his teaching career for a coaching career—not as an Ohio State graduate assistant, but as a twenty-two-year-old full-time defensive backs coach. That would never happen today. Suddenly my dad went from a team captain to now coaching his former teammates. He was basically the same age they were. Imagine walking into the staff meeting room, this time with Woody not as your coach but as your boss.

Coaching didn't pay much, not even at Ohio State. Woody's salary in 1951 was $12,500. In 1978, his final season at OSU, it was $43,000. He lived in an unassuming two-story, white-framed, three-bedroom house in Upper Arlington. According to *USA Today*, the top 55 highest-paid coaches in college football make anywhere from $3 million to $9 million per year. Just think what Woody would have made in today's market.

My dad spent two years on Woody's staff. Money was tight. If Woody made only $12,500, you can imagine what a new assistant made. There were times, my mom said, when her meager grocery allowance meant having to decide between buying a can of tomato paste or a small jar of meat. My mom chose the meat because she thought Teri needed the protein. She buttered the pasta noodles instead. To help save money, my dad ate at the Ohio State training table.

As a player and as an assistant coach, my dad revered Woody. But he was never afraid to stand up to him if he thought "the Old

Man" (that's what the players and assistants always called Woody) was wrong. Other assistants would recoil—how dare this *kid* question the legend. But Woody, said those who knew him best, appreciated my dad's willingness to make his case. My dad picked his spots, though. There were limits.

During his first season as an assistant coach, Ohio State tied TCU in its opening game and then ran the table, finishing the regular season 8-0-1, ranked No. 2 in the country, and atop the Big Ten standings. They were going to the Rose Bowl to face UCLA, the same team they had beaten in the second game of the season.

But the Ohio State faculty committee, worried that football was becoming too important at the school, voted to turn down the Rose Bowl invitation. Thousands of students protested in the streets of Columbus, but it was Woody who helped defuse the situation by having several of his team captains talk to the demonstrators.

In 1963, Schembechler left Woody's staff and returned to his alma mater, Miami (Ohio). He brought my dad along as the defensive backs coach. It was a step up in pay, and he would have more of a voice in the defensive philosophy.

Miami was known as "the Cradle of Coaches." Sid Gillman, Woody, Ara Parseghian, Bo, and later Bill Mallory, Dick Crum, and Randy Walker were all head coaches there. Weeb Ewbank, Paul Brown, Red Blaik, John Harbaugh, and Sean McVay played there. Jim Tressel, Dick Tomey, John Mackovic, Larry Smith, and Walker were assistant coaches there.

The relationship between my dad and Bo was different from the relationship between my dad and Woody. That's because Bo was different. At the time, Bo was trying to make a name for himself as a young head coach. He was a master motivator. He was also a hard-ass. He was the bad cop on the staff. My dad was the good cop.

A year later, my dad quit coaching to work for a prominent Columbus family, the Yasenoffs, who had strong ties to Ohio State and were a major presence in the business community. He stayed in the job until 1965, the year my brother John was born. Then he returned to coaching, this time at the University of Akron as a defensive coordinator.

I came along on August 19, 1969, just as my dad, now thirty years old, became Mallory's defensive coordinator at Miami. Woody played a major part in that, too. I know this now because in October 2020, I received a handwritten note from Ellie Mallory, Coach Mallory's wife of nearly sixty years (Coach Mallory died in 2018). She had found a 1969 Miami football media guide while going through some of her husband's files.

"Woody Hayes called Bill and said, 'You need to hire Jim Herbstreit as your DC,'" she wrote in the note. "Of course Bill said, 'Yes sir' and called your dad for an interview and hired him! Your folks and their then-two children lived in a house where the present Miami University football stadium is located."

At the end of the note, she wrote: "Your folks raised you right!"

It was so thoughtful of Ellie to write, and, yes, my mom has mentioned that we lived where Yager Stadium now sits on the Miami campus. To supplement my dad's salary, my mom babysat neighborhood kids in the months before I was born.

I was a big baby, almost nine pounds at birth, and my mom said I beat on her stomach throughout the pregnancy. My dad wanted to name me Tom—long last name, short first name. He was overruled.

"He's not a Tom," said my mom. "He's a Kirk."

She had decided I had a strong personality and that "Kirk" reflected that more than "Tom." So I was named Kirk Edward Herbstreit, the middle name in honor of my paternal grandfather.

After a month, I weighed nearly fourteen pounds. My mom took me to visit my grandmother, who was astounded by my size.

"I can't believe it—that's a *baby*?" she said.

At age one, I weighed thirty-three pounds, about a dozen pounds more than the average. The three kids shared a single room, and Teri says I was so big I could stand up in my crib and turn on the light in the middle of the night. Then I'd just fall back down and laugh.

The first-ever football game I attended was on September 13, 1969: Xavier at Miami. I was three weeks old. Miami won.

Sometime after the end of the season, my dad walked away from coaching, this time for good. The reason? Depends on who you ask. My mom said he quit coaching because he was unhappy. My dad told people he left in an effort to save his marriage. Whatever the reason, the decision would forever impact our lives.

In 1970 we moved to the Dayton area—Weybridge Drive in the suburb of Trotwood, to be exact. My vocabulary as a two-year old was limited. When anybody asked what I wanted for Christmas, it was always the same answer: "Candy, gum, and balls." Baseballs, footballs, Wiffle balls, Ping-Pong balls—I had a fascination with throwing them, bouncing them, hitting them, trying to catch them. I didn't understand football, but there was something about it that got my attention. Teri remembers my pulling the pacifier out of my mouth as a little kid, getting into a football position, and telling everyone, "Ready, guys!"

My dad taught me the game, or at least the basics of it: how to hold the football, how to tuck the ball into the V of my elbow, how to grip the laces, what the rules were, how to tackle. Even when I was four or five years old, I was drawn to the competition of it, to the team aspect of it. I would go outside and force my way into the games with the older kids on the block.

"Me not chicken, guys!" I would tell them.

I was the young towhead, the kid with white-blond hair . . . thick even then, sturdy, big for my age. I didn't want to get left behind. The older kids slammed me to the ground on tackles, but I never cried. I wanted to prove to them—and to my older brother, John—that I belonged. I looked up to John. In the neighborhood, on the playgrounds, and on the fields, he did what older brothers always do: look out for their little brothers. He always had my back. If a kid tried to rough me up, he'd have to answer to John.

There was no question about my favorite team. Like father, like son. My childhood world revolved around the Buckeyes. Even then, just as my dad had done when he was a kid, I dreamed of playing for Ohio State. I was like a lot of little kids in Ohio.

Some people watch a football game on TV and carry on a conversation with someone else in the room, or take a phone call. They're watching, but they're not completely locked in. My mom has a photo of me at five or six years old, and I'm sitting on my dad's lap while watching a game on TV, and I am completely locked in. I'm the same way today. There could be a kitchen grease fire behind me and I wouldn't notice it once the game began. There's another photo of me as a little kid sitting by myself on the living room couch. I've got my favorite blanket and I'm watching all the bowl games on New Year's Day. My parents couldn't get me to budge from that spot, or from the games. I fell asleep in that same spot. And they have a picture of me wearing an Ohio State shirt as the national anthem is playing before a game. I've got my hand over my heart and I'm saluting as the anthem is playing. Like I said, locked in.

My block was like a lot of blocks in Trotwood. We had a mix of nationalities, races, religions—not that it mattered to me. I just wanted to play sports. All we did in the early 1970s was go to school and then, the minute we were out of school, we played every game imaginable: four-square, freeze tag, baseball, Wiffle ball, football . . . whatever. We had mud ball fights (some kids wrapped the mud around rocks). We played on swing sets. We caught crawdads from the creek and watched them snap at each other. We caught garter snakes and, as dusk turned to night, we cradled fireflies in the palms of our hands. In the winter we'd play hockey on the ice patches. In the summer we rode our bikes everywhere.

We were like a scene from the movie *The Sandlot* or an episode of *The Wonder Years*. We played barefoot in blue jeans and T-shirts, or no shirts at all. Half the time our parents had no idea where we were—and that was okay. They just knew we were outside being kids. All the parents in the neighborhood looked out for the all the kids. They were like your aunts and uncles.

There were no cell phones, no internet, no laptops, no YouTube, no LOLs, no emojis, no Instagram, no nothing. The only phone in the house had a long curled cord, was attached to the kitchen wall, and was shared by everyone. The TV got three channels, and that's if the rabbit ears worked. Cable? There was no cable when I was a little kid. Color TV was a luxury. Your entertainment was each other. Your block, your neighborhood, your best friends—they were all right there. It was the center of your life. Well, that and football.

It was glorious. It was perfect. I wish every kid could experience it. Looking back, I wouldn't change a second of it.

My dad never forced me into sports. There was never a "You *WILL* play football!" command. If anything, he was the opposite of that. He wanted us to find our own way.

But I already knew I was crazy about the game. I loved listening to my dad tell his stories of playing for Ohio State, of coaching with Woody, of his friendship with Bo, who had become Michigan's head coach in late 1968 and had won his first game there about a month after I was born. I loved hearing about the football traditions at Ohio State, about this too-huge-to-be-believed stadium nicknamed "The Horseshoe," or "The Shoe" for short. Dad was a great storyteller.

Most of all, I loved hearing about The Game, which is what the annual Ohio State–Michigan meeting is called. It was first played in 1897, and beginning in 1917 it was played every year until COVID-19 issues ended the streak in 2020.

In our house, there was no debate about the greatest rivalry in sports. My dad had played and coached in The Game. He had lived it, and we lived it with him. Nobody—and I mean nobody—took the Ohio State–Michigan game more seriously than my dad. The Game was sacred to him, and that feeling trickled down to all of us, especially me.

On that particular game day, there was a different vibe in the house. It wasn't, "Hey, here we go. Let's have some fun today. We'll cook out, have some laughs, then settle down for a leisurely afternoon of football with the Buckeyes." Nuh-uh.

This was war. Football war. In our house, it was the USA (Ohio State) versus the USSR (Michigan) during the height of the Cold War. It was not silly. It was not cute. We all woke up in the morning and it was game on.

My dad was a good friend of Bo's. But when Bo was on the Michigan sideline, you've never seen anybody pull harder against his friend—against Michigan—than my dad. There's a reason why they called the period between 1969 and 1978, when Woody and Bo were going at it *hard* in that rivalry, "The Ten Year War." During those ten years, Michigan went 5-4-1 against the Buckeyes, and each of those losses gutted my dad. And me.

That rivalry became a centerpiece of my life. When I was growing up, we played electric football. You had a metallic playing field and there was a little motor that caused the board to vibrate. The vibrations caused your team of miniature plastic players to move against the other team. Completing a pass was almost impossible. There was a tiny piece of felt in the shape of a football. You placed the felt in the quarterback's hand, pulled a lever on the quarterback's arm, aimed, and hoped.

We had a dog (not surprisingly, his name was Woody), so there was a dent from where he walked across the board. The players would sort of drift into the dog's paw mark. Every year as a little kid I would ask Santa for a new electric football game. And every year, Santa would deliver the game. Only years later did I learn that my dad had stayed up late on Christmas Eve meticulously repainting each of the miniature players, from Pittsburgh Steelers black and gold and Dallas Cowboys blue and metallic silver to Ohio State scarlet and gray and Michigan maize and blue. They didn't sell the game with college teams, so my dad would paint the pants, jerseys, and helmets, even the jersey numbers. When I tore open the package on Christmas morning, I just assumed that's how it came: Ohio State versus Michigan. It must have taken him forever to paint everything just so.

When you're a little kid, you think your parents are perfect. But to have a dad who played for the team you worship, who played for a mythical figure in a football-crazed state, who was a team captain, who later coached for the mythical figure, well, that was next-level perfect. And my mom also loved sports. When she was growing up at her family's house in Fort Worth, she used to throw the football with her dad in the front yard. They were a Dallas Cowboys family, too.

I was five or six when my dad took me to my first Ohio State practice . . . to the Hall of Justice. It was only about an hour-and-fifteen-minute drive to Columbus. Archie Griffin, who had won the Heisman in 1974 and would win it again in 1975, let me put on his helmet, the one with the iconic I-bar face mask on the front. It was covered with Buckeye leaf stickers on the top and sides (and paint marks from opposing players' helmets), and it felt so heavy on my head. But I couldn't wait to tell the kids the next day at Westbrooke Village Elementary about wearing Archie's helmet.

Better yet, sometimes my dad would take me to the Horseshoe for a game, and if the Buckeyes won, we would go inside the locker room and Woody would let me sit on his knee as I asked him about the latest victory. It was all over for me then. Seriously, how do you beat that? It was like sitting on Santa's knee and having him ask you want you want for Christmas. What do I want? I've got it! There was nothing I wanted more as a six-year-old than to talk Ohio State football with Mr. Ohio State Football himself.

My dad occasionally took me to Ohio State functions that featured former players. Some of his old teammates would gesture toward my dad, nudge me on the shoulder, and say, "That little son of a bitch right there? Let me tell you, kid, the Old Man always said that pound for pound he was the toughest player he ever had."

The Old Man . . . Woody.

My dad was supposed to play for Miami University. That was the original plan. All that changed the day my dad helped his high school win a baseball playoff game, and then went directly to the track (he wore his track uniform under his baseball uniform), put on a pair of track cleats, and ran in the state finals of the 100-yard dash. In the crowd that day was Woody. Not long after that, my dad wasn't going to Miami University anymore.

Chapter 2

The Pact

Sometimes I would go down to the basement of our house and rummage through the boxes of my dad's Ohio State stuff. It was like being the son of two different fathers. There was my 1975 dad, now a home appraiser for a properties company. And then there was this 1960 football superhero dad: the really fast, undersized player with that undersized piss-and-vinegar attitude that I saw in the newspaper clippings arranged just so in the photo albums. I tried to imagine what it must have been like for him. I would look at his folded Ohio State varsity letter jacket—it seemed so big at the time—and treat it as if it were the Holy Shroud. It wasn't until nearly twenty years later that I actually saw footage of my dad in action. The Big Ten Network aired an Ohio State game from his junior or senior year, and there he was: quick feet, instinctive, tough, athletic. He would have thrived in today's game because height and weight don't matter as much. Today it's all about being a playmaker. He was willing to throw his body in there. He reminded me a little of former LSU defensive back Tyrann Mathieu, the Honey Badger. He was fearless.

It was quiet in that basement. It was quiet upstairs, too. Little by little, my mom and dad had begun to drift apart. There were no arguments, no yelling at each other. Instead, it had become a marriage of silence.

My mom says that she felt alone in the marriage, that she didn't exist to my dad anymore. She says she began to question herself: Was she not pretty enough? Was she not interesting enough? Why wouldn't he listen to her?

Teri did her best to shield me from what was happening in the house. She was the oldest and often took the brunt of what was happening between my parents. John had to suffer through his share, too. Teri always reminded me of Sheryl Yoast, the daughter of assistant coach Bill Yoast in the movie *Remember the Titans*. Smart. Defiant. Unwavering. Strong. And she knew football, too.

We were close, and still are. We've had one argument in our entire lives. She was thirteen, I was five. We both tried to apologize and both ended up crying.

Teri was my buddy. It wasn't unusual for me to sleep on the floor next to Teri's bed. She would make a sort of nest out of pillows and blankets, and that's where I would spend each night. We would listen to the radio, or she would tell me scary stories, or do sound effects, or tell jokes ("What do you get when you put a puppy in the oven? A hot dog!")

Teri says she kept reassuring me, telling me everything was going to be okay with Mom and Dad. I was only in second grade, so I believed her. Why wouldn't I?

But everything wasn't okay. My mom was eventually hospitalized because she felt so discombobulated and overwhelmed emotionally as her marriage dissolved. She had reached her breaking point.

My mom got the help she needed, but there was nothing to be done to help the marriage. One day my dad left. There was no explanation. Nobody sat me down and said, "Okay, here's what's happening." Instead, he just disappeared.

One day became a week. A week became a month. A month eventually became a year.

My dad had reached a breaking point, too. He would never speak a bad word against my mom. Ever. But you could see it in his eyes, I suppose. Teri says she could. Whatever my mom and dad had, it was gone—and it didn't really matter whose fault it was.

A few months after my dad left, my mom announced that we were going to move to Centerville, which was about a half hour south of Trotwood. *Move? Why? Isn't Dad coming back home? What about my friends? What about the neighborhood?* I was devastated, confused.

Teri pulled me and John into the kitchen.

"No matter what happens, our pact is that we stay together," she said. "Wherever we are, we stay together. That's it."

We promised each other in that kitchen that nothing would pull us apart. Not our dad being in and out of our lives. Not our mom's decision to move us to a new town.

When I finished second grade that spring, we moved to Centerville. As we pulled out of the driveway for the final time, that's when it hit me: this is really happening. I had this perfect kid life . . . and then I didn't.

On February 10, 1978, my parents' divorce became final. An eighteen-year marriage was done. A family wasn't a family anymore.

I didn't fully understand what "divorce" meant. All I knew was that I was leaving all my buddies. I was leaving Mrs. Whittaker, my favorite teacher at school. I was leaving my house. I wasn't upset. I was sad. I was scared. I couldn't make sense of it.

My dad now lived in an apartment in Kettering, which was a suburb just north of Centerville. I would see him periodically, but there was no set visitation schedule. Of course, none of us kids cared about that. We just wanted to spend time with him whenever we could.

My dad didn't like conflict. He didn't handle confrontation well. His solution to any sort of controversy was to ignore it, separate from it. We, his kids, were part of the conflict, so he withdrew from us. I wouldn't see him for weeks at a time. If I did see him, the meetings didn't last long. My superhero was gone.

My mom, Teri, John, and I lived together on Red Coach Road in Centerville. The pact was in place. Teri was still going to her old high school, so she commuted back and forth each day. John and I started at new schools, he at Hithergreen Middle School and me at Driscoll Elementary, where I didn't know anybody in my third-grade class. I was terrified. As I walked to school each day, I dreaded the thought of having to talk to anyone. I was super shy, so I just sat in the classroom and hoped nobody would notice me. I wanted to be invisible. If a teacher called on me, I would immediately feel self-conscious and my face would turn red. I was just born that way.

Gym class and recess were what saved me. I learned that if you were good at sports, the other kids were more accepting of you, were nicer to you. Sports became my way of coping with my parents' divorce. I was either playing sports, watching sports, or listening to sports. It was my escape from the pain of our family's disintegration. It temporarily blocked out the sadness, the sight of my mom freaking out as she tried to navigate the next chapter of her life and of our lives. When I listened to a Cincinnati Reds game on the radio . . . when I could stare at the TV as the Buckeyes played . . . when I could compete against the other kids at school—that's when I felt like the world couldn't hurt me. It was my protective bubble.

It was in third grade that I wrote a paper for class that began, "Football is the best in the world." When my teacher handed the paper back to me, she had written, "Would you want this as a job?"

I still have that paper. I've always wondered if that teacher ever saw me on TV and said, "Wait a minute—I think I remember that kid."

My mom got a job selling cars at Rubicon Cadillac in Dayton. She'd never sold a car in her life. Everything was done on commission. If she sold a car, we ate. If she didn't sell a car, we went hungry. My mom says she would have nightmares about not being able to make a car sale.

As the oldest child, Teri says she felt a greater responsibility to help. While her high school classmates and friends were going to parties on Friday nights, she often stayed home to help my mom take care of John and me. Teri's boyfriend, Jeff Johnson (who later became a football team co-captain at Navy, and then a Navy pilot and eventually a commercial pilot), would come over almost every night and eat dinner with us. Sometimes he would bring us food. He was always asking, "How can I help?"

I loved Jeff like a brother. He was a wise old soul, and he was a really cool figure in my life. He liked my dad, and he would encourage me to play football. Sometimes he would stop at the house and tell me, "C'mon, let's go do something."

Teri says she remembers days when we didn't have much food in the house. At the time, she says, our dad had chosen to keep his distance and rarely checked on us. Teri would leave countless phone messages at his office, but he would ignore them. One time, Teri drove to his apartment building at midnight, saw his car parked in the lot, and began pounding on his door.

"I need your help, Dad," she pleaded through the closed door. "We need money for food."

He was inside the apartment, but he wouldn't open the door.

When Teri did talk to him, he would tell her, "It's difficult not to have you kids all the time." Since he couldn't have custody of us full-time, he decided to barely deal with us at all.

Teri says my grandparents seemed to be more worried about my dad than they were about us. We were at their house one day and they began telling Teri how worried they were about our dad.

"Poor Jim," said my grandfather. "I feel so bad for him."

Teri says she had had enough.

"'Poor Jim'?" she told them. "Poor Jim, my butt. How about 'Poor boys in there who don't have a parent'? How about 'Poor fridge,' because it's bare? I made Hamburger Helper for the boys and there's nothing left to eat after that. 'Poor Jim'? Poor Jim needs to get us out of here."

My dad had been a bigger-than-life figure to me, but now we couldn't depend on him. I was just a kid, but I didn't know whom to trust and whom to believe. I loved my parents, but all our lives had been turned upside down. I just wanted everyone to be happy. I wanted it to be like it used to be.

My mom didn't have a college degree. She was a stay-at-home mom. Now she had to financially support three kids. My dad sent along a monthly check, but it didn't go far. She did the best she could, but our family was fractured in ways we didn't even realize at the time.

————

On December 28, 1978, Ohio State played Clemson in the Gator Bowl. Sixty-five-year-old Woody was on one sideline. A thirty-year-old interim head coach named Danny Ford was on the Clemson sideline.

There was no comparison between the coaches. Woody had won 205 games, five national championships, and thirteen Big Ten championships. He was a three-time national coach of the year, and during his watch, his program had produced fifty-six All-Americans and four Heisman winners, and his teams had played in eight Rose Bowls. Ford was an offensive line coach pressed into duty after Charley Pell left Clemson for Florida. The Gator Bowl would be Ford's first game as a head coach. He was the youngest head coach in Division I football.

And yet, with about two minutes left to play in the Gator Bowl, Ford's team led Woody's Buckeyes—*my* Buckeyes—by two points. I was watching. Every Ohio State fan was watching, including my dad.

It didn't happen often, but we were all together that night at his apartment. For a few hours, it was like the old days.

Ohio State only needed a field goal to win. It was third-and-five on the Clemson 24-yard line.

Today, we would call the play call an RPO: a run/pass option. Quarterback Art Schlichter, only a freshman, had the option of trying to run for the first down or dumping the ball to the running back, who was supposed to curl out of the backfield and settle in the middle of the field.

What was it that Woody always said about throwing the ball? Three things can happen, and two of them are bad.

In this case, there was a fourth thing that could happen: a coaching legend could suffer a meltdown.

Schlichter got too cute. He backpedaled and then tried to flip the ball over the Clemson defensive line as tailback Ron Springs circled toward the middle. Instead, the pass dropped directly into the hands of Clemson nose guard Charlie Bauman, who ran up the Ohio State sideline before Schlichter tackled him at the feet of Woody. According to an ESPN.com story years later on the game, Woody reportedly yelled at Bauman, "You SOB, I just lost my job!"

Then, in an instant, Woody grabbed Bauman and punched him just below the throat. It wasn't much of a punch. Woody was left-handed, and famous for taking swings at his own players at practice. This punch was with the right hand.

Everyone saw it except the ABC broadcast crew of Keith Jackson and Ara Parseghian. According to Michael Rosenberg, who wrote a book about the rivalry between Michigan and Ohio State and Bo and Woody, Buckeyes athletic director Hugh Hindman also saw Woody take a swing.

"If he hit that kid, Jim," said Hindman to administrative assistant Jim Jones, who was sitting next to him, "he's done."

Woody's punch sparked a brawl between the teams. Even nine-year-old me knew Woody was in trouble. So did my dad, who told me, "I don't think Woody's going to make it through the weekend."

I started crying. "Well, he can still be our friend, can't he?"

The next day, Hindman, with the blessing of the university president, fired Woody. Hindman had played for Woody at Miami, had been an assistant coach for Woody, and, thanks partly to Woody's recommendation, had been hired as Ohio State's athletic director. But when Woody wouldn't resign after the Gator Bowl incident, Hindman said he had no choice but to dismiss him.

This was a huge deal at Ohio State, in the state itself, and in all of college football. The first paragraph of Hindman's 1994 obituary in the *New York Times* referenced him as the man who "discharged the university's legendary and belligerent football coach, Woody Hayes . . ."

In our house, he wasn't belligerent. He was revered, respected, and loved. He was the Navy officer who fought in World War II. He was the military historian. He was the man who devoured American literature. He was the coach who insisted his players "pay it forward," and, most of all, that they get their college degrees. My dad would mention Woody's temper, but it was his other qualities, said my dad, that defined him.

Ohio State hired Earle Bruce to replace Woody. Earle had played briefly at OSU before an injury ended his playing career in 1951. He had been a successful high school head coach in Ohio, including a 20-0 record at Massillon, and then returned to Ohio State as an assistant coach before becoming a head coach at the University of Tampa and later at Iowa State.

But you could make the argument—and it wouldn't be a stretch— that had my dad stayed in coaching, he, not Earle Bruce, would have been named Ohio State's head coach on January 12, 1979.

I want to be clear: this is nothing against Earle Bruce. Earle did a great job at Ohio State. He was 81-26-1 during his nine years as the Buckeyes' head coach. He won or shared four Big Ten titles. He took a team that was unranked at the beginning of that 1979 season and almost won a national championship. He was 5-3 in bowl games and 5-4 against Michigan, and his coaching tree is amazing. So many of his former assistants went on to become head coaches, including Nick Saban, Urban Meyer, Jim Tressel, and Pete Carroll. Earle liked to say he bled scarlet and gray, and he did. He loved that place.

But when I say Jim Herbstreit would have been Woody's successor, I say it not to toot my dad's horn but because I'm being realistic. Had he stayed in coaching, his résumé would have read: Ohio State co-captain for Woody, Ohio State defensive backs

coach for Woody (only months after receiving his Ohio State diploma), and defensive coordinator for Bo at Miami. And when Bo
took the Michigan head coaching job in 1969, it's probably safe to
assume that my dad would have been his replacement at Miami,
or followed him to Michigan, or returned to Ohio State as an
assistant. He would have had eighteen years of college coaching
experience before his fortieth birthday. He would have been at the
front of the line to replace Woody.

Instead, he had walked away from coaching, and he lived with
the pain and regret of that decision for the rest of his life. It was
like having the winning lottery ticket, but then deciding to rip it
up instead of cashing it. That's what my dad did when he gave up
coaching. It must have crushed him.

––––––––

When I was in fifth grade, my mom remarried and my brother
John and I moved in with them at their house in Franklin, Ohio,
which is thirty-three miles north of Cincinnati (Teri was in college). We went from not having much money at all to now living in
my wealthy stepdad's house.

Franklin was a small, blue-collar town in southwest Ohio. I
started fifth grade in a public school, but when my mom saw the
level of homework I brought home, she decided it was a year behind what I had been doing at Driscoll. So I had to change schools
again, this time to a private school called the Miami Valley School
in Dayton. It prided itself on academics, not sports.

My life had been turned upside down. I was in a new town,
in a new house, with a new stepdad, and in a new school that
didn't field teams in the two sports I absolutely loved: baseball
and football. My stepdad owned a very successful graphic design

company. In fact, my mom left the car dealership to work as a secretary at his design firm.

My stepdad worked hard, and when he got home, he liked to have a few drinks, laugh loud, and talk loud. Basically, he was a life-of-the-party kind of guy. He was okay, I guess. He just wasn't my dad—and never would be. I had to fake laugh whenever I was around him and pretend that everything was normal, but it wasn't.

I will give my former stepdad credit for this: he had season tickets to the Reds. We went to fifteen or so games a year at Riverfront Stadium, and it was heaven—second row, right behind the Reds' dugout on the first-base side. Riverfront was one of those cookie-cutter, 1970s-type of stadiums. It was built next to the Ohio River in downtown Cincinnati.

As much as I loved Ohio State football and college football, I loved the Big Red Machine as much or more than the Buckeyes. The NFL was a distant third.

My stepdad had those Reds tickets, but it was my own dad, the former Ohio State shortstop, who taught me the strategies of the game as a kid: when to hit and run, when to pitch out, when to pinch hit, when to bring in a reliever . . . all the things that made the National League more interesting to me than the American League. I just loved the buildup to each game.

My dad didn't have extra money to take me to Reds games, so instead we played a board game called All Star Baseball Game. It used a real player's lifetime statistics and applied those results on a spin dial that you used to activate each play. It was one of the very first baseball simulation games and seemed so cutting edge at the time. Today if I tried to get my own kids to play the original Strat-O-Matic, they'd look at me and say, "Is that it? You're kidding."

Even as a seven-year-old in 1976—the year the Reds won their second consecutive World Series—I could recite the Reds' lineup. In fact, I can recite every MLB team's lineup from those eras.

The '76 team was one of the greatest lineups of all time: Pete Rose at third, Ken Griffey in right field, Joe Morgan at second, Tony Perez at first, Johnny Bench at catcher, George Foster in left, Davey Concepcion at shortstop, Cesar Geronimo in center. The Great Eight.

During those vintage Big Red Machine days, most people liked Bench or Rose the best. But I was a Davey kind of kid. When I would go to those Reds games with my stepdad, I watched how Davey jogged on and off the field. He just had a style about him. I saw he was always the guy who brought out the cap and glove of a teammate if that teammate was stranded on base at the end of an inning. In Little League, I would carry a cap and glove out to my teammate, just like Davey did. I patterned my closed batting stance after Davey's. I even made the sign of the cross when I stepped into the batter's box, just like Davey—and I wasn't Catholic. I didn't even know what it meant when I did it.

I grew up listening to Reds baseball on the radio. Marty Brennaman did the play-by-play; former Reds pitcher Joe Nuxhall was the color analyst. Brennaman had come to the Reds from Virginia Tech, and replaced Al Michaels on the broadcasts. In his first-ever regular-season Reds game, he called Hank Aaron's 714th home run—the one that tied Babe Ruth. Not a bad debut.

Brennaman was our Vin Scully, our Harry Caray. When I lived in Franklin with my mom and stepdad, I'd buy a large pepperoni thin crust from Star Pizza, a two-liter bottle of Mountain Dew, turn down the sound of the TV broadcast, turn up the sound of the radio broadcast, and listen to Marty and Joe. I'd sit on the couch by myself and keep score in my notebook. It was a great day if you could end it with Brennaman saying, "And this one belongs to the Reds."

———

The first time I ever played organized football was in fifth grade, when I was a running back and linebacker on my Pee Wee league team. I loved it. Every time I touched the ball, I thought I was going to score. There was something about running the ball that came easily to me. I also loved hitting people on defense. I played again in sixth grade, but I don't ever remember my dad coming to any of my games. By then he had started a new life of his own, remarrying and moving to Mason, Ohio, which is a suburb of Cincinnati.

Once in a while, my dad would bring me to his rental house, which was on a huge farm. He had a stepson who was my age.

It was a very strange experience to walk into your dad's house and feel like a complete outsider. His wife, who was younger than him, was clearly the boss. She had an "I-run-this-show" mentality. I instantly felt uncomfortable. You half-wondered if you should ask her permission to open the fridge and get a glass of milk or to open a cupboard and make a peanut butter and jelly sandwich. It was like you were an intruder.

When the visit was done, my dad would drive me back to Franklin and my stepdad's house. I'd get out of the car and wave to him as he drove off, all the time thinking, "I wish he wasn't leaving."

I didn't play football as a seventh grader because Miami Valley School didn't offer that sport. The only thing I did was move again. My mom and my stepdad got divorced at the end of my school year, which was fine with me because it also meant no more stepdad. Not long after that, my mom called my dad and said, "I'm scared. I don't want the stress. You need to take your boys." She was a single mom again and was looking for a job.

My mom moved into an apartment in Cincinnati, while John and I moved in with my dad, stepmom, and stepbrother in Wyoming, a suburb of Cincinnati. My stepmom didn't get along with

John, and she eventually kicked him out of the house. (He was okay; he found another place to live.) Now it was just me.

I shared a room with my stepbrother. We had bunk beds and we became friends. I kept the fake laugh with my stepmom and enrolled at yet another school, this time at Wyoming Middle School. I went out for football, and when the coach asked what position I played, I said, "Running back."

"Nah, you're a big kid," he said. "We're going to put you on the offensive line." So I played offensive line as an eighth grader. I didn't have much of a choice.

I was probably naïve, but I also wanted to be with my dad. I loved him and I missed him. Despite all that had happened, he was my dad, and I wanted him in my life.

I was a pleaser by nature. I wanted my dad, my mom, my teacher, my coach to say, "Hey, I'm proud of you. You did a real good job today." I also was a survivor. I just weathered the storm. Did I have clothes to wear? Was there something to eat? I was a day-to-day kid. I never really asked for a lot of information about what was going on. I didn't have any resentment toward my dad. There was hurt, but it wasn't the same thing as anger. My brother John, who had experienced more of the family dysfunction than I had, did develop a level of resentment and anger. It was understandable.

One day I came home and there was a guy at the house with my stepmom. My dad was out of town for his job. He traveled a lot.

Not long after that—with my dad out of town again for work—I walked into the house and that same man was there with my stepmom. They were watching a movie together.

I told my mom about it.

"Don't say anything yet," she said. "That's going to be your ace in the hole. Just hold on. Eventually, that's going to be a breaking point."

I continued to gather intel about my stepmom and this other man. I was very controlled and calculating about it. Now I was going to use this information to my advantage.

Even though I had met some great friends in Wyoming, including my girlfriend, I wasn't happy there. I had already wasted a year of football as an offensive lineman, but more important, I was unhappy with my home life. I didn't like my stepmom, and my dad was out of town most weeks.

One day I said, "Hey, Dad, I need to talk to you." Then I calmly explained what I had witnessed at home while he was on the road in Cleveland.

I wanted him to leave her, and sure enough, he did. In early 1984, my dad divorced his second wife and then told me, "You've moved a lot. You've seen us get married and divorced. We're done moving. Where do you want to go to high school: Centerville, Moeller, or Princeton?"

I felt a combination of happiness and relief. I didn't have to live in the same house with that woman anymore. I didn't have to pretend we were getting along, or try to ignore the man she invited to the house when my dad was gone. Finally, I had a voice in my life.

Archbishop Moeller was a private Catholic high school in Cincinnati, and its football program was one of the best in the country. Under Gerry Faust, Moeller had won five state championships and four mythical national championships, and had gone 174-17-2 during his eighteen seasons there. He went directly from Moeller head coach to Notre Dame head coach in 1981. Even without him, Moeller won the state championship in 1982.

Princeton was a public high school in Cincinnati, and had just won the state championship in 1983.

Centerville High School had never won a state championship. Its coach was Bob Gregg, who ran the triple option and who had a reputation as a no-nonsense, super-demanding kind of guy.

My mom also was doing some high school scouting work. She looked into Kettering Fairmont, as well as Centerville High. She talked to a few of the football moms at Centerville, and they complained about how tough Gregg was on his players. The more they complained, the more my mom became convinced that Centerville High was the right place for me.

Early that spring, we all decided that Centerville was the best fit for me. If you're keeping track, it would be my seventh different school in eight years. Of course, there was always a twist with my family. My dad and I had moved into an apartment in Centerville. My mom moved into the same Villager Apartments complex.

It was a strange setup. I was fourteen going on twenty-five. I would cook and clean for myself. I was still in eighth grade and basically on my own. My dad worked in Cleveland, which was a three-plus-hour drive from Centerville. When he was home, it was awesome. He was the chef of the family. He loved to cook. And the weekends were a blast. It was like the old days: father and son watching the Buckeyes on Saturdays, the NFL on Sundays.

When he wasn't home, I'd go hang out in my mom's apartment. Back and forth I went. If I wasn't there, I was at Elsa's, a Mexican restaurant that was located next to our apartment complex. I would walk over with a handful of quarters, sit in the nearly pitch-black restaurant bar, and spend hours playing a golf video game called Golden Tee. During the afternoons, it usually was just me, the bartender, a few customers, and then Harry Caray and the Chicago Cubs on the TV. The whole restaurant staff knew me. They would bring me chips, salsa, and a Coke, and never charge me.

Late that spring or early summer, my mom made a proposal to my dad: instead of her and my dad each paying monthly apartment rentals, she would buy the same house we had rented years earlier on Red Coach Road in Centerville, and we would live under one roof. It would be a way to help each other financially, and help provide some sense of normalcy as I began high school. We would try to be a family again.

My dad did a very sweet and unselfish thing: he said yes to this unusual proposition. So we all moved into the small, four-bedroom ranch house. We each had our own small room. Teri said we were the "pretend" family, but there was nothing pretend about it to me. I was all in. I loved the idea of all of us being together. And who knew—maybe my mom and dad would patch up their fractured relationship.

A kid could hope, right?

Chapter 3

Elk Pride . . . and the Art of the Puke

Near the end of our school year, an announcement was made over the intercom system.

"If you have any interest in playing ninth-grade football next season," said the voice, "Centerville High School coach Bob Gregg will be here after school to answer any of your questions."

I didn't know very much about Coach Gregg, other than that my mom said he was tough. She liked that about him.

She was right. When I showed up for the after-school meeting with some other kids, there was no question who was in charge. Coach Gregg stood at the front of the room like a Marine drill instructor welcoming a busload of recruits to boot camp. The way he carried himself, the way he talked—the guy was scary. He was only 5-foot-8, but he acted taller. I found out later that he had served in the Marines.

This wasn't a friendly meet-and-greet with freshly baked cookies and group hugs. Instead, Coach Gregg challenged us that day—and we didn't even play for him yet! But that was his style, to challenge you in every aspect of your life. I was good with that. Sign me up. The Pleaser wanted to please.

The Pleaser also wanted to play, but when I arrived for my first-ever Centerville High Elks team event late that summer of 1984, I knew that was going to be a challenge. For starters, the varsity team had won nine consecutive Western Ohio League championships under Coach Gregg. They were calling it the "Decade of Domination." They had finished 10-0 in 1983 and fourth in the state rankings. The 1984 team was loaded, too.

To the coaching staff at my new school, I was just a nothing freshman quarterback who had played offensive line as an eighth grader. Our first workout actually took place at the high school track, where I met a handful of kids who would become some of my best and most trusted friends in my life: Deron Brown, Troy Hutto, Craig Schmidt, Dave Rosenbaum.

Deron had just moved to the area from Cleveland, but had grown up in Middletown, which is a steel mill town in southwest Ohio. He wore the latest Nikes and started leading us around the track. We had to run the 400-yard dash, and Deron beat us all. It was like he was trying to prove a point: the new kid wasn't going to be intimidated by the locals. Deron's family was wealthy compared to mine. He lived in a really nice house and had things we didn't.

About 80 of us tried out for the team as freshmen. By the time we were seniors, fewer than 20 of us were left from the original 80. Coach Gregg—the drill instructor—made no secret of his coaching methods. The concept was simple: grind us down to nothing and then rebuild us into football soldiers. He had graduated from Centerville in 1951, and had played on the school's first team as a 110-pound running back. He was legendary for his four-letter words, for the occasional midnight practice that would cause someone in the neighborhood to call the police, for his willingness to line up against us in a drill and show us exactly how he wanted it done. One time, he suffered a double hernia during practice.

At school I kept to myself, especially in my classes. I took freshman English, and was doing fine until I noticed that one of the requirements in the class was to give a speech. The idea of public speaking paralyzed me.

Week by week, month by month, the teacher called on different students to recite a paper or give a short speech on a topic. But she never called on me. I had escaped. She had forgotten about me!

Then one day I heard, "Kirk, why don't you come forward and tell us about the paper you've written."

I sat frozen at my desk.

"Kirk?" the teacher said. "Come on up, please."

I walked slowly to the chalkboard. In the front row, only a few feet away from me, was Lael Oosthuizen, a freshman cheerleader and the most beautiful girl in our school. I was so self-conscious that as I started to talk, my face turned red. Then I started to sweat. Lael began to giggle as my meltdown reached Defcon 1, and I heard her whisper to someone, "Look how red he is." It wasn't mean-spirited on her part; I'm sure I looked ridiculous with my bright red face.

I stumbled through my speech, and then made the walk of shame back to my seat. As I sat down, I said to myself: "I'm never doing this again. Mark it down. This is the last speech of my life."

Meanwhile, I played quarterback, running back, and linebacker on the freshman team. Our varsity team won another league title, beat national No. 1 Cincinnati Moeller, reached the state playoffs for the first time in school history (Centerville lost in the semifinals), and finished 11-1 and 22nd in the national rankings.

In early 1985, Teri said she wanted to talk to me. She had made a decision: she was going to Europe, and she didn't know when she'd be back. She had no idea where she was going, where she would live, or how she would support herself. She had a one-way ticket and three hundred dollars in her pocket. But she had to escape, she said. She had to do this for herself.

For years, Teri had sacrificed her own dreams in order to look after me and John. She was like George Bailey in *It's a Wonderful Life*. She never complained. She just did what she thought a big sister should do: help take care of her younger brothers.

Now, she said, she needed to experience happiness and success without the weight of being the big sister. She told me that so much of her life—and she was only twenty-four at the time—had been spent as a safety net for our parents. She said she had been forced into adulthood before she was an adult. Now she wanted to live the part of her life she'd missed by taking care of us.

Teri would later say that conversation with me was the hardest thing she'd ever done. But I understand why she had to leave. It was hard for me, too. She had been out of my life on a day-to-day basis for a few years as she worked her way through college. But to know she wasn't going to be a phone call away, or a car ride away . . . that was tough for me, but liberating for her.

———

Going into my sophomore year, I wanted to make the varsity roster. Of course, you first had to convince Coach Gregg you were worthy of a place on that roster.

During the summer, we had 5 a.m. weight-lifting sessions on Monday, Wednesday, and Friday. Schmidt rode his bike six miles to get there. I got up at 3:30 or 4 a.m., made pancakes, and then carpooled with some buddies to the weight room. I wanted to be among the first guys there. I wanted to outwork everybody.

The workouts were brutal, borderline cruel. I'm not sure you could get away with it today in this age of everybody gets a participation ribbon. There were two weight rooms: the larger free-weight room (bench presses, barbells, squat racks, etc.) that we used on Mondays and Fridays, and the much smaller Nautilus weight-machine room, which we used on Wednesdays for circuit training.

You went to bed on Tuesday nights crying out of fear. Hell awaited you first thing Wednesday morning.

The Nautilus room was claustrophobic in size, about 25 yards long and 10 yards wide, with two metal doors at the end of it. There were one hundred players, and the coaches rotated half of us into the room at a time. Before long, our collective body heat would turn us all into one big sweat stain.

There were garbage cans placed throughout the workout room. As the temperature increased, as the yelling of the coaches intensified, and as their relentless whistles (every thirty seconds) signaled a rotation to another Nautilus machine, guys started throwing up. Sometimes you made it to the garbage can in time. Other times, you puked on the floor, or accidentally puked on someone's arm. The thing is, your brain was so gone by then that you didn't care if there was puke dripping off your arm. It didn't even disgust you. There was so much puke pouring out of everyone that it almost seemed natural. Whistle . . . lift . . . puke. That's how it went.

It was miserable—and then it got worse. As demanding as the weight-lifting sessions were, the final phase of the workouts was what we dreaded most.

Conditioning drills.

"This is death," Schmidt would mutter to us, as we made our way to the field in the early morning darkness.

We were split into four groups. We all knew what was coming: 44 40-yard dashes . . . if we were lucky. And we never were.

We would run seven or eight 40-yarders and then we'd hear Coach Gregg.

"Ross, you loafed on that one! Everybody back on the line! We're doing it all over again!"

We'd groan, stare a hole through Ross, and start the sprint count over. We'd get through another six or so gassers and we'd hear Coach Gregg again. He had found another player to blame.

"Get on the line! Back to zero!"

By the time we were done, we had run nearly 100 40-yard gassers. Guys would peel over to the side of the track and puke out the remainder of their breakfast meals.

Forty-four 40-yard sprints equaled only a mile in distance. One hundred 40-yarders equaled only 2.27 miles. Easy, right? Except that we had just spent hours in the weight room, followed by sprints covering every inch of those 2.27 miles. Your lungs screamed. Your legs begged for mercy. The morning pancakes had no chance.

"The mind is way stronger than any muscle," Gregg would tell us. "Elk pride! We're going to be in the best shape of any team in the state."

I'm convinced that no other high school team in Dayton, Cincinnati, Columbus, Cleveland, or anywhere in Ohio got up at 4:30 a.m. for summer workouts. They sure as hell weren't running 100 40-yarders. Schmidt's younger brother played at Centerville and later joined the Marines. He said our conditioning drills were harder than what he went through at Parris Island for boot camp. I don't doubt it.

Practices weren't any easier. Coach Gregg was a disciple of Vince Lombardi, the legendary coach of the Green Bay Packers. Lombardi famously said, "Fatigue makes cowards of us all." Coach Gregg decided there would be no fatigue on our team.

It didn't happen often—maybe a half-dozen times a season— but Coach Gregg was known to look up at the sky and talk to the ghost of Lombardi.

"Vince," he would say, disgusted with one of our drills, "what am I going to do with these kids?"

When that happened, Schmidt would shoot me a look and a quick warning.

"Coach is talking to Vince today," he'd say. "This practice is going to be brutal."

And it always was.

Schmidt was convinced Coach Gregg had lost his mind. After all, who talks to an imaginary Lombardi? But I didn't mind. Coach Gregg was tough, but caring. He was trying to develop us as young men, and he used discipline as a way to wring everything out of us, even if we didn't think there was anything left to give.

Centerville, at least parts of it, was affluent. It had a little bit of a rich-kid reputation. Coach Gregg wanted to change that perception. He set standards: team first. You were going to sacrifice everything for the team. Not everyone bought into the philosophy. Each day as we walked into the locker room, we could see a blackboard in the coaches' office that listed the names of the players who had quit the team. Each week the list grew longer.

I started at quarterback for the 1985 JV team and later got called up to the varsity as a backup to our senior starter, Rob Carselle. I had a few good moments running Coach Gregg's signature veer offense (split back, triple option, read the defensive linemen, pitch or keep), including a backup appearance in a 58–7 blowout win against Dayton Carroll. I remember everything about my first varsity score. The play was called "38 Counter Trap" and I ran 75 yards for the touchdown.

My mom and grandmother—we called her "Mimi"—were sitting together at the game. My mom says that when I broke a few tackles and barreled into the end zone, my grandmother was in shock.

"Who was that?" she said. "Was that Kirk?"

She was used to seeing mild-mannered Kirk. Deferential, shy, quiet Kirk. But on the field, I felt transformed. At times, I felt more comfortable inside those lines than outside them. I was the ultimate gym rat. I spent hours alone as a kid and teenager practicing baseball and football. I made up games and competitions with myself. It was nothing for me to spend part of an entire afternoon throwing a ball against a wall and catching it hundreds of times until I could close my eyes and do it. Sports came naturally to me.

———

Teri returned from Europe in the spring of 1986 with a crazy collection of personal experiences. My sister, the one who had always been so responsible, so buttoned up, had done as she had promised: she had let loose across the pond.

I could barely believe the stories as she told them. The short version: She had met another young woman on the plane on the flight from the States to Paris. The woman had befriended her and offered her a place to stay in the city. By chance, a Frenchwoman at the Paris airport had suggested that a great way to learn French and the history of Paris was to tour all the churches in the city. The woman had also said that au pairs were in demand, in case she needed a more reliable housing option. During that search she had somehow ended up with the entourage of a Saudi Arabian prince and his son, who occupied the entire top floor of the ultra-exclusive George V Hotel near the Champs-Élysées. The prince had offered her a chance to travel the world with them. As part of the group, she had attended the birthday party of Princess Stephanie of Monaco. There were nightclubs, international actors and actresses, royalty—and then there was Teri.

It was almost impossible for me to comprehend. Princess Stephanie? Who is that? And why was my sister at her birthday party?

Saudi princes? World travel? Movie stars? We were lucky if we could afford HBO in our cable package.

Teri returned home exhausted and without any money. She

said she felt guilty that she had left me and John behind. But I never felt betrayed by her. If anything, I was happy for her. She deserved to experience a different kind of life.

Still, I was glad she was back. Our four-bedroom ranch wasn't the George V Hotel, but Teri now had a place to live for free. She quickly found a job working at a French restaurant (of course), and later returned to Wright State and eventually earned her college degree.

As for me, I worked out and played baseball for Centerville that spring. I was the starting third baseman, and we had a huge ball game coming up against Wayne High School. A week or so before the game, I kept having a sharp pain in my lower right abdomen. It felt like someone was sticking a knitting needle in my gut. I couldn't go to the bathroom, it was so painful.

My mom took me to the urgent-care doctor, who examined me and diagnosed the condition as gastritis. He gave me a prescription. I was sixteen and thought, "I've got the medicine. I can play with the pain."

I took the meds each morning, but the pain never subsided. If anything, it got worse.

When game day finally arrived, I was a mess. I knew something was wrong with me, but I didn't want to let my team down. I felt awful and looked awful. In fact, a few of the other players alerted my head coach, Tim Engleka. He called me into his office before the game.

"How you doing?" he said. "You okay?"

"I've got this pain in my side and it really hurts," I said.

"I'll tell you what—we won't put you in the starting lineup and we'll see it how it goes. Maybe we won't need you."

In the sixth inning, with the score tied 5–5, we had runners on second and third with two outs.

"Coach, if you need a pinch-hitter, I think I can pinch-hit," I told him.

He looked at me, not entirely sure this was a good idea. I insisted.

"Okay, you're in," he said.

I lined a hit to the outfield and stretched it into a double as two runs scored. As I slid headfirst into second base—just like Pete Rose did with the Reds—I felt a jolt of pain that overwhelmed my entire body. I honestly thought I was going to die in the middle of the infield.

I staggered up, raised my hand, and waved for Coach to jog out to second base.

"I gotta come out," I gasped.

I made my way to the dugout and found a spot at the end of the bench, where I sat shivering uncontrollably, even though someone had draped a heavy coat around my shoulders. We won the game, but by then I was as pale as a ghost. One of my buddies drove me home.

When I walked in, my mom couldn't believe how bad I looked. I told her I just needed to eat some dinner and then lie down for a while. I'd be okay.

After I ate, I struggled to get back to my room. I got in bed, but the pain was unbearable. I tried to call out to my mom or sister through the closed bedroom door, but I could barely manage a whisper. I was beginning to lose consciousness.

I had an idea. I reached for the phone on my bedside table and somehow dialed the number of my buddy, Dave Rosenbaum.

"Call my house," I told him, my voice fading out. "Tell my mom and sister to come back to my room. Fast."

Then I hung up the phone and hoped. I was this close to passing out.

The phone rang a few moments later, and then I heard footsteps running toward my bedroom. My mom and sister burst into the room, saw my condition, and rushed me to the hospital.

I wasn't there long before I was on an operating table for exploratory surgery. That's when the doctor discovered that my appendix had ruptured. He met with my mom and sister after the operation.

"I don't know how he's alive," the doctor told them. "He must have ruptured it when he slid into the base."

Pools of now-poisonous pus had been collecting in there so long that my system had been compromised. He said it was the worst case he'd ever seen.

I had a scar on my abdomen about a half-foot long. There was a drainage tube. They told me that the incision had to heal from the inside out, not the other way around. Once I got home, I had to take three baths a day to allow the incision area to remain clean and heal properly. They were insistent: three baths a day.

I followed the instructions on the first day. And on the second. But on the third day, I decided I was sick of taking three baths. So I took one, and everything seemed okay. The next day, I did the same thing. The incision area looked fine to me.

What I didn't realize is that the skin had begun to close up around the incision. There was no drainage. I had to go back to the doctor's office, where they lanced the skin. Pus flew everywhere.

I spent most of the next three months on my back as I recovered from the surgery. My weight dropped from 180 pounds to 160. Meanwhile, I kept hearing about a new quarterback, Jason Cantrell, who had transferred to Centerville from another school. Some of my teammates raved about his throwing arm, about his athleticism.

Great. I was stuck in bed. I had lost twenty pounds, and now there was some new hotshot quarterback.

During the off-season, Coach Gregg had traveled to the United States Air Force Academy in Colorado Springs, Colorado. He wasn't there to see its gorgeous campus, but to see Coach Fisher DeBerry's gorgeous wishbone offense.

For years, Centerville High had run the triple option through the veer formation: a quarterback under center, split backs in the backfield. We ran it to perfection, but our opponents had so much film on us, so much experience facing us, that Coach Gregg decided our offense needed to evolve. So he brought home the wishbone from Air Force, which featured the quarterback under center, a fullback, and two running backs in the backfield.

One way or another, I was going to be that quarterback. All I could think about was getting out of that bed and back onto a football field.

By the time training camp arrived, I had gained back most of the weight I had lost after the surgery. The triple option wishbone offense meshed perfectly with what I did as a quarterback. I was a physical quarterback who could run and was very comfortable with play-action off the option-based system. I loved the nuances of the option. Our offensive line wasn't big enough to block 235-pound defensive tackles. Instead, the triple option wishbone was built around reading the actions of the defensive tackles and ends. If they did one thing, we did this. If they did that, we did something else. Running the wishbone made it even more confusing for the defense.

In the middle of August, we had a scrimmage against Chaminade Julienne High School at Dayton's Welcome Stadium. The temperature on the artificial turf had to be close to 120 degrees. You could see the heat rise from the ground.

We wore down Chaminade with our running attack and played relatively well. Or, at least we thought we did.

After the scrimmage, Coach Gregg called us together and started cussing us out. He said we had made too many mistakes and began listing them one by one. He got so worked up he finally said, "Take your shoulder pads and helmets off. We're running a mile."

We had just played a full scrimmage in the sweltering summer heat. Our shirts were drenched with sweat. But nobody said a word. We were programmed robots. We took off our pads and helmets without complaint and moved to the starting line of the track that encircled the Welcome Stadium field.

The Chaminade players looked at us like we were crazy. But to us, the extra work was spinach, and we were Popeye. We were all about mental and physical toughness. Run a mile after a full scrimmage in August? No problem. We proudly ran the four laps in that heat.

That's how Coach Gregg worked. In 1986, that type of account-ability was acceptable. Today, they'd lock up a coach for doing that. But to us, it wasn't torture. It was a badge of honor.

Before I played for Coach Gregg, I thought I was a hard worker. I thought I knew about making a commitment. But this dude took me from what I thought was my max effort to a different strato-sphere. What I considered my limits weren't even close to what Coach Gregg brought out in me and our team. Without him, I would never have known the true meaning of hard work, of push-ing yourself to a place you didn't think you could reach, especially when it came to mental toughness. I still apply those lessons and principles decades later as a father, a husband, an employee. That's why all these years later I still have such love and respect for him. He helped me become the person I am today.

I won the starting job, and my debut at Centerville came against one of the three high schools I had considered: Cincinnati Prince-ton. Princeton was coached by Pat Mancuso, a Hall of Famer so respected that the school named the field in his honor. They were ranked as one of the top teams in the state and had more than a dozen major college prospects on their roster. They had speed all over the field. If Vegas had put a betting line on the game, Prince-ton would have been 21-point favorites.

We were undersized. I was bigger than our center, Craig

Schmidt, who was 5-foot-10, 185 pounds. In fact, when we stood in the huddle, I was taller than most of my offensive linemen.

But that was the great thing about the triple option wishbone attack. It was built for rosters like ours: average-sized players who were grinders, offensive linemen who crab-blocked, football soldiers who were willing to run through two walls for each other and Coach Gregg. We had good football players, but overall, we weren't the most athletic team. That's why the option offense worked at the service academies, where they couldn't recruit the best football talent. It emphasized decision making, deception, ball control, toughness, commitment. It forced a defense to be disciplined and smart. Coach Gregg always reminded us that we had guys who ran 5.0 40s—slow by football standards. "The other team might run faster than us in the first quarter," he said, "but by the fourth quarter they won't be able to catch us. We'll wear them down."

Princeton had no clue we were going to run a triple option wishbone. They had expected our usual veer formation. Its defense had a hard time finding the ball that night.

Instead of them beating us by three touchdowns, we trailed 21–14 with about three minutes left in the game. My man Schmidt, who was making his first varsity start, too, had to block a Princeton linebacker who would end up getting a full ride to Michigan State. I could actually hear the linebacker snorting in anger before each snap. But Schmidt found a way. We all did.

We drove down the field and scored with about forty seconds remaining. The conventional decision: kick the extra point, tie the game, and try to win in overtime.

Coach Gregg had other ideas. He gathered us together near the sideline.

"This is all you, boys," he said. "This is up to you. You want to go for the tie or for the win?"

It was the quickest vote in football history. We were going for two.

Even now, I can close my eyes and remember everything about the play: triple option to the right. I put the ball in the fullback's stomach as we moved down the line—would the defensive lineman positioned on the outside shoulder of the right guard move upfield toward me, or crash down toward the fullback? If he took me, I could hand it to the fullback off "the ride" for the possible score, or I could pitch it to the trailing running back, or keep it myself.

The defensive tackle moved upfield toward me. If I had read it properly, I would have handed the ball to our fullback. Instead, I made a mistake and kept it. Worse yet, they had our running back covered on the pitch play. So I faked a pitch, which caused the defensive tackle to freeze just for a moment, and then cut underneath him and dove into the end zone at the last moment for the huge 22–21 upset win.

I'm in my early fifties, but that touchdown and that win remain one of the top five favorite moments of my athletic career. It wasn't because I scored the touchdown but because of what that win meant for us as a team: huge underdogs against one of the best teams in the state, a new offense, a new starting quarterback.

My parents were at the game, but they didn't sit together. My mom stayed in the stands, and my dad watched from the sidelines, hands on knees, in full former-coach mode.

Afterward, my family, friends, and teammates piled into our house and watched the late local Dayton news shows, especially *Operation Football* on Channel 2. On a Friday night in Dayton, high school football usually was one of the top sports stories, along with the Buckeyes, the Reds, and the Bengals. That night, after that upset victory, we were one of the lead stories.

On Monday—and this was pre-internet days—I walked into our locker room and there was a telegram taped to my locker. Jon Berger, a senior on our team who was being recruited by multiple college programs, had put it there.

On the outside of the envelope was the Ohio State football logo. Inside was this: "Congratulations on the big win against Princeton. We'd like to offer you a scholarship."

I couldn't believe what I was reading. It blew me away. I was only a couple of days removed from my first start, a big win, and now this showed up? It was incredible. We had a 3 p.m. practice and I floated out to the field. It was such a cool moment. Ohio State wanted me!

Chapter 4

The Best Damn Fan in the Land

You have to understand that my life revolved around Ohio State football. My bedroom was painted scarlet and gray. The bedsheets were scarlet and gray. The light switch in my room read *Ohio State turns me on. Michigan turns me off.* I had a photo in my room of Woody talking to my dad on the sidelines when my dad was a player at Ohio State. I had Big Ten banners hanging on the wall.

As an eighth grader, I would watch an Ohio State game on TV and then afterward go into the backyard and re-create the key plays. Me and my dad did that together, or if he wasn't around, I'd find a neighborhood kid. If the game wasn't televised live (and pre-1984, before the Supreme Court ruled against the NCAA's iron-fisted hold on college football, there were only a couple of games on national television each week), I would intentionally not listen to the radio broadcast and instead wait until late Saturday night and watch the rebroadcast on WOSU with Paul Warfield as the game analyst.

I was the kid who knew every Ohio State player, every jersey number, every stat. I was the kid who, every Saturday morning before a Buckeyes game, played a record album made by the

Ohio State Marching Band. If it was a big game, I cranked that son of a gun up. I knew the introduction by heart:

"Allow us to introduce you to our musicians by section. First, the basses: the lowest-sound instruments in the band . . ."

And the sousaphones would play the first few notes of a song.

"And now the baritone horns, the next-higher voice to the basses . . ."

Then they'd play for a few seconds.

"The F horns have this unique sound. . . ."

And the F horns would play.

On and on it would go: the flügelhorns, the second cornets, the E cornets, the snare drums, the bass drums, cymbals, and tenors.

"Building layer by layer, when you put them all together, they sound like this . . ."

Then TBDBITL (The Best Damn Band in the Land—Woody coined the phrase) would belt out the "Buckeye Battle Cry." I got goose bumps—and I must have listened to that album a million times. It never got old. Still doesn't.

The weird part about that recruiting telegram? I never got another piece of recruiting correspondence from any school, including Ohio State, the rest of the season. But what a season . . .

We kept winning and winning. Better yet, our family was having a great time. My dad would work and stay in Cleveland during the week, but would return to Centerville in time for my Friday night lights and stay through the weekend. Sometimes he'd get back there on a Thursday night and help my mom cook a big pasta meal for a dozen or so of my teammates. There would be cardboard cutouts of our next opponent hanging from the ceiling and we would take turns taking playful punches at them.

In the kitchen area, we had a chalkboard that everyone would use as a message board. You know, *At the grocery store, be home by 4 . . .* that sort of thing.

My dad commandeered the board, and every Saturday morning, after he made a huge breakfast for everyone, including some of my teammates who had spent the night, he would stand there in his robe and break down the game on the chalkboard for me. This is what the nose guard did, this is where the linebacker went . . . he was in his coaching glory. He just loved the chalk dust flying up as he diagrammed the Xs and Os—and I loved it, too. At dinner he would sometimes pull out a pen and start diagramming a play on a paper napkin. He wasn't wearing me out. This was my wheelhouse. He was speaking my language. I couldn't get enough football from him.

Our house became the hangout house. All my friends loved my mom and dad. My dad was a nerdy kind of guy, super friendly, jovial, a rule follower, but always very welcoming. He read the latest cookbook by the famous chef Emeril Lagasse and then served up some sort of New Orleans–style dish to my teammates. He almost always had a pot of homemade chili on the stove, or some sort of stew, or steaks on the grill. It got to the point where my buddies would ask me, "Is your dad home this weekend?"

After all the crap we had been through growing up, my parents were incredible during my high school years. They really tried. They were involved in all facets of my life. It was as if we had come full circle.

My parents were friends. They were cordial. If my buddies were at the house talking football with my dad, it wasn't unusual for my mom to listen in, or even bring my dad a beer. When I got my driver's license, I had the same conversation that other teenagers had with their parents:

"Hey, Dad, where's the car keys?"

"They're on counter. Remember, be home by midnight."

As I'd walk out of the house, Mom and Dad would be sitting in the family room watching a movie together. It felt . . . weird and normal at the same time. Those are great memories for me.

I told a few of my closest friends about the arrangement, but everybody else thought my mom and dad were married. I let them think whatever they wanted to think. My buddies would come over to the house, see my parents, say, "What's up?" and then head back to my bedroom.

We finished the regular season undefeated and ranked No. 1 in the state. We also were the No. 1 seed in the state playoffs, but were upset in the first round by Dayton Dunbar. They had some dudes on that team.

After the season, Coach Gregg asked me to stop by his office. When I got there, he handed me a stack of mail. There were recruiting letters, dozens and dozens and dozens of them, from every major program. Now I knew why I hadn't received any more letters after the initial Ohio State note at season's beginning. Coach Gregg had become my mailbox. He didn't want me to have any distractions.

My dad said I could pick ten schools and fill out their recruiting questionnaires. I chose Penn State, Tennessee, Iowa, Florida State, Notre Dame, Pitt, Oklahoma, USC, Michigan, and, of course, Ohio State.

Throughout Ohio, but especially in Centerville, high school football meant everything. On a Friday night when we played a home game, it was like that scene in *Hoosiers* where the local stores closed and the town came to a complete standstill. If we played an away game, there was always a caravan of cars following our team bus. They loved their Elks.

Because of the success of our team, we got a lot of local newspaper and TV coverage. And because I was the quarterback and was being recruited by all the major programs, I received a lot of attention in the media, in the halls of Centerville High, and even in my own house.

I'm not a boastful person. I'm the complete opposite of being boastful. I understood why the quarterback of one of the best high school teams in the state was featured in headlines and stories—and I was fine with that, because it reflected on our whole team. I was being singled out, but for the right reasons. I had worked hard—our whole team had worked hard—and the positive attention was part of the reward. It wasn't going to change me. If anything, it was a reminder of the responsibility I had. I welcomed that role.

Inside my own house, there was a different kind of attention. Even though Mom and Dad were getting along great and there was a positive vibe in the house, I occasionally had to deal with being portrayed as the golden boy. My mom, like all moms, was extremely proud of her kids. In my case, she wasn't shy about mentioning my sports accomplishments to her sisters when they'd visit. She meant well, but it put me in an awkward position, not only with my aunts but with my brother John. He could have resented the attention paid to me, but instead he always seemed proud of me.

I prided myself on being a good kid. I didn't want to add any more stress to our family situation. My mom says I was the barometer of the family. If I was happy, then everyone else was happy. The thing is, I could sense them looking at me, waiting to see how I would react. I felt that pressure of not wanting to create any more tension. So even if something did upset me, I pretended it didn't. I absorbed the pain, rather than saying how I actually felt.

Over the years, having those antennae up all the time created stress. But eventually it also turned me into a piece of granite when it came to dealing with parent or family issues. If there was a problem, I flatlined emotionally. I didn't get upset. Instead, I stayed exactly in the middle, never too high or too low. I did that as a way to protect myself. I identified the problem and then took care of it. I've been that way for nearly the last forty years. As an adult, I live in the far right lane of the highway. I go 55 when it comes to living my life. I have my routine. I'm dependable. That was, and still is, my way of dealing with complicated situations. Turn off the emotions, turn on the problem solving.

————

On March 12, 1987, Woody Hayes died. He was seventy-four. His health hadn't been good for a number of years, but the news was still a shock in our house, and across the state of Ohio. It was personal to us. My dad had played for him and coached for him. You can't measure the impact he had on my dad's life—on a lot of lives, including mine.

I had sat on his knee as a little kid. I had heard my dad tell countless stories about him. I had watched dozens of his 205 career wins at Ohio State. I always remembered one of his favorite sayings, about how hard it is to pay back those who have helped us and loved us, but how easy it is to pay forward. In fact, that saying is engraved on the stone next to his statue at the Woody Hayes Athletic Center, which is where the football facility is located. And every Ohio State fan remembered the time a reporter asked Woody why, after scoring a touchdown in a 50–14 rout against Michigan in 1968, he went for a two-point conversion instead of kicking the extra point. Said Woody: "Because I couldn't go for three."

Despite his unceremonious firing, Woody still loved Ohio State until his last day. A year earlier, in the spring of 1986, his health failing, Woody gave the commencement speech at Ohio State. This is a man who had won more games than any Buckeye football coach (nobody else is close), who had won national championships, Big Ten titles, Rose Bowls, and coach of the year awards. But he called giving that commencement speech "the greatest day of my life."

That was Woody. People can forever connect him with that punch at the Gator Bowl, but my dad, our family, and all those players who played for Woody remember the fuller version of who he was and what he stood for.

That same spring, Bo Schembechler came to Centerville High on a recruiting visit. Michigan had beaten Ohio State seven of the last eleven games, including the last two in a row. The Wolverines had played in the Rose Bowl a few months earlier. Michigan was a perennial national force, and it was because of Bo.

Dad and I had taken an unofficial visit to Michigan after my junior season. Bo had pulled me aside and said, "I want to recruit you, but I want to know if I have a chance."

He also talked to my dad.

"Jimmy, let me know if you're uncomfortable with this," he said.

"Nah, I'm fine," my dad said. "This is his decision, not mine."

I had all but made up my mind to go to Ohio State, but I respected Bo so much that I wanted to be recruited by him. I didn't do it out of vanity. I wasn't one of those recruits who needed their ego stroked every day. I was legitimately intrigued and interested in the program.

First of all, Jim Harbaugh was my guy. I had watched him during his entire career as Michigan's starting quarterback. His senior season there was my junior season at Centerville. He played with such intensity, such passion, such toughness. I admired his style. That's how I wanted to play. His Michigan teammates fed off that intensity.

Michigan was a 1,000 percent perfect fit for me. It was a turnkey situation. They ran an offense that fit my skill set. Harbaugh was a senior. I trusted Bo and could see myself playing for him.

Bo was such an honorable man. In Woody's last months, it was Bo who had constantly checked on Woody and his wife, Anne. He was a friend until the very end. I also knew Bo was somebody my dad looked up to. Forget all the bullshit about the Ten Year War and the rivalry itself. Yes, my dad and Bo were fiercely competitive in football, especially when it came to Ohio State–Michigan. But they were friends first. Always friends.

When Bo came to Centerville High that day, our entire school buzzed with excitement. Everyone knew who Bo was. All my buddies wanted to meet him, including Schmidt.

"How you doing, young man?" Bo said to Schmidt. "What's your name?"

"Craig Schmidt, sir."

"What position do you play, son?"

"Coach, I'm a center."

Bo broke into a smile. He turned to me and said, "Damn, Herbie, that's why you need to come to Michigan. We've got real linemen up there."

My undersized center stared at his shoes.

"I'm just kidding with you, son," Bo said to Schmidt. "I'm sure you're a fine center."

Our senior season was a challenge. I was bigger than three of our starting offensive linemen. We were a team in transition and struggled early, losing our first three games, two of them by 34 and 30 points, respectively. But each week we got better. The losing streak ended and a winning streak began.

During my junior year, I had been hesitant to be a vocal leader. Time and time again, Coach Gregg had told me to take more responsibility, to take charge. But that wasn't my style. I always felt you had to earn the right to be a leader. It wasn't until later in that junior season—when I challenged one of my teammates during a game—that Coach Gregg said I had experienced a breakthrough.

My senior year was different. I wasn't hesitant to take charge, to lead. I was buddy-buddy in the locker room, but I picked my moments to yell at someone. If you were dogging it in practice or in a game, I wasn't afraid to confront you. But I preferred encouraging a teammate, motivating him. Most of all, I wanted to lead by example.

We won our remaining seven games (including three consecutive shutouts) and by the end of the 1987 season we were better than our No. 1–ranked team of a year earlier. In the days leading up to a late-season game against one of our biggest rivals, Fairmont, its star defensive player called me at home.

"Hey, Herbstreit, nobody is going to want you after this game," he said. "I'm tearing your knee up."

A Fairmont team hadn't beaten Centerville since 1975. But now, because we had struggled early, this guy thought he could call me at home and threaten to injure my knees so nobody would recruit me? You don't think I was counting the seconds until I got to play against *that* guy? I couldn't wait.

During the game we ran a play called "18 Counter Option." My job on the play was to read the defensive end, who happened to be the guy who had called my house that week. I took the snap, did a reverse pivot—and bam!—the defensive end was coming at me at 100 miles per hour, and with bad intentions. He wanted to hurt me.

Coach Gregg had taught us how to absorb a hit. If you want to survive as an option quarterback, you have to go limp as a wet rag the moment you're hit. A millisecond before he tackled me, I pitched the ball to our fullback, Deron Brown, and then relaxed my body as the defensive end stuck his helmet into my chest.

As soon as I had pitched it, I knew Deron had room to run. I rolled off the ground and started sprinting down the field after my fullback. Deron, who was built exactly how a fullback should be built—thick neck, stocky, cankles—rumbled down the field for 10, 20, 30, almost 40 yards before he was brought down. I nearly beat him to the spot. When I got there, I helped pull him up and started yelling, "See! You got this! That's what I'm talking about! We're going to whip their ass!"

And we did, 39–0. That Fairmont defensive end had been chirping at me early in the game, but now it was my turn. I didn't usually talk trash at the other team, but this guy had threatened me. Turns out he was kind of soft, a fake tough guy. As we kept piling on the touchdowns, he got quieter and quieter.

A week later, as we took the field against Springfield North, some of their fans held up a homemade sign that read, "Nightmare On Herbstreit." It was a play on that Freddy Krueger horror movie *A Nightmare on Elm Street*. Turns out the nightmare was on them; we won, 36–0.

That senior season was also when I gave my mom a football present for her birthday. During the season, I didn't have a job, and our family didn't have much money. There were no weekly allowances.

Her birthday was the same late October week as one of our games. Before I left that Friday for the field, I told her I was going to give her a touchdown as a gift. Later that night, after I scored in the game, I pointed up to the stands where she was sitting. It wasn't much, but I knew it would matter to her. She cared about me, and I wanted her to know I cared about her. I couldn't afford to buy her a real present, so I tried to do the next-best thing.

There is a tradition at Centerville High called Senior Talk, in which each senior addresses the coaching staff before the last regular season game. For me, it was a chance to thank Coach Gregg and his assistants for their commitment, their love, their encouragement, their time. That night I thanked them with tears running down my face. I poured out my heart because they had done the same during our four years at Centerville. Decades later, I still talk to my former teammates about Elk Pride. I talk to my own sons about the values taught to me by Coach Gregg.

Coach Gregg retired after the 1999 season. In twenty-seven years at Centerville, he won 301 games. The victories are impressive, but his real impact goes deeper than that. It's the reason why so many of us returned to Centerville for his eightieth birthday in 2013, and why we'll keep coming back to honor the man who meant so much to us.

Unfortunately, we didn't make the playoffs in 1987. Because of the way the postseason was structured, we missed out. But in many ways, it was such a satisfying season because of how we improved and what we overcame. That's what I've always loved about football. It makes things hard for you and then gives you a choice: Are you going to fight through an obstacle, or not fight at all? Playoffs or no playoffs, our team fought.

At season's end, I was named to the *Parade* Magazine High School All-America Team. That was a big deal back then. Todd Marinovich, a quarterback from Capistrano Valley High in Mission Viejo, California, was also on that team. He was a classic pocket passer who had thrown for a then–national high school record 9,182 career yards and 73 touchdowns (the last time I looked, the career high school passing record was 18,932 yards). That was mind-boggling to me. I threw for 874 yards and seven touchdowns my senior season and rushed for 445 yards and 15 touchdowns. But we were a triple-option team and I was an option quarterback, or what they would call a "dual threat" quarterback in recruiting language today. You're either a "pro style" quarterback or "dual threat."

Quarterbacks Tony Sacca, Darian Hagan, and Bret Johnson were also on that team. Running backs Raghib Ismael, Kevin Williams, O. J. McDuffie, and Rodney Culver were on that team. The wide receivers included Derek Brown and Carl

Pickens. Chester McGlockton was one of the defensive linemen. The team was loaded with elite talent.

When the recruiting process first started for me, it was a cool experience. The college coaches would call my house on our landline and I would talk to them about their program, their roster, their academics, their facilities, their campus—you name it, they talked about it. After a few months of that, I'd had it. I quit answering the phone. Instead, I let my parents field the calls. It got to the point that when the phone rang, I'd give my mom and dad the "I'm-not-here" gesture.

Even though everyone assumed I was going to Ohio State, there was a part of me that wanted to keep people guessing. Sometimes I would wear a Michigan ball cap to school, just to plant the seed that I was having second thoughts.

As our season ended in late fall, Ohio State's season still had a few weeks left to go. As usual, Buckeyes fans expected nothing less than a Big Ten title and a Rose Bowl appearance. But Ohio State lost to Michigan State at the end of October, and then lost at Wisconsin. The Buckeyes were 5-3-1 and 3-3 in the Big Ten. They weren't going to the Rose Bowl, but they still could go to a bowl game.

My buddies were at my house for the November 14 home game against Iowa. Dad made his usual pot of chili, and we sat in the living room as Ohio State took a 27–22 lead with 2:45 left to play. Iowa had beaten Ohio State only once in the previous twenty games. Now they had to try to put together a game-winning drive at the Shoe, and against a Buckeyes defense that hadn't given up a passing touchdown in fourteen quarters. Good luck with that.

Somehow Iowa got to the Ohio State 28-yard line, but it didn't have any timeouts left and faced a fourth-and-23. Quarterback Chuck Hartlieb took the snap and found tight end Marv Cook at the 10-yard line, and Cook dragged Ohio State's Ray Jackson and Sean Bell into the end zone with six seconds remaining in the game.

We couldn't believe what we had seen. The miracle finish meant Ohio State had lost three in a row for the first time since 1971. Worse yet, it meant Earle Bruce, the guy who had first offered me a scholarship as a junior at Centerville, was on the hottest of hot seats. His critics—mostly disgruntled fans—called him "Eight-and-Three Earle," a reference to four of his nine years when Bruce finished the regular season 8-3. At almost any other program, eight regular season wins would be considered a success. At Ohio State, you got blasted on the local talk shows and in the newspapers.

That loss set into motion a chain of events that would cost Bruce his job and affect my life in ways I wasn't aware of at the time.

A few days after the Iowa defeat, which dropped the Buckeyes to 5-4-1, Ohio State president Ed Jennings told athletic director Rick Bay to fire Bruce. Bay refused and said he would resign in protest. Bay thought the firing was unfair: Bruce had an 80-26-1 record at the time, had led the Buckeyes to Big Ten championships and Rose Bowls (and eight consecutive bowls in all), and had run the program with integrity. To fire him, said Bay, would send the wrong message, that Ohio State was only concerned about wins and losses. Remember, this is the same school that didn't allow the 1961 team to accept a Rose Bowl bid because it was worried about the balance between football and the university's academic mission.

It didn't matter. Bay announced his resignation at the same news conference that he announced the school's decision to fire Bruce ("It's a dark day for OSU," Bay said of Bruce's dismissal).

Jennings took a lot of heat for the firing, and deservedly so. Bruce wasn't universally loved by Buckeyes fans (if they could turn on Woody, they could turn on anybody), but he was respected. It wasn't just that he was fired, but it was when (the week of the Michigan game, and with a year left on his contract) and how he was fired (Jennings didn't have the nerve to attend the press conference). As the news spread, members of the Ohio State Marching Band gathered in front of Bruce's house and played "Carmen Ohio." When Bruce saw them play, he was moved to tears.

There were two twists to Bruce's firing: 1) he would still be allowed to coach in the season finale at Michigan, and 2) I was going to be at that same game, not as an Ohio State fan but as a Michigan recruiting prospect.

On November 21, 1987, I was at the Big House wearing a Michigan recruit sticker on the front of my coat. My dad had driven me and Deron up to Ann Arbor for the recruiting visit. When it came time for the game, Michigan seated us in the stands with the rest of the Wolverine recruits.

Michigan and Ohio State were both unranked, but the Wolverines were favored. They were headed to a bowl, win or lose. The Buckeyes were headed nowhere. The administration had even canceled the annual football banquet.

It was weird sitting in the Michigan section of the stadium. I saw the players take the field, and the Buckeyes were all wearing headbands. Word trickled up to the stands: the Ohio State players had written "EARLE" on the headbands.

Michigan was up, 13–0, in the second quarter and was dominating the game. But Ohio State scored after a turnover and trailed at halftime, 13–7. Then it took the lead when true freshman running back Carlos Snow took a short pass and turned it into a 70-yard touchdown.

Michigan tied the game late in the third quarter, but Ohio State kicked a field goal midway through the fourth quarter and held on for the upset win.

I know I was a guest of Michigan, but I couldn't help myself. Deep down, I was still that seven-year-old kid who lived and died with Ohio State. As the final seconds ticked off the clock, the Ohio State players put Bruce on their shoulder pads and carried him off the field. Most of the Buckeyes fans who had made the trip to Michigan Stadium began to storm the field. Deron and I looked at each other.

"I'm going down, too!" I said.

Deron was right behind me.

So, yes, I might be the first Michigan recruit to celebrate an Ohio State victory at midfield of the Big House. But I couldn't help it. At one point, there were so many Ohio State fans on the field that Deron literally got swept away by the crowd. His feet weren't even touching the ground.

We eventually made our way to the main stadium tunnel. The Michigan locker room was on the right, the visitors' locker room to the left. As we stood there, Carlos Snow saw me and said, "Hey, man, we need you at Ohio State."

My dad walked us to the door of the Michigan locker room and told the security guard, "Can you let Bo know that we're out here?"

A few moments later, the guard let us into the locker room, where the dejected Michigan players were peeling off their uniforms. We met Bo in a separate room. It was just me, my dad, and Bo.

Bo started breaking down the game.

"Jimmy, what'd you think?" Bo said to my dad.

My dad was more excited about the Ohio State win than I was. But once a coach, always a coach. He and Bo talked about certain plays and momentum shifts.

Suddenly the door to the room burst open and it was freakin' Earle Bruce, wearing his signature fedora and suit coat outfit. He started yelling at Bo, telling him about the circumstances of his firing.

"The president at Ohio State had it out for me!" he said.

Bo, who had publicly criticized Ohio State for the firing, said, "I hear you, Earle. I know. I know."

Earle was beside himself as he vented to Bo. His lips were quivering with anger. He pounded the desk. He looked like he could run through a cinder-block wall.

Then he saw me and my dad sitting on the couch. He stared at my Michigan recruit sticker in disbelief.

"What the *hell* are you doing in here?!" he said. And then he stormed out of the room.

Just thinking about his reaction, I get scared again.

Bruce won 81 of his 108 games at Ohio State for a 75.5 winning percentage. Woody won 76.1 percent of his games. Bruce won five of the eight bowl games he coached. He was a Buckeye through and through. And he got fired.

There was a lawsuit brought by Bruce against Ohio State and lots of ugly accusations after his firing. A settlement was quickly arranged, and Ohio State began its search for a new head coach.

I liked Earle. I would have been proud to have played for him. But it didn't really matter to me who Ohio State hired as his replacement. They could have hired Elmer Fudd or one of the band's sousaphone players, and I was still going to Ohio State.

Instead, on December 31, they hired Arizona State coach John Cooper.

I didn't know a thing about Cooper. Nothing. He had coached on the other side of the country in the then Pac-10 Conference. His ASU team had beaten Bo and Michigan in the Rose Bowl a season earlier (that, I watched). When he was hired by Ohio State, he was fresh from a 7-4-1 season and a win against Air Force in the Freedom Bowl.

Cooper flew from Southern California to Columbus at midnight, arrived early that morning, met with the school's board of trustees, and had his introductory news conference at noon. There were about five hundred people at the news conference. I watched on TV.

According to the media reports, Cooper beat out West Virginia's Don Nehlen and Kent State's Glen Mason (an Ohio State alum) for the job. Ohio State had reached out to Nebraska's Tom Osborne and UCLA's Terry Donahue, but both coaches said they weren't interested. Cooper received a five-year contract for about $400,000 a year. His overall package at Arizona State was slightly higher than the one he got at OSU, but as Arizona State athletic director Charles Harris told *Sports Illustrated* when he lost Cooper: "Ohio State is Ohio State. They still dot the *i* there."

One of the first things Cooper said at the press conference: "I feel we can win a national championship at Ohio State. It's better to aim for the sky and hit an eagle than aim for an eagle and hit the ground."

Ohio State hadn't won a national championship since 1968, so this was music to the ears of Buckeyes fans.

Cooper made a point of mentioning a sheet of paper he had with him that day. He had told the new athletic director, Jim Jones, that he would interview any of Bruce's assistant coaches who were interested in staying at OSU. He asked each of those assistants to submit a list of Ohio State's top recruiting targets. My name was on all those lists.

Cooper put together a master list, and that's what he brought with him that day to the news conference. Of course, Cooper knew as much about me as I knew about him.

A few days earlier, my dad had called Jones and told him that I was done with the recruiting process.

"He's ready to become a Buckeye," he said. "I just wanted to let you know that, in case you think it might help with recruiting."

Only a few minutes after the news conference was done, the phone rang. It was Cooper.

We talked for a few minutes and he officially offered me a scholarship. I committed then and there. It had to be the easiest and quickest recruiting commitment of Cooper's career. He didn't even have to drive to our house from Columbus for an in-house visit. I was that easy.

I had dreamed of that moment my entire life. I had a one-track mind, and Ohio State was the only school on the track.

It was like Cooper handed me a contract and I didn't care about reading any of the fine print. What kind of offense did he run? I didn't care—I'd figure it out. Who was his offensive coordinator? Got me. Was Cooper the right head coach for me? Well, if he was good enough for Ohio State, I guess he was good enough for me, right?

Nothing was going to stand between me and my dream. I wanted to wear scarlet and gray. I wanted to play at the same school as my dad. So on Cooper's first day on the job, he was able to put a check mark next to my name on that recruiting list.

My decision wasn't a surprise to my friends, my family, or to any of the other schools recruiting me. My teammates and family were happy and excited for me. It wasn't until years later that I learned that my parents had secretly wanted me to play for Bo. True to their word, though, they had left the decision up to me. Even if they had told me their secret wish, I still would have committed to Ohio State. I loved Bo, but I loved Ohio State more.

My commitment was important to Cooper. I was a five-star, in-state recruit. Cooper got a late start on recruiting, so he needed to keep as many of the top Ohio high school players as he could. He ended up with three top-100 in-state signees: me, offensive lineman Corey Pargo, and running back/defensive back Buster Howe, who was Ohio's Mr. Football that year.

But Cooper missed out on two *Parade* All-Americans: Chuck Webb, a running back from Toledo who signed with Tennessee, and O. J. McDuffie, a running back from suburban Cleveland who signed with Penn State. A lesser-known running back from Cleveland, Desmond Howard, signed with Michigan. He was interested in Ohio State until it fired Bruce. Like me, he didn't know anything about Cooper or the offense he planned to run. Unlike me, he was also concerned about being part of a rebuilding program with a coach who came from outside the program. Instead, he went to Ann Arbor without taking so much as an unofficial visit to Ohio State.

After I officially signed with Ohio State in February 1988, Cooper said: "I'm excited about Herbstreit. He's a good athlete. He came out of a good program and he wants to play here. Any coach in the state who played against him will tell you how good he is."

The truth is, Cooper had never seen me play in person. It's doubtful he saw film of me before he offered me a scholarship. And I'm not sure he knew Coach Gregg's name at the time. He has said it himself in the past: he had no idea what kind of player I was. He only knew that I had been recruited heavily and that I was an Ohio State legacy recruit. I guess we both took leaps of faith with each other.

With football done and my recruiting officially finished, I tried to enjoy the home stretch of high school. I played baseball, but unlike my junior season, when I hit .505 (I could run a little bit—eight triples, 13 doubles), there weren't any major-league scouts evaluating me this time. As soon as I verbally committed to Ohio State and later signed my National Letter of Intent, the scouts disappeared.

I hit .472 as a senior, and Coach Engleka is convinced I would have been taken in the 1988 MLB Amateur Draft if I hadn't decided to play football at Ohio State. Who knows, right? I had good range, was faster than I looked, could play defense, had a strong arm, and loved to hit. Had I been drafted, Engleka says I would been moved to first base or left field. (By the way, in 1988 my *Parade* All-American teammate Marinovich was drafted in the forty-third round by the then California Angels as a pitcher. Nineteen rounds later, the Los Angeles

Dodgers took Mike Piazza, future Hall of Famer.) Somewhere—maybe my mom still has it—is a home run ball I hit during my senior season. It shattered the window of a woman's car. She brought the ball to the dugout. It still had pieces of glass in it.

Do I think about baseball sometimes? Sure. Human nature. I loved baseball. Still do. Some of my favorite memories are from playing high school baseball, or going to old Riverfront Stadium with some of my teammates to watch the Reds play. We would buy "Top Six" tickets, which cost only three dollars but were located in the top six rows of the stadium. As the game would move from inning to inning, we would sneak from our Top Six seats down to the red seats, which were a little lower, then down to the yellow seats, then to the green seats, which weren't bad, and then finally to the blue seats, which were the prime seats at field level. You had to have a blue ticket stub to get past the ushers for those seats.

I always kept in my wallet a blue ticket stub I'd found from a previous game. As I approached the usher, I'd flash him the ticket—just long enough that he could see it was blue, but brief enough that he couldn't read the date. The key was to project an air of confidence, like you belonged in the blue seats, that you were a blue seats kind of guy. You didn't want to make the mistake of hesitating and saying, "Am I okay with these?" No, no, no. You had to sell it. You looked at the usher's name tag and confidently said, "Hey, Bob, good to see you again." And you kept moving.

We'd get about six steps past the usher and start high-fiving each other in celebration. There was an air-conditioned area behind the home plate seats that had a bar and concession stand. That's where I liked to hang out. No sweating there.

Before I graduated from Centerville, there was one last bit of drama. It came in English class, and it involved public speaking and my teacher, Ms. Jeri Neidhard.

Everyone in the class was required to give a speech. Ms. Neid-hard had worked her way alphabetically from A through G. When she got to H and Herbstreit, there was an impasse.

"Kirk, it's your turn, please," she said. "Go ahead."

I had made a vow as a freshman that I would never give another speech. I had embarrassed myself that day, and I wasn't going to do it again. I made a stand.

"I'm good," I said to Ms. Neidhard.

Ms. Neidhard was perplexed.

"What do you mean, you're good?" she said.

"I'm good," I said. "I'm okay. I'm not going to give a speech."

"Kirk, you realize this speech represents twenty-five percent of your grade. You realize you're going to get a zero, don't you?"

"Doesn't matter what you say. I'm good."

I got a zero on the assignment. It was worth losing all 25 percent of that grade *not* to give a speech. I still passed the class and received my Centerville High School diploma later that spring.

If not for sports and the full scholarship to Ohio State, I wouldn't have gone to college. My parents couldn't afford to send me to school. My mom put it bluntly: she said I had to take care of it, that it was "my job." And it wasn't just me. Teri paid her own way through college, and had student loan debt into her forties.

Instead of college, I would have enlisted in the Marines or the Army. I didn't have a plan. Sports was always my plan. Ohio State was always my dream. And now, the two of them were going to intersect in the fall of 1988.

With the exception of a freshman English class speech, my high school years were great. Coach Gregg and Coach Engleka were everything you could want from a head coach: fair, disciplined, tough, compassionate, consistent. I still hear their voices today in my own life, and I apply their lessons to my own sons.

———

As I got in the car that August day to drive to Ohio State with my dad, I was overwhelmed with a sense of excitement, a touch of anxiety, and maybe a little sadness, too. During my four years of high school, the truce between my mom and dad had held firm. They had coexisted, and the result was a form of normalcy that made me think, "So *this* is what it's like to have a family."

I hugged my mom hard the day I left. That was a tough one. I said goodbye to my friends, such as Hutto, who was like a brother to me. I said goodbye to Teri.

As we pulled out of the driveway and I waved goodbye to my mom and then glanced at my dad next to me, I wondered, "What are my parents going to do? Are they going to stay together, or drift apart now that I'm gone?"

We hadn't talked about it, but I was pulling for them and some sort of reconciliation. I was pulling for us. Deep down, I think my mom wanted things to work out between them. She was still that girl from California who had come back east to marry my dad decades earlier. She still cared for him.

Even though Ohio State was only seventy-eight miles from Centerville, it seemed like 1,078 that day. When we got to campus, my dad could sense my apprehension.

"Kirk," he said, "you're going to walk into that locker room and you're going to see twenty-one other freshmen kids, and just like you, they're all going to have credentials: all-state, players of the year. But mark my words: at the end of four years here, there won't be more than thirteen of them that end up playing."

"You're crazy," I said. "They're all great players."

"You watch," he said. "Some of them will get homesick and leave. Some of them will flunk out. Some of them will get their girlfriends pregnant and leave. Some of them will get tired of football and leave. So don't be intimidated when you walk into that locker room."

More than thirty years earlier, my dad had walked into the Ohio State locker room with far fewer football credentials than I had. He was an undersized kid from a small town in Ohio. He wasn't scared then, and he was telling me not to be scared now.

In that car, at that moment, he spoke to me as a former Ohio State team captain to an incoming Ohio State freshman quarterback. But when it was time to part ways that day, we shook hands and hugged not as ballplayers separated by generations, but as something more meaningful to me.

As father and son.

Chapter 5

Nobody's All-American

O nly a few days into my Ohio State football career, I knew I had a major problem.

I was in the wrong offense, playing for the wrong coach, trying to fit in at the wrong time. I even got the wrong jersey number. I wanted No. 14 (my Centerville High number), but they gave me No. 19 as a true freshman. It matched my age.

If you listened to the local sports talk stations in Columbus, Cleveland, or Cincinnati—there were Ohio State fans everywhere—the general narrative was this: "We got this kid Herbstreit out of Centerville; he'll take us to three Rose Bowls."

I was the *Parade* All-American. I was all-everything on the *USA Today*, *Street & Smith*, and *Sporting News* teams, and the Ohio Player of the Year. But it became abundantly clear after only a couple of practices at fall camp that I had no chance to compete for the Ohio State starting job. In fact, I wasn't sure I was going to be listed among the top three quarterbacks on the depth chart.

I wasn't getting any reps in practice, and when I did, it was obvious that I lacked confidence. You can't fake football. You either produce or you don't, and I wasn't producing at all.

Cooper and his offensive coordinator Jim Colletto ran the I-formation, but with an emphasis on more passing than previous Ohio State teams. Seven-step dropbacks, five-step dropbacks, read what the strong safety is doing, identify the middle linebacker, figure out if the secondary is in zone or man-to-man, determine the pass protections—my head was spinning.

I ran the triple option my entire high school career. I *never* dropped back in high school. I ran down the line; I didn't drop back behind it. I read the defensive line, not the secondary. If we had a three-hour practice at Centerville, we spent thirty minutes, tops, on our passing game. It wasn't a priority to Coach Gregg.

Now I'd parachuted into a completely different offense, with different coaches, who had different sensibilities than Coach Gregg. It was like speaking English your whole life and suddenly you have to speak fluent Hungarian. Mentally, it was almost like playing football left-handed.

Imagine asking Tom Brady to run the wishbone triple option. He wouldn't have a clue. But I had run the option ten thousand times. I understood its every nuance. I appreciated its underrated sophistication. You put the ball in the belly of the fullback—he's holding it 50 percent, I'm holding it 50 percent, and we're both reading what the defensive end and tackle are doing. Then, depending on how they act, we react.

I knew that world. Running the option was like breathing to me. It just came naturally, almost involuntarily.

Now as I settled under the center for the snap—that is, when I actually got a rep in practice—I was *thinking*, not playing. Worse yet, I was worrying. There was no rhythm, no consistency to my play.

By the time fall camp ended, I was buried low on the depth chart. It didn't come as a surprise when the coaches told me I was being redshirted.

"This way you can learn the offense," they said.

I was disappointed in myself, rather than frustrated with the Ohio State coaches. I had made the decision easy on them. Cooper had said when he took the job that he intended to redshirt more freshmen as a way to build roster depth. I just didn't think I'd be one of them.

We finished 4-6-1 that year (2-5-1 in the Big Ten), the worst Ohio State record since 1959, my dad's junior year, when the Buckeyes were 3-5-1. Cooper's honeymoon period didn't last long. The same people who had ripped "Eight-and-three Bruce" were suddenly looking at those days with fond memories.

My season was spent on the scout team. I was designated as a nontraveling player, which meant no road games for me. I watched them on TV just like everyone else.

On the night before home games, we didn't stay in the team hotel like the rest of the players. We stayed in our campus dorms and then reported to the stadium fifteen minutes before the team bus arrived. We dressed in a separate locker room than the rest of the team, too. But we did get to go out onto the field for warm-ups, which was a huge deal as a redshirt freshman.

Sometime during my true freshman year, my dad moved back to Cleveland full-time. There would be no reconciliation with my mom. He had said he would live with us during my high school years, and he had kept that promise. But his departure was devastating to all of us, especially to Mom. It was like a second divorce. I'm not sure any of us ever got over it.

He had met a woman in Cleveland who had three children of her own. Once again, we were a family split in two.

———

Football was my escape, but my second season at Ohio State wasn't much different than my first, though I did dress and travel with the team. I also wore a different jersey number: No. 4, in honor of my favorite player, Jim Harbaugh. Of course, that wasn't something I mentioned to our equipment manager when the number became available.

Cooper made some changes to his coaching staff, including one change that would almost eventually drive me from the game I loved. Colletto remained as the offensive coordinator, but Cooper switched Ron Hudson from running backs coach to quarterbacks coach. I didn't know much about Hudson, but I would learn.

I still was struggling to find my way in Colletto's offense. Greg Frey, a junior who threw for 2,028 yards and eight touchdowns in Cooper's first season, was our undisputed starter. In the 1989 media guide, where it detailed the season outlook, there was no mention of me. I wasn't listed in the two-deep on the preseason depth chart. Instead, another redshirt freshman named Nick Cochran was designated as the backup.

Complicating matters was the arrival of Kent Graham, a big-armed, big-bodied (6-foot-5, 236 pounds) transfer quarterback from Notre Dame. Graham was a huge get for Lou Holtz two years earlier, but he sat behind Tony Rice in 1988 as Notre Dame won the national championship.

"I like what Cooper and his staff are trying to do there," he told a UPI reporter.

I didn't like what Cooper was doing by having Graham transfer in. Graham would have to sit out the 1989 season, but he would be eligible in 1990.

Meanwhile, my media guide bio was polite in its description: "One of three redshirt freshmen vying to back up Greg Frey . . . excellent runner . . . ran a wishbone attack in high school, but has a good arm and throws particularly well on the move . . . good ballhandler with excellent fakes . . . has the athletic ability to scramble out of trouble . . . very highly recruited in high school . . . John Cooper's first recruit."

For the record, Cooper's first-ever Ohio State recruit made his first-ever Ohio State appearance on September 16, 1989, in our season opener against Oklahoma State. The Cowboys' starting quarterback was future Oklahoma State head coach Mike Gundy.

We won, 37–13, and I got a few minutes of garbage time. I completed two of four passes for 17 yards. The Ohio Stadium stats crew was so impressed by my performance that they spelled my name *Herbstriet* in the official postgame sheets distributed to the media.

We were ranked 25th in the AP poll after the win and then traveled to Los Angeles the following week for a game against No. 12 USC at the Los Angeles Coliseum. I had been on an airplane once, maybe twice, before I boarded our team flight.

As we began our descent into LAX, I was amazed by the sheer size of the city and the urban sprawl that stretched as far as the eye could see. On the way in, we flew over the Coliseum, and I felt like a kid as I stared down at the famous stadium. It was like football Disneyland to me.

I knew Ohio, or most of it. That was my backyard. California was like a foreign country. I grew up watching Notre Dame play USC in the Coliseum, but the day that mattered most to us was New Year's Day: the Rose Bowl. We'd watch the parade in the morning, then wait for the game to begin. You'd see that gorgeous stadium, the blue skies, the San Gabriel Mountains, the sun beginning to dip below the peaks. Maybe the blimp would show the Pacific Ocean in the distance. Then we'd look out our front window and there would be two feet of snow and a bag of rock salt on the front stoop.

The Coliseum wasn't the Rose Bowl, but it was historic and impressive. It was a perfect 74 degrees and sunny when we took the field. I looked over at the Trojans' marching band, which calls itself the Spirit of Troy, and it seemed like every member was wearing sunglasses. There were the USC Song Girls in those iconic white sweater tops and, well . . . we weren't in Columbus anymore.

On the other sideline was Marinovich, who was USC's starting quarterback as a redshirt freshman. I watched him during warm-ups. He was so cocky. He just knew he was good.

We took a 3–0 lead, and then Marinovich and the Trojans scored the next 42 points. Their band never quit playing. And I think their horse, Traveler V, got exhausted running around the outer track after every touchdown.

Marinovich picked us apart, throwing for 246 yards and four TDs. He had the time of his life out there.

By the end of the third quarter, USC led 35–3, but it felt like 80–3. They were so much faster, quicker, and more athletic than we were. They would go on to win the Pac-10 and beat Michigan in the Rose Bowl that season. They were an all-star team.

As I stood on the sidelines and watched the carnage, I prayed that I wouldn't get into the game. But when it became obvious there was no chance for a comeback, one of the coaches told me to warm up.

Oh my god, really? You sure?

With 8:05 left in the fourth quarter and USC still leading by 32 points, I replaced Frey in the lineup. He was angry he'd been taken out of the game. I wanted to tell him, "It's okay with me if you want to stay in." A few other backups also entered the game.

We had a holding call on the first play, gained two yards, then five yards, and then faced a third-and-13 from our own 17.

The play came in from the sideline: the coaches wanted me to run a play-action pass, because, you know, down by 32 points, USC's defense is going to be terrified by the threat of a fake handoff by a redshirt freshman quarterback midway through the fourth quarter of a game where our offense would finish with 88 net rushing yards. Yeah, that'll work.

I walked up to the line, and there was consensus All-American safety Mark Carrier—No. 7. I was staring right into his eyes. Tim Ryan, an All-American defensive tackle for USC, was on the field, too.

Then I glanced to my left and there was the scariest sight known to opposing quarterbacks: USC outside linebacker Junior Seau—No. 55. Seau would be named the Pac-10 Defensive Player of the Year, as well as a first-team All-American in 1989. In 1990 he would be selected as the fifth overall pick in the NFL Draft and, years later, be voted into the Pro Football Hall of Fame.

On that day, he looked like a football god and ran like a running back. He was everywhere. I was in awe as I watched him from the sideline. We didn't have *anybody* like that.

Now I was on the same field as him. On third-and-13 late in the game, Seau didn't try to disguise what he was going to do. As I settled under the center, Seau inched up to the very edge of the line and positioned himself on the outside shoulder of my left offensive tackle, second-stringer Roy Nichols.

Two thoughts crossed my mind: "Why in the hell is the USC first-team defense still on the field?" And, "Roy Nichols is not going to be able to block this guy." Nichols was a converted defensive lineman who backed up our starting tackle, Joe Staysniak.

Had there been time for a third thought, it would have been, "Our Father, who art in heaven, hallowed be thy name . . ."

The snap count was on the sound of a color, in this case "Blue." The ball was snapped, and I moved to my right to fake a handoff to our running back. Then, after the fake handoff, I was going to set up for the pass. That was the plan.

Out of the corner of my eye I saw Nichols. He hadn't moved. He was still frozen in his stance!

Nichols apparently had thought the snap count was going to be on a number, such as "Ready, set, hut one!" In that nanosecond that I saw Roy standing motionless like a terra-cotta soldier, I knew I was already dead.

You know how you can hear a train in the distance? And then suddenly it's there, 3,000 horsepower bearing down upon you, air horn blaring, the power of the machine beyond comprehension. That was Seau. After his first step, Seau was already by Nichols. Nichols literally never touched him.

I had barely completed my fake handoff when Seau hit me. He was the freight train, I was the penny on the track. He flung me to the ground like I was an empty water bottle. Had I been more confident, more experienced, I would have felt the pressure and known to cut upfield. Instead, I was a mechanical redshirt freshman, thinking instead of playing. I was so concerned about executing the fake to the back, setting up on the inside leg of the right tackle as I dropped back, looking downfield . . . that I had no chance escaping Seau, who came around the corner like his cleats were on fire.

As I stared up at the beautiful blue Southern California sky that afternoon, a shadow appeared over me for an instant. It was Seau again, his arms outstretched in victory. He pranced around after the sack, acting like a badass, which he was. I just wanted to go home.

As I got to my knees and then stood up, Seau glanced back at me. He had a look of triumph and satisfaction. I stared back at him and said with the utmost respect, "Yessir, you're the Man."

And he was.

I didn't play again until four games later, just long enough to complete a pass to one of our guys, and to one of Purdue's. There was another DNP (Did Not Play), mop-up duty against Northwestern, Iowa, and Wisconsin, and then I sat on the bench during our loss to Michigan (Bo's final regular-season game as head coach) and also during our bowl loss to Auburn. We finished 8-4, and as usual, I was frustrated with my lack of progress.

I had played only 27 total minutes in 1989, completing four of nine passes for 48 yards and zero touchdowns in six games. I did my best to learn behind Frey, but it was obvious that Colletto was not a big fan of mine. I didn't fit his West Coast offense.

Meanwhile, Cooper recruited over me, signing Joe Pickens, a five-star-type, classic pocket passer from St. Ignatius, just outside Cleveland. That was in addition to Cooper's decision to bring in Graham from Notre Dame.

Much like me several years earlier, Pickens had been recruited by every major program in the country. He had led St. Ignatius to consecutive state titles and had never lost as a starter. Ohio State actually sent a university plane to Cleveland to bring Pickens and another big-time recruit, Euclid High School running back Robert Smith, to Columbus for their official visit.

There was nothing subtle about what Cooper and Colletto were doing. If they had been confident in the way I was trending, they wouldn't have encouraged Graham to transfer in. They might not have signed Pickens—or Pickens might not have signed with Ohio State early in 1990. My status as QB2 was in trouble.

I did what I always did: I worked harder. I worked on my technique, my reads, my dropbacks. I got bigger, stronger in the weight room. From the time I was a little kid watching Ohio State football on TV, I had dreamed about wearing the scarlet and gray. I don't know how many times I had said to myself, "Oh my god, I'd do anything to play for that team." I'd come all this way, dedicated myself to the game, become one of the most recruited players in the country, been the first high school player to commit to Cooper, and now it's an offensive system that's stopping me? Nuh-uh. *C'mon, Kirk, you've got to figure this system out.*

Frey had been named second-team All–Big Ten after the 1989 season. When he decided to play baseball rather than spring football in 1990, it not only annoyed the coaching staff (especially Hudson) but it also gave me and Graham more practice reps, more scrimmage reps, and more playing time in the spring game.

I came out of the spring game feeling as if I had locked down the No. 2 spot on the depth chart. The offense still wasn't second nature to me, but I felt more comfortable running it. Frey would be our starter and team captain—he had earned that—but I felt I was ready to step in now if something happened to him. Even Cooper agreed: "We can win with any of the three [quarterbacks]," he said. "We didn't have that luxury a year ago." The 1990 media guide added that I had made "dramatic strides as a passer and may have been the most improved player in the spring."

There was still a problem, though. When you're entering your third season, you never want your bio in the media guide to have more high school highlights than college highlights. It was almost a tie between Centerville High accomplishments and Ohio State appearances. That wasn't a good thing.

For the first time since I had been at Ohio State, we had some real roster depth. We were ranked No. 17 in the preseason AP poll, and someone even picked us to win the national championship. Our recruiting classes were getting stronger, too. The 1990 class included wide receiver Joey Galloway, running back Butler B'ynote', Smith, and Pickens, the consensus high school All-American.

The roster also included one other name: Deron Brown, my former teammate at Centerville.

Like me, Deron had come to Ohio State in the fall of 1988. He was the first person in his immediate family to attend college. And also like me, he loved the Buckeyes.

Deron had been lightly recruited coming out of high school. Several Mid-American Conference programs, as well as a handful of Division III schools, had encouraged him to walk on. Instead, he decided to try to walk on at Ohio State.

It didn't go well. He attempted to make the team during the 1989 winter conditioning drills, but got cut. Cooper said he could join the staff of team managers. Deron politely declined the offer. He wanted to wear the uniform, not wash it.

In 1990, he tried again. When he checked back to see if he had made it, his name was on the bottom of a list of thirteen walk-on candidates. Next to his name it said, "See Coach Kennedy." Coach K was the team's strength coach.

Kennedy told Deron that his workout times were below qualifying standards. He hadn't made the team. But . . . if Deron wanted to try the next day when the varsity players reported for conditioning drills, Kennedy would give him one last chance.

Deron returned the next day, lowered his times, and made the team. It meant so much to Deron to become a Buckeye, to be part of a program he'd idolized when he was kid. Deron would go on to earn varsity letters in 1991 and 1992 as well as a full athletic scholarship.

———

As fall camp began, it became pretty clear that the coaching staff had brought in Graham not only to challenge me for the backup spot but also to challenge Frey. Hudson used Graham as a motivating tool for Frey. He thought Graham's presence would bring out the best in Frey. Instead, there was frustration and resentment on Frey's part.

With each fall practice, my number of meaningful reps decreased. It was a Frey/Graham battle in 1990. I was out.

Every day I would look at the depth chart and see the jarring reality: third string, behind Frey and Graham. The only time I got onto the field was as a holder on extra points and field goals. It was like the coaches had nothing else for me to do, so they said, "Hey, let Herbstreit hold on kicks." In practices, I covered kickoffs as part of the scout team.

We started 2-0, including a win at Boston College, where I bobbled a snap on a field goal attempt on our first possession. As I scrambled around looking for a receiver, the TV play-by-play announcer referred to me as "Mark Herbstite." I threw the ball toward the end zone, but it was intercepted. The sad thing about it: my season got worse.

At one point, the coaches asked me to cover kickoffs as a scout team player during practices. Think about that: the former five-star recruit was now a scout team kickoff coverage guy. My job was to be a wedge breaker, to run down the field as fast as I could and blow people up. I was like a human bowling ball. It's where I took out my rage and frustration.

I always wanted to hit people as hard as I could. I never minded being hit, and I loved hitting people. Covering kickoffs and hurling myself at the blocking wedge was not a stretch for me. In fact, it was the only thing that felt natural to me: run fast, hit someone.

Cooper called me into his office after a Monday practice.

"Hey, listen," said Cooper, who had noticed me covering kickoffs on the scout team, "you're an athletic guy, and we want to get you on the field. We feel like we have a better chance to win if we can get you out there. How would you feel about switching to safety? Is that something you'd do?"

"If it will help me get on the field, then all right, sure," I said. "Let's do it."

But even as the words came out, I knew my heart wasn't into it. I was defeated. I was broken.

Tim May was the Ohio State beat reporter for the *Columbus Dispatch*. He had been covering the team since 1984, and would cover it for years to come. The guy was good.

He was standing in the Woody Hayes Center, leaning against one of the Heisman trophies out there, when Cooper and I walked out for practice that week. Cooper motioned to May.

"Tim, I just want to tell you that we've been talking about it, studying it, and Kirk is going to try to play safety now," he said.

May didn't say much, but you could see the skepticism in his eyes. He had covered football long enough to know what the position change meant for me. I had become irrelevant.

Ron Zook, who would later become the head coach at Florida and Illinois, was our defensive backs coach. He had come to Ohio State from Virginia Tech, where he was the defensive coordinator. Zook was an absolute lunatic at that stage of his career.

As I got dressed for my first practice as a free safety, the equipment guys gave me gloves and different pads.

"What the hell are these?" I said.

"Put 'em on," said the equipment manager. "You'll need them."

I reported to the defensive backs meeting room, where the other DBs greeted me with looks of amusement.

"What's Herrrrb doing in *here*?" said one of the cornerbacks. That's what they called me: Herrrrb.

I asked myself the same question.

The first seven or eight minutes of the practice were individual drills: working on our backpedal, hitting each other, catching balls. I was a fish out of water. I hadn't played defense since sixth grade. And now I was going to play free safety in the Big Ten? There wasn't one moment when I thought I could play the position.

Some of the guys tried to help me. Bo Pelini, who would go on to be a head coach at Nebraska and Youngstown State, was our starting free safety. He was from Youngstown, Ohio, and had played at the same Cardinal Mooney High School program as Bob, Mark, and Mike Stoops. Bo was a tough dude, but he also had played quarterback and safety at Mooney. So maybe there was a part of him that related to what I was going through. Every day he tried to coach me up. Thirty-plus years later, I still appreciate how Bo took a genuine interest in helping me.

The other DBs? They just clowned with me. They'd watch me struggle through a drill and yell, "I see you, Herrrrb!" I think some of them almost felt sorry for me. They could read the depth chart. They saw that I had tumbled behind Frey and Graham. They saw that Cooper had signed Pickens. In other words, they knew I was the answer to the question "What's wrong with this picture?" The coaching staff didn't know what to do with me.

I was about 6-foot-3, 225 pounds, ran a 4.6 40. I was a good athlete, which is why Cooper was willing to take a flyer with the position change. I wasn't afraid of physical contact, but I didn't have the instincts for the position. Plus, we were moving toward our fourth, fifth, sixth games of the season. Nobody—not Zook, not Bo, not the other DBs—had a lot of time to teach me anything. They had to concentrate on their own preparation.

Joey Galloway saw me over there and couldn't believe it. To this day he tells me he would have paid money to get a shot at me at safety. It would have been bad.

I was still the holder on PATs and extra points. I also covered kicks for a couple of games. But that was about it.

We lost to Illinois at home, and then tied Indiana to drop to 2-2-1. After two weeks at safety, I told Coop that I wanted to play quarterback again. He was fine with the switch. Truth is, I think he had given up on me. *What, you're still here? Sure, go back to quarterback.*

To him and everyone else, I was no factor in our team's success or failure. I was just a name on the roster. I figured I'd rather sit in the quarterbacks room—even with the sarcastic Hudson there—than be a fake defensive back. I dreaded seeing Hudson again. He was a former Notre Dame assistant who always seemed to give the benefit of the doubt to the former Notre Dame quarterback, Graham. It wasn't just me who felt that way. There was resentment toward Hudson—and Graham—from some of the other quarterbacks.

When we beat Purdue the next week by 40—and I didn't get a snap at quarterback—that's probably the day I mentally went into the tank. My youth and immaturity began to get the best of me. I became cynical. All my football dreams and goals were gone.

On every roster there are a handful of players who are misfits. They're usually in the back of the meeting room being silly, not paying attention, acting like goofballs. That was me that season.

I became a misfit. My way of dealing with my reality was to say, "F— it." I didn't take coaching. I was resentful. I was immature. I was ready to give up. I was a time bomb.

In practice I would count the minutes until we were done for the day. If a coach said something to me, I'd mutter under my breath, "Whatever." After all, what were they going to do to me? Drop me to fourth string?

It was a toxic way to live my daily life. Some of my buddies on the team—Deron, kicker Jon Berger, long snapper Jim Borchers (these days, *Dr.* Borchers, the Ohio State team physician)—were all walk-ons. They would have given anything to experience my worst football day. I was brought in on a pedestal. Deron, Jon, Jim . . . they had to scratch and claw just to get on the team.

They were nearly invisible to a lot of the scholarship guys. Here I was, bitter at my situation, and then there was Deron, who was grateful to be in the running backs meeting room, to be part of the team in whatever small way possible. Everything is seen through the lens of your own situation.

We beat Minnesota by 29, and I couldn't get into the game at quarterback. In the days leading up to that game, I didn't feel right. My energy level was down. Early that next week, I went and saw our team doctor, who sent me to get some blood tests. The next day he said, "No wonder you're not feeling well. You tested positive for mononucleosis. You're out this week."

In a weird way, I was so excited that I didn't have to go to practice. I almost felt like I hit the jackpot by testing positive.

Near the end of the week I started feeling better. On Saturday, rather than watch our game against Northwestern, Schmidt and I drove back to Centerville. I vented to him during the drive about my frustration level, how Hudson had handpicked Graham from Notre Dame, how they had kicked me to the curb when they had decided I wasn't worth the effort anymore.

"I'm never going to play here," I said.

I was in a bad place.

The Buckeyes didn't miss me. We beat Northwestern by 41. The following week we won at Iowa (I was back at placeholder) and then at Wisconsin (our fifth consecutive victory), where I made an unassisted tackle. Sadly, it was one of my season highlights, another few words to be added to next year's media guide bio.

By then, I had decided I would get through the season and then go play baseball for the Buckeyes in the spring. I was at the end of my rope with Hudson. He didn't respect me, and I couldn't stand him. It wasn't just that I never got into the game, it was this feeling that it had become personal with Hudson, that he *enjoyed* that I didn't play. Almost single-handedly, Hudson had taken away my love for the game.

Years later, as an adult, I understand that he was trying to motivate me in his own way. But I got tired of being the brunt of his jokes in the film room and practice field. I started to lose face with my teammates, and it was partly because of Hudson's constant verbal jabs.

To me, it was like being in a prizefight. I got knocked down as a true freshman, as a redshirt freshman, and now as a redshirt sophomore. I was trying to hang on for dear life. Every time I got up from the mat, I'd get punched in the face, hit in the ribs, hear the seven, eight, nine count . . . I was just trying to get to the bell, to get to the end of the season.

We lost at home against Michigan (Cooper's third straight loss to the Wolverines) and accepted a bid to play Air Force in the Liberty Bowl. The give-a-crap meter of the seniors was at an all-time low. Unranked Air Force? Memphis and the Liberty Bowl? They didn't care.

I might have been the most excited player on the team. When I found out we were playing Air Force, I asked the coaches if I could run the scout team against our No. 1 defense. Why? Because I had run Fisher DeBerry's Air Force wishbone offense at Centerville. At last, I was going to have some fun as quarterback.

Deron and Berger, another former Centerville teammate, were my running backs. Galloway, who was redshirting that year, was my wide receiver. When you're on the scout team, a grad assistant or assistant coach will hold up a play drawn on a card. In this case, it was card after card of Air Force's option attack.

This time, I told the assistant, "You don't need to show me any cards. I'm reading this shit."

I became a quarterback/grad assistant for our scout team. Our first-team defense wanted a good look at Air Force's option? Okay, be careful what you wish for.

Suddenly I felt like a quarterback again. It felt natural, real. I didn't think, I just played. Deron and Jon knew what I was doing. I read the defensive line and either pitched, kept it, or handed off. Once in a while, I threw it to Galloway, who had world-class speed.

We kicked our first-team defense's ass. Gashed them. Lit them up. They couldn't stop us. Zook got so mad that I heard him tell Pelini, "Go kill Herbstreit."

I outweighed Bo by thirty pounds. When he came up to make a play, I carried out my fake, then grabbed Bo by the face mask and threw him as far as I could. He got up ready to fight—and so did I.

The defensive coaches were pissed. The defensive players were mad at the scout team offense.

"Hey, man, chill out," they told us. "What are you doing?"

What were we doing? We were doing our jobs, which was to show them exactly what to expect from Air Force's option. But Zook didn't like to be embarrassed by an irrelevant quarterback, a walk-on fullback (Deron), and a second-team kicker (Jon).

Air Force beat us 23–11. It wasn't a surprise. If our scout team could run over our first-team defense, I knew Air Force was going to be a real problem. Those guys weren't afraid of Ohio State. They were going to fly fighter jets in combat situations. They were trained for high-pressure, high-adversity moments. You think they were intimidated by a Buckeyes team that played with zero motivation?

We were bigger, stronger, and faster, but they were more committed, more invested, more everything. They attempted and completed just one pass, for 11 yards. But they rushed for 294 yards on 61 carries. They imposed their will on us.

I played in the game on kickoff coverage and kickoff returns. It was a fitting end to a forgettable season, where we lost our third consecutive game to Michigan and our second consecutive bowl game. The fans were all over Cooper.

After the game, some of the seniors sat in the back rows of the team bus and waited for the rest of us to take our seats. As we boarded one by one, the seniors unloaded on just about every player. Galloway, who was a great college and NFL player, says he's never seen anything like it before or since.

Through it all, my dad had been an encouraging voice. He had told me to stay positive, to hang in there, to not be one of those guys he warned me about when he dropped me off at school in 1988. But the Air Force game was my version of the finish line. I had run the good race, fought the good fight, and made it through three years of Hudson, of a new offense, of bench warming, of being asked to switch positions, of scout teams and kickoff coverage. Now I couldn't wait to tell my dad that I was playing baseball in the spring (I had only missed a couple of seasons) and then transferring to another program for football—or maybe quitting football and just concentrating on baseball.

I had come to Ohio State as a five-star freak who was going to start for three, maybe four years. When it didn't happen, when the expectations weren't met, I would go back home and people would say, "What happened to you? I thought you were going to start. What's going on?"

There was part of you that felt like a failure, like you had let them down. They didn't know what I was going through. All they knew—and these were people who cared about me—was that I wasn't the starting quarterback when they turned on their TVs on Saturdays for Ohio State games.

I had heard these kinds of stories before: the top-10 recruit who turns out to be a complete bust. But I never thought it would be me. A lot of players have had to deal with that reality, and now I was living it.

I had these mental conversations with myself. I second-guessed my decision out of high school. Had I allowed my lifelong dream to be the quarterback at Ohio State to cloud my judgment when it came to signing with another program? Did I screw up by not going to Michigan, where I could have plugged right into their offense? When you're coming out of high school, you're not looking at the big picture. At least, I didn't.

Despite all our family troubles, I still respected my dad's opinion, especially when it came to football. He had played the game, excelled at the game, and coached the game. His experiences—and what he had overcome himself as a player—gave him even more credibility with me.

When we finally talked, I told him I was quitting the team. I had had enough.

Some dads, especially those dads who live through their sons, would have said, "Bullshit. No you're not! You're staying there!" But my dad understood what it was like to be in a locker room, to be on the field, to be doubted, to compete. He understood the struggle. He knew how easily a player could get lost in a program as big as Ohio State's.

His tone was gentle and heartfelt. He didn't yell at me. He didn't go macho dad on me. Instead, he asked me to not to give up on my dream just yet.

"You've got a chance to compete and win the job next year," he said. "Why don't you see how that plays out? Keep battling. Keep competing."

As frustrated as I was, I valued my dad's wisdom. I trusted his opinion. It was true that Frey had finished his career at Ohio State. Graham would be the favorite to win the job, but I was still ahead of Pickens, at least.

I thought long and hard about my conversation with my dad. I easily could have been spiteful and turned it around on him and said, "Why should I stick it out? You didn't stick it out with us and Mom." But I knew he was coming from a good place, that he had my best interests in mind. I respected him, and his advice carried a lot of weight.

A few days after our talk, I decided, "Okay, let's go do this. Let's give football another chance."

Year Four awaited.

Chapter 6

End of the Misfit

In retrospect, if I'm brutally honest with myself, I had no business being on the field my first three years at Ohio State. I simply wasn't ready. I didn't want to admit it then, but I can admit it now.

In 1991, though, I was ready. I had a new attitude and a new offensive coordinator. Colletto was gone; he was the new head coach at Purdue. In his place was Elliot Uzelac, who had come to Ohio State from Indiana and had previously coached with Bo at Michigan. The reviews were mixed on him. He had head coaching experience at Navy and Western Michigan. He also had a reputation for being a hard-ass.

Regardless, the offensive philosophy wasn't going to change. With running backs Raymont Harris, Carlos Snow, Butler B'ynote', and Robert Smith, who was the Big Ten and national freshman of the year, we were going to be a ground-oriented, power offense.

At our very first quarterback meeting in the spring, Hudson stood in front of us and declared an open competition between Graham, me, and Pickens.

"I don't want to hide anything," he said. "We want to be transparent on this. We're going to track every rep you get: on seven-on-seven drills, in scrimmages . . . everything. You'll see your numbers every day. Those numbers are going to dictate who we choose as the starting quarterback."

This was a surprising but welcome development. I looked at it as a *Dumb and Dumber* moment: "So you're telling me there's a chance?" Even though I was hell-bent on winning the job, I had assumed Graham would be the favorite because the coaches liked his size and his strong throwing arm. I figured I'd be the one holding the clipboard while Graham started. But at least this had the appearance of a fair competition.

I competed my ass off that spring. My throwing mechanics, my accuracy, my arm strength, and my dropbacks all improved. It was the first time in my career there that I had an actual grasp of the offense. Cooper didn't declare a winner after the spring game, but I felt like I was ahead.

That summer, in the stifling Columbus humidity and heat, I worked out almost every day with dozens of players. We would run for about an hour and then everyone would leave except me and wide receiver Brian Stablein, a former walk-on who had earned a scholarship before the 1990 season. Stablein had great hands, ran precise routes, and knew how to get open. He was a big-time player.

I would do rep after rep after rep of seven-step drops while Stablein ran a 20-yard out cut, or an 18-yard dig route, or a skinny post, or a short drag route, or a fade, or a corner route. I started consistently hitting those throws, partly because I had become comfortable with those seven-step drops. Plus, Stablein could make a lot of quarterbacks look good. By the end of summer, I felt confident about the progress I'd made. Even my teammates noticed a difference in the way I threw.

As fall camp began on August 15, our coaches, the players, and the local media were fixated on the quarterback competition. Graham had a huge arm, there was no doubt about it. He could make throws I couldn't. But he had consistency issues. He would thread a pass between two defenders for a completion and you'd go, "Yeah, that guy is going to the NFL." Then on the next play he'd throw an interception to a linebacker.

But it was on the night of August 15 that Uzelac and Robert Smith would have a confrontation that eventually would become a national controversy. As we all would read later in the *Sports Illustrated* account of the incident, it began in classic style: a tone-deaf coach more interested in enforcing a rule than actually trying to understand a player's situation.

According to *Sports Illustrated*, Smith was reading a textbook for his inorganic chemistry class when Uzelac opened the dorm room door for bed check and ordered him to turn off the lights. When Smith told him he first had to finish his schoolwork, Uzelac yelled, "Lights out!" Smith didn't budge.

Smith was in the premed program and his summer school final exam was in two weeks. Uzelac didn't care.

On August 23, Smith quit the team. He said Uzelac had told him on multiple occasions, "You're here to play football. . . . You take school too seriously," and had encouraged Smith to skip classes so he wouldn't miss team meetings or practices. He also accused Cooper and Uzelac of not caring about the players' health and dignity, and said Ohio State's football coaches valued a player's eligibility more than a player's education. Cooper denied the allegations and said his reputation had been compromised by Smith.

This wasn't your ordinary player/coach disagreement. This was public. This was heated. This was one player—Smith—taking on

Ohio State, a coaching staff, and the football establishment. This was no small thing, especially in the early 1990s, when players were more reluctant to take a stand. He said he wouldn't play at Ohio State as long as Cooper and Uzelac were there.

Smith had been a prized recruit, and his performance as a true freshman had been historic. He broke Archie Griffin's freshman rushing record. He had the kind of talent that could win a Heisman, just like Archie did. But football wasn't everything to Smith. That sort of thinking, especially at Ohio State, bothered some of our coaches, our fans, and even some of the players. Our senior nose tackle, Greg Smith, who also was a premed student, told the Associated Press, "I think he lost much more by quitting football than we lost by losing Robert Smith."

Smith addressed the team the day after he quit. I know there were players in that room who were mad at him, who thought he was quitting on them, who didn't understand or care about his motives. I'm not sure I completely understood. But I know this: Robert was the only one on our team with the *cajones* to do what he did, to stand up to Uzelac. The other players might not have admitted it publicly, but it seemed almost everyone wanted to boycott Uzelac. We all talked openly about it in the football facility. Uzelac and Hudson were two of the biggest schleps to ever coach football at Ohio State.

Smith was kind of a loner on our team. He made his decision and was willing to live with the consequences. I respected that. He remained on scholarship, but now as a track athlete. His football locker was cleaned out. It was as if he didn't exist anymore.

————

Midway through camp, Graham started getting most of the snaps with the No. 1 offense. It felt almost as if the coaches had been humoring me, or probably using me to push Graham. I think it was predetermined that Graham was going to start. They said it was going to be an open competition, but it wasn't.

And yes, I know this sounds like sour grapes, but that isn't the case at all. Going into that 1991 season, I had come to a point where I was productive, even confident again. I had the ability and the mobility to create something. I could drop back and throw, but I could also scramble, or be used on QB-designed running plays. Graham didn't have that kind of agility or speed. I could open up the offense, which is something my teammates were excited to see.

Instead, the coaches chose Graham. As much as I hated the decision, I knew I was only a twisted ankle away from being The Guy. I knew now I could do the job. My misfit days were done. I was listening now in the quarterbacks room. I soaked up the game plans. I was ready.

Part of my transformation was the result of a new addition to the football support staff, Dr. Budd Ferrante. He had been introduced to the team as camp began. His official title at Ohio State: Psychologist for Athletics.

"I'm here to be part of the team," he told us. "Look at me like a trainer, a team doctor. I just got added to the staff and I'm here to help you be your best. I'm not going to judge. Whatever we talk about will stay between us."

You could hear a few snickers, a few disparaging comments. Football players pride themselves on their mental toughness. Plus, how did anyone really know if this guy wouldn't run to the coaching staff with what we told him?

I fell into the first category: I didn't want to be seen by anyone, especially my teammates, as mentally weak. I had overcome so much to get to this position that I kept telling myself, "There's nothing wrong with me. I've handled everything on my own and done just fine."

Deep down, though, I knew I wasn't completely fine. You couldn't experience what I had experienced during my life without having suffered some form of emotional damage. There was scar tissue built up over the years.

One day—and I can't tell you exactly why—I decided to make an appointment with Dr. Ferrante.

At first, I didn't open up to him. I was protective of my story. As time went on and I became more at ease with him, he slowly gained my trust. He was a little quirky, but, true to his word, he was also nonjudgmental. He knew nothing about me, so I had to coach him up about my personal journey. He would sit there and just listen. No rushed conclusions, no lectures from him.

Every so often I would see him out at practice. I'm sure he was talking to a few other guys, too. He stood off to the side, just watching, observing. Maybe he came out there to show he was part of the team. Maybe he wanted to observe how we dealt with the pressure of playing at one of the premier football programs in the country. Whatever the reason, it was comforting to see him. I began to think of him as part of my team. Once I crossed that bridge in my mind, Dr. Ferrante became a powerful resource for me.

With each session, more details of my life began spilling out. I opened up to him about everything: first my football frustrations, the anger I had related to my playing status, the constant struggle to cope with it all. Then I eventually told him about my family, where I had grown up, how I had grown up, what I had witnessed, how those events had affected me. I was slowly dissecting my own life to him. It was difficult, but also liberating in a way.

I didn't tell anyone about my visits with Dr. Ferrante. I definitely tried to hide them from Hudson. Somehow, though, Dr. Ferrante's presence came up, and Hudson's response was to roll his eyes. His attitude—"Why do you need to see *him*?"—was what you'd expect from a conventional coach who was unconvinced, maybe even suspicious, about the value of a team psychologist.

To me, when people in that position tear down the notion of your seeing someone like Dr. Ferrante, it shows weakness and vulnerability on their part, not yours. They feel threatened by that person's potential role in your life. It's a control thing—and coaches like control. The smart coaches, the ones capable of evolving, understand the difference between a threat and an asset. Dr. Ferrante was an asset, but Hudson saw him as a threat. Ridiculous.

There was pressure, of course. Always pressure. Every day you fought for your place on the depth chart. You fought in games. You dealt with injuries. You tried to satisfy the demands and expectations of yourself, your coaches, your teammates, the fans, the media, even your own family and friends. There's a standard at a program such as Ohio State's, and you tried to meet that standard every day. That's fine. That comes with the territory of playing major college football. But add in the academic demands, the training, and whatever family and financial issues you're dealing with. Maybe you have girlfriend problems. It can add up, and as a teenager or early twentysomething, it can sometimes be overwhelming.

I was at a point where I wanted help. I needed help. That was thirty years ago, and the demands and the pressures on college athletes, on young people in general, haven't lessened. If anything, they've increased exponentially. Look at the rising numbers of teenage suicides. In college football, we've learned of the tragic consequences when a player feels he has no option other than suicide.

To those athletes, to those young people who wonder if they should seek help, who question whether it's safe to reach out to others, I would say it's not only safe but it's a lifeline. I'm thankful that Ohio State made Dr. Ferrante available to us. He made it okay for me to vent years of frustration, hurt, anger, and confusion.

Not long ago I was listening to a talk by someone who said, "As I'm speaking to you right now, you're likely in the midst of a storm. And as you come out of one, you'll eventually head into another. How will you handle that?"

As a player late in my career at Ohio State, I handled that with Dr. Ferrante. He became part of my coaching staff. He was my life coach. He helped me navigate those storms. He had no agenda, no skin in the game. His only mission was to build a relationship and level of trust where he could try to help me. Looking back at it, I can see what an incredible opportunity that was for me. There's no need to feel ashamed or embarrassed about seeking that help. Honestly, I would have been more embarrassed with myself if I hadn't taken advantage of his expertise and kindness. Or think of it this way: I had coaches throughout my life who taught me how to throw a football, how to run the option, how to drop back, how to read a defense, how to check to an audible, etc. So why wouldn't I want to take advantage of a coach who could teach me how to deal with the pressures, with the mental aspects of the game and life? Making that first appointment to see Dr. Ferrante was one of the best things I've ever done.

———

We beat Arizona to open the season, and then squeaked by Louisville to climb to No. 16 in the rankings, but not before Graham suffered a concussion early in the fourth quarter against the Cardinals. I came in and finished the game, and on September 21, more than three years after my dad dropped me off at school, I made my first start as an Ohio State quarterback.

We played Washington State at home, and the Cougars' quarterback was Drew Bledsoe, who would go on to be the No. 1 overall pick in the 1993 NFL Draft. I didn't care about Bledsoe's bona fides.

I didn't waste time reflecting on my own past and how far I'd come. I was 100 percent focused on the game: *I'm starting. What's the plan? Let's execute it.* That's where my head was. If this was going to be my chance to make a statement, then I wanted to make the loudest statement possible. I didn't have the luxury of being nostalgic.

If you've never been in a huddle, if you've never been on a team, I'm not sure I can fully explain what it's like when you *feel* the confidence of your teammates. My running backs believed in me. My offensive line believed in me. Guys like Stablein, who had sweated through the summer running routes on empty practice fields, believed in me. Their belief gave me confidence. I felt like they felt I could do this for them.

Since the beginning of the season, Uzelac had installed a small package of option plays in our offense that we had run about ten times a game. We weren't Air Force, but it gave opposing defenses something else to prepare for. Graham could run it, but I could run it better.

It was a game of firsts for me: my first Ohio State start, and on the first drive and on my first pass attempt of the game, I threw my first-ever Ohio State touchdown: a 39-yarder to our flanker Bernard Edwards. The TD came off an option play.

As the game moved on and we took a 14–0 lead and then a 21–0 lead, I let my emotions spill out. We rushed for 321 yards, and after a Snow touchdown run or a B'ynote' TD run, I'd dap a guy up. In return, some of my teammates who had seen me struggle over the years got in my face: "I told you, boy!" they'd say. "I told you! You got this!" They knew what this game meant to me.

We won, 33–19, to improve to 3-0. Bledsoe completed 26 of 43 passes for 237 yards. I completed 8 of 13 for 158, and rushed for 43 yards. In a way, I felt my performance proved a point, and I said so in the postgame interviews, telling reporters, "My passing is equal to anyone else in Division I football."

Making the day even better: Deron played, too. You should have seen the smiles on our faces that day. You should have seen the smile on my dad's face.

He talked to longtime *Dispatch* columnist Dick Fenlon after the game.

"If he never starts another one, he's my son, he came here and started and had a pretty good day and beat Washington State one Saturday afternoon," he said. "He made me feel important again."

Afterward, the beat reporters asked Cooper about the possibility of my starting against Wisconsin in our next game. Cooper said I was still the backup, but told May of the *Dispatch*, "I think a lot of people questioned whether he could throw it or not, and I think he proved he can throw it."

The headline in the *Dispatch* read: "Herbstreit hasn't passed Graham as QB." In his follow-up story, May wrote: "But sometime within the next few games, expect a possible controversy. Because, after playing competently most of the time and brilliantly on a couple of plays, Herbstreit has risen from mop-up guy to legitimate relief pitcher."

I felt reborn. I was finally contributing to the team. That's all I had ever wanted to do.

My issues had never been with Kent. I didn't dislike him. I just disliked the situation. I had a bitter feeling toward Hudson because of the way he worshipped Kent. If anything, I had a professional relationship with Kent. He was a good guy, but he didn't have many relationships with guys on the team. He had transferred in; he was married and had a child. He didn't have the time to hang out with us. He had a family, and it came with time demands and responsibilities that we didn't have. He was almost more like a coach than one of the guys.

As promised, Cooper started Graham against Wisconsin, and I was back to being 1B on the depth chart. We were ahead, 17–2, with about six minutes left in the game, when Cooper sent me in. Our drive stalled at Wisconsin's 32-yard line, but Cooper decided to go for it on fourth-and-seven.

I took the snap, faked a handoff, was chased left by three Badgers, slipped through a tackle, reversed all the way to the right, ran down the sideline, and leaped over another Badger at the two-yard line and into the end zone for the score. My guys grabbed my face mask and yelled, "Way to show those mother-f'in coaches!" The student section in the Shoe yelled, "Herrr-bie! Herrr-bie!" I was the quintessential backup quarterback whom the crowd loved. It blew me away when they chanted my name.

We moved up to 11th in the AP poll, but then lost at Illinois, 10–7. I came in late during the third quarter, as we drove from our 25 to their three-yard line. On second-and-goal from the three, I pitched it on an option play and we fumbled it away.

After that, I didn't play much at quarterback the rest of the season (I was still the holder on PATs and field goals): a few drives in a win against Northwestern, a 72-yard touchdown run late in the third quarter of a blowout win at Minnesota, some quality time in a close win against Indiana. We were 8-2 and ranked 18th in the polls when we headed to Ann Arbor to play No. 4–ranked Michigan. The Wolverines had already clinched the Big Ten championship, but that didn't lessen the intensity of the rivalry. Nothing would have been more satisfying than to send them off to the Rose Bowl with a loss.

Late in the second quarter, trailing 17–3, I stood on the Big House sidelines as we punted after another failed drive. Graham was struggling, and our defense was spending way too much time on the field.

The punt dropped into the arms of a kid from Cleveland.

Desmond Howard caught the ball at his own seven-yard line, toward our side of the field. He was by five of our punt coverage guys in a single burst, then split through two more would-be tacklers, then outran three others on his way to the end zone. He went right by me in a blur of maize and blue, and I thought, "That son of a gun is gone . . . Damn."

That was the play when Keith Jackson, who was doing the play-by-play for ABC, said, "Hello, Heisman," as Des sprinted into the end zone. That was the play when Des did his iconic Heisman pose. That was the play that ended any chance of our winning the game and, as usual, prompted the Michigan band to play that damn fight song, "Victors."

Des had come to Michigan the same year I had come to Ohio State. During Michigan's freshman camp, he played defensive back the first day (he had also played free safety in high school and led the state in interceptions), running back the second day, and wide receiver the third day. After the third day, they asked Des if he would switch to wide receiver. He said yes, and red-shirted that year, just like I had.

If only that position switch had worked out for Des . . .

I replaced Graham to start the second half against Michigan, but I didn't do any better. In fact, I got knocked out of the game with a concussion late in the fourth quarter when a Michigan defensive lineman decided to do a belly flop on my head. I woozily headed back to the sideline.

Des won the Heisman by a landslide in 1991. I would have voted for him, too. He was the first Big Ten wide receiver to lead the league in scoring. He wasn't big—only about 5-foot-9, less than 180 pounds—but he was instinctive, fast, quick, and so confident in himself. He had an innate understanding of how to play the game. He was his own man then as he is now.

Michigan went to Pasadena for New Year's Day; we went to Tampa to play Syracuse in the Hall of Fame Bowl. Rather than start Graham, the coaches decided to give me the start and see what I could do. I was coming back in 1992; Graham wasn't. It was a way to get me more practice reps and playing reps with the first-team offense, and give me a springboard into the next season.

We lost 24–17, but had fought back from being down two touchdowns and had made it a game. I blamed myself for the loss. I told the reporters afterward, "I'm so disappointed in myself. I'm going to throw in the off-season until I can't throw anymore."

Chapter 7

Worth the Wait

On the flight back to Columbus, I did some soul searching and reflected on my journey up to that point. I had been to football hell and back. I had one year left in my Ohio State career, and I decided on that plane that I was going to do everything in my power between that moment and the opening of fall camp in 1992 to get myself right and my team right.

There was negativity surrounding our program. We hadn't beaten Michigan under Cooper. We hadn't won a Big Ten championship. We hadn't won a bowl game. The Robert Smith controversy had not only put more pressure on Cooper but it had also cost us maybe our best player.

Despite it all, I was convinced we could win the Big Ten and even a national championship in 1992. I decided I was going to put all five years' worth of effort into one season. I was going to be the best teammate we had. I was going to be the best leader. Bring in whoever you wanted to challenge me, I was going to be the starter.

There would be one other difference in 1992: Uzelac wouldn't be the offensive coordinator. After one season, he resigned near the end of February. Good riddance. He was finally out of all our lives. Joe Hollis became our new coordinator.

As we began spring practice, Cooper asked each player to write down his choices for team captains—one on offense, one on defense. Weeks later, the day before our spring game, he called the entire team together.

"I want to announce our team captains," he said. "On defense, Steve Tovar will be one of our captains. And on offense, we're going to have Kirk Herbstreit as our other captain."

Steve was an All-American linebacker. He had played in every game as a true freshman, had started every game as a sophomore and junior, and had led our team in tackles in 1990 and 1991. He was a star.

I wasn't a star. I was barely a starter. I was mostly a career backup with two starts to my name. I had been redshirted, asked to switch from offense to defense, covered kickoffs, contemplated quitting, been a misfit, heard myself described as a five-star washout, and seen my childhood football dreams crushed. The closest I came to being an All-American was standing next to Tovar.

But as Cooper said my name that day, I was filled with an indescribable pride. I had grown up with such an appreciation of what it meant to be an Ohio State captain. My dad had cherished that honor as a player, and cherished the Captain's Mug that came with it. Now I got to follow in his footsteps, and in the footsteps of so many great players at Ohio State. Nobody appreciated it more than me. On some level, it was a miracle, especially given where I had been eighteen months earlier in my career.

For my teammates to vote for me—the non-star, the grinder, the guy who had lived and died Ohio State football since I was a kid—made me feel like I was ten feet tall. It gave me such incredible confidence. They believed in me, even though my career stats weren't very impressive. I promised myself that I wouldn't let them down.

During that off-season, I asked Hollis if he would consider putting in a package that would include the triple option. We could use it for short-yardage situations, or on the goal line. I argued that defenses wouldn't know what hit them. You can't play a base defense against it because it's so assignment based. We would have an instant advantage.

Hollis gave his blessing, and I started working with our freak of a fullback, Jeff Cothran, on mesh zones and reads. During the same time, I was also working out with Stablein on pass routes and timing. We were workaholics in May, June, and July.

One afternoon, Brian and I were out there by ourselves in the summer heat and humidity (rarely did anyone else stay to throw with us after our team workouts) when someone walked out of the Woody Hayes facility and started making his way toward us. He was wearing gray workout shorts, socks and cleats, but no shirt. He was eighty to ninety yards away, but from a distance, he looked like he was chiseled out of marble. I thought he was an NFL player.

"Who *is* this dude?" I said to Stablein.

When he finally walked up to us, I couldn't believe how incredibly well built he was. I could have sworn he had negative body fat.

"Hey, man, how you doing?" I said.

"Good," he said. "Is it okay if I take some handoffs and run with you? My name is Eddie George."

Eddie George? I didn't know any NFL players named Eddie George. Then I remembered he was on our roster: Eddie George—true freshman tailback from Philadelphia . . . had played at Fork Union Military Academy in Virginia . . . track star . . . a grown-looking man. He was part of the same recruiting class that had included Korey Stringer, Luke Fickell, Lorenzo Styles, Juan Porter, and a walk-on wide receiver named Terry Glenn. He had been lightly recruited, enrolled early, gone through spring practice, played in the spring game.

But given the depth we had at running back, and that I was a fifth-year senior and he was a true freshman not getting many reps, I hardly noticed him that spring.

I damn sure noticed him now.

Here he was, confident enough as a true freshman to approach two seniors—one of them a team captain—shake their hands (vise-grip handshake, by the way), and ask if he could work out with them.

"Can you take some handoffs?" I said. "Sure, big fella. Abso-f—-ing-lutely."

He was great. I'd explain a play to him and he'd get it correct on the first try. There was no half speed with this kid. He took the ball and *ran*. I looked at Stablein and said, "This son of a gun is crazy. Look at this guy." I loved his work ethic and his attitude.

Just before fall camp started, Robert Smith contacted Coop about returning to the team. Uzelac was gone. Robert had had a year to think things through.

Cooper called me, Tovar, and a few other players into his office. "What do you guys think?" he said.

Robert's talents were undeniable. He was incredibly gifted, and I liked him as a person. But the last thing we needed was a repeat of the sideshow from 1991. I told Coop that I would support a decision to let Robert back on the team, but only if Robert was coming back to be *part* of the team. At that stage in his life, it was hard to predict what Robert would do.

There was a vote of sorts: we said bring him back. Cooper agreed.

As a quarterback, my skill position players were now Raymont Harris, Butler B'ynote', Robert Smith, and Eddie George at tail-back; Jeff Cothran at fullback; Joey Galloway and Chris Sanders at flanker; and Brian at split end. Robert, Joey, and Eddie would go on to be first-round NFL draft picks. Jeff and Chris would later become third-round selections, while Raymont would be picked in the fourth round, Butler in the seventh, and Brian in the eighth. In other words, we had ourselves an offense.

Late in training camp, near the end of our grueling two-a-days, the Ohio State University Marching Band came to our practice fields. As a kid, I had always loved that band. It wasn't any different now that I was a player. I can't tell you how many times I watched in awe when they came down the stadium tunnel, marching the way they marched, the drum major coming through the middle of the formation, the precision of each of their steps, the way they took over a field. It gave me chills. I got so fired up as a player. Years later as a broadcaster, I still act like a seven-year-old when I see the band emerge from the tunnel. I take my headphones off and watch them do their thing. I get charged up just talking about it.

The band—and I'm sure it's this way with marching bands in every program (except maybe, well, Stanford's band)—worked as hard as the players. It was hot in August, and we could hear them practicing all day, every day.

It was such a cool thing when they came to our fields. It was a break for them, and a break for us. The offensive linemen grabbed the sousaphones and the band members showed them how to march with those instruments on their shoulders. The running backs grabbed the trumpets. Each position group was paired with a section of the band. I was assigned to the drum major, which was a thrill.

Each player walked next to a band member as the band began the Script Ohio formation. We started in a square and slowly un-wound into the script O-h-i-o. Some of the players were being silly, but not me. This was serious stuff. At the very end, I got to walk out and dot the *i*. I know it wasn't the same as dotting the *i* in an actual game (it's very rare for a non–band member to be invited to dot the *i*—Woody Hayes, John Glenn, and Jack Nicklaus are part of a very exclusive club), but it was one of the highlights of my time at Ohio State. I have so much admiration for the band. In fact, I was so excited that day that I called my mom and told her about dotting the *i* at practice.

There was another Ohio State ritual in the fall: the annual Captain's Breakfast. The only people allowed in the room are the previous Ohio State captains, the current head coach and coaching staff, and the latest captains. As a kid who spent hours in the basement going through my dad's Ohio State clippings and photos, who watched countless Buckeyes games, who used to pretend I was certain OSU players, who sat on Woody's knee in the locker room, who considered only one football program out of high school, I was blown away by the breakfast. Almost all the living captains from the 1950s, '60s, '70s, and '80s were there. My dad was there, too. I walked around the room shaking their hands like a fanboy.

Tovar and I were presented with our mugs, and then said a few words to the other captains. We were part of their fraternity now. It remains one of the greatest days of my career.

Meanwhile, I still worked with Dr. Ferrante. He came up with different ways to try to help me with my approach to football. Back then, we listened to Walkmans and cassette tapes before games. This was almost ten years before Apple invented the iPod.

Dr. Ferrante asked me to put together a playlist of the top twenty pregame songs that got me in the right football mood. Then he asked me to record my dad, my mom, my sister, and my brother as they each gave me a positive thought to take out onto the field. I took all the recordings to a local radio disc jockey, who was nice enough to mix them together on a cassette tape for me.

I would sit in the locker room preparing for kickoff, my headphones on, my favorite songs playing, and then I would hear my dad giving me encouragement. There would be a few more songs, then my mom would say something. A few more songs, and then I would hear Teri's voice. And so it went.

We were 19th in the preseason rankings, but I thought we were capable of winning the Big Ten and making a run at a national championship. Our season opener was at home against Howard Schnellenberger's Louisville team. Jeff Brohm, who is now Purdue's head coach, was Louisville's quarterback. For two dollars, you could buy an official game program that featured me on the cover (an Ohio State first for me) wearing those big 1990s-style shoulder pads, those thick thigh pads, and hip pads that stuck up four inches on each side of my game pants. Adding to the one-of-a-kind look: at Ohio State we wore Pony cleats and Champion jerseys. Cutting edge, we weren't.

We were 17-point favorites, and we played like we had read too many of our press clippings. I listened to my custom pregame cassette tape, but I was still a nervous wreck early on. "Jello legs" is how I described to reporters how I felt at the beginning of the game.

Louisville had a chance to win the game on a two-point conversion, but Brohm's pass was incomplete with 33 seconds remaining. I finished 16-of-20 for 180 yards, but also threw two interceptions. We lost Smith to bruised ribs in the third quarter.

My family was there to see the game. George Strode, the *Dispatch* sports editor, interviewed my dad.

"I get more nervous as a father than I ever did as a player because of the unknown," he told Strode. "You worry about it as a father. . . . I'm more relaxed now because he seems more relaxed."

We beat Bowling Green the following week, 17–6, but didn't look good doing it. Joey hurt his knee in the second quarter. Robert wore a flak jacket to try to protect his injured ribs. I had to leave the game in the first quarter with torn ligaments in my left ankle and a very tender Achilles, but returned in the second quarter. We

improved to 2-0, but that didn't stop the Ohio State fans from booing us off the field. I don't know if the boos were meant for us or
for Cooper, but it didn't matter. I had seen my teammates leave bits
and pieces of themselves on that field, and in return they got booed.
Afterward, I told reporters that I was looking forward to going on
the road to Syracuse and to a stadium where the fans were involved
in the game. (School hadn't started yet, so the students weren't on
campus for the first two games. There was no energy.)

Even inside the football facility there was a lack of compassion.
When Joey showed up a day or so later to get the results of the MRI
on his right knee, the trainer was busy taping a player's ankle. The
trainer looked up for a moment and said, "Yeah, you're done for the
season," and then went back to taping the ankle.

Joey stood there stunned by the news and the dispassionate way
it was delivered.

Welcome to big-time college football.

We had circled Syracuse on the calendar. It had beaten us in
the bowl game, was ranked No. 8 in the AP poll, and had one
of the better quarterbacks in the country, Marvin Graves, who
ranked first nationally in pass ratings. The game was on national
television, and even attracted the attention of ESPN's *College
GameDay* analysts.

Oh yeah, we watched the show in our team hotel that morning
in Syracuse. Our game wasn't until that night, so we had plenty
of time to hear Craig James and Lee Corso explain how the big,
slow, underdog team from the Big Ten was going to get crushed
by Syracuse—a Corvette, they said, compared to our plodding
semitruck offense. Syracuse had too much speed, too much talent.
We were overmatched. As ten-point underdogs, we had no chance
on the artificial turf of the Carrier Dome. That's what Corso said,
and we remembered every word of his prediction.

My ankle was a mess. I couldn't put much weight on it. Before the game, I got it shot up with a painkiller and did what I could. I can tell you there's not a lot of fatty tissue around the ankle for a hypodermic needle. But there was no way I was going to miss that rematch.

Just to make a point to the Ohio State fans who had booed us off our field a week earlier, to the media that covered our team on a weekly basis, and to the national media—all of whom thought Syracuse was going to beat us—Tovar and I led the team out by twos, side by side, holding hands as a symbol of us against everyone else. There is no more powerful motivator in sports than being told you don't have a chance, that you're too beat up, that your talent doesn't match their talent. We beat Syracuse 35–12.

Take that, Lee Corso.

George had three touchdown runs. Good luck tackling that human bicep. Smith had another one. Our defense picked off Graves four times. I threw a 46-yard TD to Stablein. We made a statement to the country.

The touchdown throw came on our second series: ball fake to Smith . . . see if the safety bites on the fake . . . throw it as far as you can . . . watch Stablein make a great catch. That was the play in a nutshell. The Carrier Dome crowd went quiet, but we were going nuts. *Holy shit, we're going to do this today.*

Then someone told me Hudson wanted to talk to me. He was upstairs in the coaches' booth. I grabbed the phone behind our bench.

"Why didn't you look for the tight end earlier in the drive?" Hudson said.

What? We had just taken a 7–0 lead on a 46-yard bomb and Hudson wanted to bust my balls about not finding the tight end?

"F— you," I said, and hung up the phone.

Syracuse was tough enough as an opponent, but now we had

to overcome the Orangemen *and* Hudson? That guy could make Woody Hayes hate football.

As always, there were a series of TV timeouts during the game. During one of those timeouts, I jogged over to the sideline to talk to Coop and Hollis. Hands on hip pads, I stood there as Hollis looked at his play sheet and discussed what we should run against Syracuse's defense.

As Hollis was talking to me, I noticed an Ohio State cheerleader in the background. She was just over his right shoulder in my direct line of sight. Suddenly I found myself listening to Hollis but looking at her. And whoever she was, she was a stunner.

Her back was to me as she did the cheers. Then she turned around and it was obvious she was athletic, tall, and very pretty.

I nodded as Hollis talked, but I was actually thinking, "I wonder if she's dating anybody?"

Then Hollis gave me a play and I turned and ran back onto the field.

On the flight back to Columbus, I talked to Bryan Niemeyer, our third-team quarterback. Niemeyer was dating one of the Buckeye cheerleaders, so I figured he'd be able to do some intel for me.

"Hey, man, can you inquire who the blond cheerleader is?" I said. "Find out what her status is?"

Niemeyer later told his girlfriend that I wanted to know about the blond cheerleader, but nothing ever came of it. That was fine. My longtime girlfriend and I were taking a break at the time. I wasn't dating anybody, mostly because I was determined not to have any potential distractions in my life. I wanted to concentrate entirely on my final season at Ohio State.

When we got back to Columbus, every Ohio State fan loved us again. We had a "how-do-you-like-us-now?" mentality, moved up to No. 12 in the AP rankings, and had a bye week before we traveled to Wisconsin. During those two weeks between games, we read the press clippings again. Years later, Alabama coach Nick Saban would call it "rat poison," which is when you chow down on the poisoned bait of backslaps and compliments. You start to believe that you're as good as everyone tells you.

Barry Alvarez was only in his third year at Wisconsin, but he had already built the foundation of his program: a physical offensive line, a fundamentally sound defense, running backs who left bruise marks on tacklers. It was a formula he would use with great success during his long and successful career there.

Our Syracuse game had kicked off at 6:35 p.m. Eastern. Our game against Wisconsin was scheduled for 11:35 a.m. Central. Because of a dairy convention (only in Wisconsin, right?) the closest hotel we could get was located an hour outside Madison. Our wake-up call was 6 a.m. that day.

I had a bad feeling on the bus ride to Camp Randall Stadium. Guys were sleeping and snoring in their seats. We were half-awake during warm-ups. Whatever hype and buzz we had for the Syracuse game, this was the exact opposite.

Later, as we waited in the locker room, the game officials knocked on the door and said it was time for the team captains to come out for the coin toss. At Camp Randall, the trip from the visitors' locker room to the field is sort of a maze. Everything is dark, almost medieval. The stadium is more than one hundred years old.

Tovar and I grabbed our helmets and made our way up and down stairs, through a concourse, and finally toward the light of the tunnel at a corner of an end zone. At the edge of the field, just as we emerged from the tunnel, there was a chain link fence above and to the side of the exit. Students, dozens and dozens of them, were pressed against the fence, yelling and snarling at us. These were bleacher creatures, and they were intimidating.

"What in the *hell* is this?" I said to Tovar.

Near the tunnel exit were two Wisconsin state troopers dressed in full riot gear. One of them turned to us and said, "I suggest you put your helmets on."

I put my helmet on.

We won the coin toss, but that was about it for victories that day. One of the creatures hit me with a marshmallow packed with quarters. Later, someone threw a tomato from the stands that exploded on the back of my neck and jersey. Alvarez should have signed the guy to a scholarship. It was a direct hit.

Gary Casper, Wisconsin's senior linebacker, was wearing war paint. The stadium was shaking. We had beaten the Badgers four consecutive times, and they were without their best running back for the game, Terrell Fletcher. But you wouldn't have known it by the vibe in the place. Meanwhile, we acted as if we were going out to play in a spring game. Our attitude was, "Why is Wisconsin so serious?" We had no fire.

Somehow we led 10–3 at halftime, but they scored the next 17 points. We scored late to cut their lead to 20–16, but turned it over on downs on our last possession of the game.

I couldn't run. It was like trying to play football on one leg—and it would be that way for the rest of the season. But the Badgers might have beaten the Green Bay Packers that day. They were *ready*.

Football teaches you harsh lessons. Two weeks earlier, we had the same attitude against Syracuse that Wisconsin had against us: motivated, angry, disrespected. But when we showed up at Camp Randall, we did so with sleep in our eyes. We thought, "Man, it's Wisconsin, we've got this."

It was Wisconsin's first win against a ranked opponent in seven years, and its first win in a Big Ten opener in eleven years. Alvarez, who would become the winningest football coach in school history and lead the Badgers to three Big Ten and Rose Bowl championships, once told me that the win against Ohio State was one of the most important of his career. It gave his young program hope.

He also told me one other thing. Remember those state troopers who suggested Tovar and I put on our helmets? Alvarez had told them to say that. It was a genius move by a guy who, next to my own dad, Coach Gregg, and Coach Corso, has become one of the most trusted voices in my life.

We lost the next week at home to unranked Illinois, and fell out of the rankings ourselves the next day. Eddie George had fumbled twice on the Illinois one-yard line (one of the fumbles was returned 96 yards for a touchdown). We missed two field goals, including a 44-yarder that would have put us ahead with 48 seconds remaining in the game. We had more rushing yards, more passing yards, more total yards, and more first downs than Illinois, and we lost.

Two weeks and two defeats to two teams we should have beaten with ease. I remember standing on the sideline as Illinois ran out the clock. Eddie stood next to me, and he was crying.

I put my arm around him and said, "Eddie, keep your head up. You're a freshman and you're going to learn from this. Don't let this crush you. You're going to be fine. You're going to get other chances."

Another football lesson: the distance between hero and goat isn't as far as you think. Eddie had gone from scoring three times against Syracuse to fumbling twice against Illinois. Years later, even after he had won a Heisman, won the NFL Rookie of the Year, been inducted into the College Football Hall of Fame, and had his number retired at Ohio State, Eddie still talked about how pivotal the Illinois game was to his career. Maybe it was a coincidence, but when Eddie set an OSU single-game rushing record of 314 yards in 1995, he did it against . . . Illinois. The record stood for twenty-five years until Trey Sermon broke it against Northwestern in the 2020 Big Ten Championship.

Of course, the fans turned on us. I told one of our beat reporters: "I'd much rather get into the business world—just eat a hot dog and drink a beer and be a fan, just like the rest of the people."

One of my escape spots was Teri and Bryan's house in Centerville. I can't tell you how many Sunday mornings those two would wake up to find me, Joey, Butler, and a few other teammates or friends sleeping on the living room couch, on the floor, in a chair, or wherever we could stretch out. There would be a stack of empty Cassano's pizza boxes in the kitchen.

Teri and Bryan were the best. Teri would walk over the obstacle course of sleeping football players, grab her car keys, and go buy bacon, sausage, fruit, bread, juice, and a couple dozen eggs and then sneak back in and make breakfast for all of us. After breakfast, Bryan would return to the grocery store and buy food for a Sunday cookout. His specialty: "Holmes Chicken."

Everybody loved Teri, Bryan, and Holmes Chicken. And Teri and Bryan loved football. They had gotten married on a fall Sunday instead of a Saturday—they didn't want to miss an Ohio State game.

Despite an 0-2 start in the Big Ten, I was still Mr. Optimistic. *Let's play it out and see what happens.* We beat Northwestern, then trailed 14–3 at Michigan State before winning that one. Afterward, I told May of the *Dispatch*: "I think it will show some people what we're capable of doing. And if not, we don't really care, because we're going to go up to Iowa and win again."

And we beat Iowa.

We won our next five games, including a shutout win against Minnesota where I really took one for the team. They had a feisty defensive end from New York named Dennis Cappella. Every time I carried out a fake on a handoff, he popped me. I said a few things to him, he said a few things to me. We kept talking shit to each other quarter after quarter.

We controlled the game, but were up only 10–0 with about five minutes left to play. By then, Cappella had sacked me twice and helped on another sack. And he had chirped every time. This guy was looking to hurt people. He was trying to get in my head.

On one of our first two plays on the drive, I carried out a fake and—bam!—Cappella hit me hard again. I'd had it with this guy. We were flat, and I was tired of his act.

On the next play—a first-and-10 from their 30—I handed off to Cothran and then looked for Cappella. We were like two battering rams. I hit him, he hit me. We were pushing each other, and I got bent backward in the pile of bodies. I could hear whistles blowing, but all I could see was Cappella's fist hitting me in the face. My helmet had been pushed up, allowing an opening for the punches.

There wasn't much I could do. I was pinned on my back, and it was open season on my face. Flags flew. The benches cleared. It was a brawl.

Eventually the officials got everything under control. It took five personal foul penalties and the ejection of one of their linebackers. Cappella stayed in the game. He even came up to me after the fight and said, "It's cool."

It's cool? Tell that to my lower lip, my right cheek, my chin . . .

When we huddled up for the next play, I had blood streaming down my face. One of my linemen saw the cuts.

"Who did that to you?!" he said. "What's his f-in' number?"

They were furious. On the next play, they went after him. Three plays after that, Smith scored on a 15-yard run.

I admit it: I tried to amp up the moment by going after Cappella earlier in the drive. I didn't know it would start a brawl, but it was time to stand up to their defensive end.

My mom, my dad, and Teri and Bryan were at the game. I told you about Teri having a football mentality. During the game, a couple of Ohio State fans seated nearby started yelling, "Get Herbstreit out of there!" Bryan had to keep Teri from going after them. And during the brawl, when she saw her kid brother getting punched, she stood up and yelled, "Get off of him!" She was fired up.

She was still upset when I saw her outside the locker room after the game. When we were away from the other parents, I told her, "Here's what happened: my offensive line was flat, and we weren't doing anything on offense. I'm the one who picked the fight."

"Really?" she said. "I'm going to kill you. I was so worried."

"I had to do it," I said. "Nothing else I said to them was working."

She thought about it for a moment.

"Man, you're awesome," she said. "You're even more awesome now that I know the story."

That's Teri. Always looking out for her kid brother.

After the game, Cooper was asked about multiple local radio reports that said he was going to resign and become the next head coach at Arkansas. Kansas coach Glen Mason, who had played for Bruce and later coached on his staff, would replace Cooper, according to the report.

Cooper said the report was untrue and basically told them to stick it before walking out of the press conference.

We had come together as a team. We would literally fight for each other. It hadn't always been that way, especially when it came to the relationship between the black dudes and white dudes on the team.

When I first got to Ohio State, we were a fragmented program. I noticed that when we would go to a team movie, all the white dudes gravitated over here, and all the black dudes would sit over there. It was the same thing during team meals. There was a division, intentional or not, that remained during each of my first four seasons on the team.

It also didn't help that we had a handful of players on those teams who had created a cynical, negative atmosphere. When we won, the victories helped mask the internal negativity. But when we lost, the cynicism was in plain sight.

I had white friends on the team, of course: Deron, Borchers, Stablein, Berger, to name a few. By the time I was a senior, I had built up a circle of friends that was predominantly black. It wasn't done on purpose. I wasn't trying to make some sort of statement—that's just who my buddies were.

As co-captains, Steve Tovar and I wanted to try to change that team dynamic of division. During those dog days of summer training camp, we began building a culture of encouragement. If, say, cornerback Foster Paulk was struggling to finish the sixteen 100-yard dashes we had to run, we'd circle back to him, pat him on the back, tell him, "You got this. You can make this."

Day after day we tried to support each other, love on one another. Little by little it began to make a difference. The veteran players, who were tired of mediocrity, began connecting with the younger players. The black dudes began connecting with the white dudes. The starters began telling the scout team players, "I really appreciate what you're doing, man. You gave us a great look out there today." We all wanted to win, but the only way we were going to do it was if we bonded together.

As the season progressed—and this was the result of everyone on the team being more conscious of the previous divisions—we knocked down a lot of the stereotypes and barriers. It wasn't forced. We built friendships that remain even today.

The other seniors on that team and I wanted to be a positive light. I felt like I could relate to a lot of the players on that roster. I had been the big-time recruit. I had been buried on the depth chart. I had been on the scout team. I had been a backup. I had switched to defense. I had wanted to quit. I had fought my way to a starting position. Maybe my experiences, good and bad, could help others.

––––––

We went to Indiana the following week. If we won and Michigan lost to Illinois at home, then we'd play the Wolverines for the Big Ten championship and a Rose Bowl invitation. Problem was, Michigan had beaten Illinois 23 of the previous 25 times and was a 28½-point favorite against the Illini.

Our kickoff was scheduled for 3:30 p.m. Meanwhile, there were rumblings about the Illinois-Michigan game, which had started at noon. During our warm-ups, we first heard that Michigan was losing late in the game. Then we heard that Michigan had lost. The news got us fired up—Michigan lost! We still had a chance to win the Big Ten!

No, wait—Michigan was losing, we were told by the Ohio State Network sideline reporter, but there was still time left in their game. A few moments before I walked out to midfield for the coin toss with Indiana quarterback Trent Green, the sideline reporter told us that Michigan was lining up for a game-tying field goal with sixteen seconds remaining. I was only a couple of steps away from shaking Green's hand when we got the sign from our sideline: the kick was good . . . the game had ended in a tie . . . Michigan had clinched the Rose Bowl berth.

One minute we thought we still had a chance at the Big Ten title, the next minute we got kicked in the shorts. I was proud, though, that we kept it together and beat IU, 27–10.

We learned later that Michigan coach Gary Moeller had chosen to kick the game-tying field goal—which would guarantee them the conference title—rather than go for the win on fourth-and-15 from the Illinois 23-yard line and keep their national championship hopes alive. The tie, Michigan's second of the season, eliminated it from the national title picture.

Maybe it was Moeller's decision to go for the tie and end their national championship hopes, or maybe it was Michigan's ten fumbles (four lost) and two interceptions, but we read later that the Big House crowd booed the Wolverines and Moeller as they walked off the field. As a player, your first instinct is to play to win. I know Moeller was doing what he thought was best, but ties stink.

In 1990, we were at Indiana and had the ball at our own 20 with a 1:04 left in the game. The score was 27–27, and it ended that way when Cooper decided to shut down our offense after an incomplete pass on first down. We ran a couple of nothing off-tackle plays and then punted. Afterward, one of our team captains, Bo Pelini, was so upset that we didn't try to score in that last minute that he started pointing and yelling in Cooper's direction. He was fired up. We all were.

That was Cooper's third season at Ohio State. A tie against Indiana wasn't going to jeopardize his job status. But as we prepared to play Michigan in our last regular-season game of 1992, the ground had shifted under Cooper. Two days before the game, the *Dispatch* reported that Cooper likely would be fired if we lost to Michigan and lost our bowl game (we had accepted a Florida Citrus Bowl invitation). Citing "high-placed university officials," the *Dispatch* said he still could lose his job if we lost to the Wolverines and won our bowl game. It came down to this: if he/we didn't beat Michigan, Cooper was probably gone, despite his signing a three-year extension that summer.

We were used to the constant local debate about Cooper's job status. But this time it seemed so definitive. According to the newspaper, we controlled his future at Ohio State. And how about this for irony: among the players strongly defending Cooper against the calls for his dismissal was Robert Smith. He told a reporter from the *Cleveland Plain Dealer*, "I think he's done a great job," and added that Ohio State should keep Cooper regardless of the Michigan game's outcome.

The whole thing was crazy. I tried to stay away from the Cooper controversy, but there was no escaping our record against Michigan since his arrival.

"I don't want to leave here having never beaten Michigan," I told Bruce Hooley of the *Plain Dealer*. "It's something you can't understand unless you grew up a Buckeyes fan."

During our practice on Thursday that week, I noticed Terry Smith standing on the sidelines. Smith was the radio play-by-play announcer for Buckeyes games. He did his homework, too. I saw him out there at least once or twice a week for the entire length of the practices. He spent a lot of time with Cooper and talked to lots of players.

When the Thursday practice ended, I jogged toward Smith and said, "Mr. Smith, I'm going to tell you right now that we're going to beat Michigan on Saturday."

He seemed surprised.

"I'm glad to hear that," he said. "I hope you're right."

Smith never went public with my prediction. He could have, and it would have been a big deal that week. *Herbstreit Guarantees Win Against Michigan*. It would have found its way onto every bulletin board at Schembechler Hall at Michigan. And if we lost, I'd be blamed for firing up the Wolverines.

Instead, he kept it to himself.

On November 21, shortly before the 12:12 p.m. kickoff at the Shoe, I was introduced by the stadium announcer, shook hands with Cooper, and then ran onto our home field for the final time in my Ohio State playing career. I was bawling like a baby. I couldn't help it. In the time it took me to join my teammates, a dozen different thoughts and moments flashed through my mind: watching games at the Shoe as a little kid . . . knowing my dad had played on that very same field . . . becoming Cooper's very first recruit . . . what could have been that season, and in my career. I cried so hard that I still had tears running down my face as I called our first play in the huddle. That stadium, that school, that uniform, those teammates, that rivalry, most of those fans . . . it meant everything to me.

I tried. We all did. I threw for a career-high 271 yards and completed 28 of 46 passes (at the time, those completion and attempt numbers were second highest in school history) on a cold, rainy day. On fourth-and-five from Michigan's five, I threw a TD pass to Greg Beatty with 4:24 left to play. Cooper chose to kick the game-tying extra point instead of going for two. With that much time left, it's hard to argue with the decision.

There was no happy ending for us. Once again, when it mattered most, we didn't take advantage of our opportunities. The Game ended in a 13–13 tie, but we could have, should have won in front of one of the loudest crowds I've ever heard at Ohio Stadium. I missed some throws. There was a blocked field goal. With 1:03 left in the game, Michigan's all–Big Ten wide receiver Derrick Alexander muffed a punt at his own eight-yard line . . . and despite having three Buckeyes near the ball, Michigan somehow recovered the fumble. It wasn't meant to be.

I wish there was overtime back then, but there wasn't. Instead, we had once again failed to beat Michigan.

As I walked slowly off the field, I started to cry. I didn't care who saw me. These were emotions that couldn't be contained.

As it turned out, Hooley of the *Plain Dealer* had watched from the south end zone as I left the field. He would tell me years later that he had never forgotten that image, that it gave him a deeper and better understanding of what that game and that rivalry meant to me and to those who played in it during that era. He had seen firsthand, he would tell me, the emotional weight of giving your all in that game and coming up short. He said he had never seen a more dejected football player in all his days of covering Ohio State.

I just felt a sense of sadness. Sad that we didn't beat them in any of the five seasons I had been at Ohio State. Sad that we couldn't figure out a way to get it done. Sad that I had played my last game on that field. Sad that I'd never get another chance to play there with my buddies and teammates. I would have done anything for my teammates.

I guess these days it sounds old-fashioned to say that. I would have cut off my left arm to play one more game with my buddies. That's why I'll never fully understand why players skip bowl games. I understand the NFL and money aspect of it, the injury possibilities. But to me, I couldn't put a dollar figure on being with my guys. Maybe that's because I knew I wasn't likely to play in the pros. This was my last regular-season game. There is nothing that compares with being part of a team like that.

Afterward, the reporters asked Ohio State president Gordon Gee about the final score.

"A tie is one of our greatest wins ever," he said. "You don't have to read between the lines to figure out this guy [Cooper] is doing a hell of a job."

It didn't feel like a win to me. It felt like a loss, and I said so after the game. "I haven't beaten Michigan yet," I told the reporters. "And now I'll never be on a team that beats them."

Decades later, it still feels like a loss.

Gee took a lot of grief for that quote about the tie. In retrospect, I think he felt such relief that we didn't lose that he simply misspoke. To him, it was a win because we didn't lose for a fifth consecutive time. Plus, a tie with Michigan was the only scenario that wasn't discussed in the *Dispatch* story earlier in the week. What would Gee do now?

After the press conference, I stayed in the locker room until it was almost deserted. I hugged and thanked as many of my teammates as I could. I just sat there, unwilling to admit I'd never be in there again as a player. It was a jarring reality.

I finally peeled off my uniform, but kept the scarlet home jersey, grass stains and all. I showered, got dressed, and waited a little while longer. I was hoping the crowd had thinned out by then. I didn't want to be around people. I didn't want to hear "We're so sorry."

It was always awkward after home games because both my mom and my dad would usually be waiting in separate areas just outside the locker room. It sucked to be a child of divorce, because you had to choose which parent you went to first. I didn't want to hurt either of their feelings. For some reason, I always felt I needed to go see my mom before I talked to my dad. She was always worried about me, always asking if my spirit was okay.

I didn't know it at the time, but my mom had cried as she waited for me to come out of the locker room. Rex Kern, one of the greatest quarterbacks in Ohio State history (an All-American who helped lead OSU to the 1968 national championship), saw my mom in tears and walked over to her.

"Mrs. H, I have to talk to you," he said.

My mom knew Kern. Everyone did.

"Don't let that boy see you crying," he told her.

"But you don't understand," she said. "He's always wanted to beat Michigan."

"Mrs. H, that boy gave everything he had," Kern said. "We don't always win in football. So don't you dare let him see you crying. He gave his all."

Then he walked away. And my mom quit crying.

I didn't, though. When I walked out and saw everyone, I started tearing up again. I kept repeating one phrase over and over to my mom.

"I love these guys."

The rivalry has changed over the years. It's still hyperintense, still must-see viewing, but the composition of the rosters is different than it was years ago. In 1992, only 22 players on our nearly 100-man roster came from outside the state borders of Ohio and Michigan. In 2020, the Buckeyes' roster had more than 60 players from states other than Ohio and Michigan. The 2020 Michigan roster featured 76 non–Ohio/Michigan players.

Back in Woody's and Bo's day, even back in my day, those rosters were primarily Ohio and Michigan kids who went to bed thinking about that rivalry. On that Saturday in November, they wanted to kill each other. But after the game was done, there was a bond between those opposing players, a respect forged because of that rivalry. Even today, if I run into a Michigan man, I'll say, "You played at Michigan? What's up?"

Today's players respect the rivalry, but many of them don't grow up with it like I did, like Desmond did, like the Ohio and Michigan high school kids do. Plus, the rivalry has become a feeding ground for internet trolls who live to blame somebody for something. Their day isn't complete without spreading their toxic negativity. They're mad because their team lost. They want the coach fired, the offensive coordinator demoted, the starting quarterback replaced, the referee punished. They're less interested in supporting their team than they are in finding reasons not to support it. And if their team wins, they turn their negativity toward the opposing team and its fans. Those people have undermined the class and stature of the Ohio State–Michigan rivalry.

I'm an Ohio State guy, and I want the Buckeyes to beat Michigan every year. But I'm also a Big Ten guy, so I want Michigan to do well in the bowl game. I want all the Big Ten teams to do well. In the 1970s, '80s, '90s, that was accepted. Now some of the fans think it's wrong to root for your league rivals. I don't.

Two days after the Michigan tie, we had our annual football appreciation banquet in front of a crowd of about 1,200. Cooper got a standing ovation, and deserved it. I got a standing O, too. In many ways, Cooper and I were the Perseverance Twins.

Cooper presented me with the team MVP award. I also received the Archie Griffin Award for offensive MVP, the Woody Hayes Award for outstanding player in the Michigan game, and the Bo Rein Award for most inspirational player.

The *Dispatch*'s May came up with his own awards in a story he wrote for the next day, including, "The Kirk Herbstreit 'Your Time Will Come' Award." I took it as a compliment. It was no accident that I told the audience that night: "In my five years here, if there's anything I've learned . . . is just because things aren't going your way right now, don't let up. Keep working, keep pushing, keep the fires burning, because it will work out for you."

Had you told me in 1990, when I was on the verge of quitting the team or transferring, that in 1992 I would receive those four awards, I would have laughed at the absurdity of it. Me? No way.

But for whatever reason—my dad's encouragement, my mom's love, my family's support, my teammates' trust—I stayed put and eventually came out the other side. Even though I'm in my early fifties, I feel like I can relate to today's players because I've lived some of their experiences. I've seen the bottom of the roster, the middle, and the top. I know what it's like to feel irrelevant, to look at the daily depth chart and see your name below everyone else's. I know what it's like not to travel with the team. I know how it feels to be on the fringes of a game, to be on the team but not really be part of the team, to hold for kicks and maybe get a few minutes of garbage time, but that's it.

As I've gotten older, I look at things more objectively than I did when I was eighteen, nineteen, and twenty. Generally speaking, I've never been a fan of players transferring because I think you learn different kinds of lessons by fighting through a situation rather than leaving a situation. There's no hard-and-fast rule to it—sometimes the circumstances almost demand that a player transfer to another program—but I'm glad I stuck it out. It helped define who I am. It made me a stronger person and, years later, a better father.

During that team banquet, I tried to remember to thank all the people who had helped me through my Ohio State journey. There was one person who deserved special mention. He wasn't family, a boyhood friend, a teammate, or a coach. Instead, he was a listener, a support system, a dependable ally.

His name was Dr. Budd Ferrante. That night, I wanted to give him a standing O.

Chapter 8

Now What?

The 349th and final pass of my football playing career was an interception—a Hail Mary pass . . . a prayer that had almost no chance of being answered. It was an unsatisfying end to an unfulfilled playing career.

We lost to Georgia, 21–14, on New Year's Day. That was a Georgia team with Garrison Hearst, Andre Hastings, Eric Zeier, and Will Muschamp.

Late in the game, with the score tied 14–14, ABC play-by-play man Roger Twibell tossed to sideline reporter Mark Jones, who did a quick interview with my dad on the sideline.

"What's going through your son's mind right now?" said Jones. "What should he do?"

"I hope he slows down a little bit in throwing the ball," my dad said nervously, in what had to be his first and last national television appearance. "We're up against a great football team in Georgia."

When Jones tossed back to the booth, Twibell said, "In other words, Dad said, 'Keep it on the ground.'"

As Twibell finished the thought, I did the exact opposite, running a counter bootleg and throwing back to Smith, who ran 45 yards to Georgia's 15. We were going to win this thing, I just knew it.

And then three plays later, Cothran and I collided on a handoff and fumbled the ball. I had checked off at the line of scrimmage, but there was a miscommunication. Georgia recovered the fumble and scored on its drive, and that was that.

On the last play of the game, I heaved a 50-plus-yard desperation pass into the end zone that was intercepted by Georgia's Mike Jones. It was such an empty, helpless feeling.

We finished the season 8-3-1. As usual, it was another *If* loss in another *If* season.

If we hadn't fumbled on the handoff exchange midway through the fourth quarter against Georgia . . .

If we hadn't missed an opportunity to close out Michigan after outplaying them the entire game . . .

If we hadn't fumbled away scoring chances against Illinois . . .

If we hadn't shown up half-awake against Wisconsin . . .

If we hadn't made those mistakes—and our three losses were by a combined 13 points—we could have been undefeated.

If . . .

My five seasons at Ohio State were like a quilt, a patchwork of frustration, anger, and unfulfillment. I don't regret going to Ohio State. After all, how can you regret a dream come true?

But this is my football reality: We didn't beat Michigan during my five years on the team. We didn't win the Big Ten or go to the Rose Bowl. We didn't win a bowl game. We didn't finish in the top 15 of the rankings, not once. There were three seasons when we didn't finish in the top 25 rankings at all.

We were a could-have-been, should-have-been kind of team. At times I was its could-have-been, should-have-been kind of quarterback. So when I say my Buckeyes career ended with a sense of unfulfillment, part of it was my own fault.

In retrospect, Michigan would have been a better football fit for me. By 1988, my true freshman year, there was a Michigan quarterback controversy involving Michael Taylor and Demetrius Brown. Would I have been in that mix? Could I have started as a true freshman? Could I have started in 1989, when Taylor and redshirt freshman Elvis Grbac both played in what would be Bo's final season at Michigan? Could it have been me in 1991 who threw those passes to Desmond?

Ifs, ands, and buts, right? Grbac, for example, went on to have a brilliant career at Michigan and spent eight years in the NFL, where he earned a Super Bowl ring and Pro Bowl honors. So I'm not about to take anything away from those other players. But I do know this: Michigan's style of offense would have given me a better chance to compete for the starting job.

It killed me . . . *killed* me to watch Michigan reach the Rose Bowl in four of the five seasons I was at Ohio State, and to win or share Big Ten titles in each of my years in Columbus. You have to understand that I was never driven by "Man, I want to win a Heisman Trophy." Not even close. I was driven by "Man, I want to wear an Ohio State jersey with a Rose Bowl patch on it."

There's a tradition at Ohio State: when you beat Michigan, each player and coach receives a Gold Pants pin. Each pin is inscribed with the date of the OSU win, the score of the game, and the player's or coach's initials. My dad had enough of them to make a charm bracelet out of his Gold Pants. They're a big deal, and were inspired by the words of coach Francis Schmidt, who was hired by Ohio State in 1934. A reporter asked Schmidt about Michigan's domination of the Buckeyes in the previous twelve years. Schmidt said, "As for Michigan, those fellas put their pants on one leg at a time, the same as everybody else."

Schmidt beat Michigan the next four times in a row.

In the end, I was born a Buckeye, raised by a Buckeye, spent every day as a kid and teenager hoping one day to be a Buckeye. It was my team then, and it's my team now. It will be my team forever.

As much as I respected Bo and would have been honored to play for him, as much as I respect the Michigan football history and the players who competed there, and as much as I wanted to run that offense, I could never have put on that Michigan uniform. I'm not sure, as an Ohio kid who dreamed of playing for Ohio State, that I can even imagine wearing a Michigan uniform while playing a game in Columbus against Ohio State. As it was, I felt funny just wearing a Michigan recruit sticker during my visit there in 1987.

The truth is, Ohio State and I are the married couple who took vows for better or for worse. At times during my career—too many times—better lost out to worse. But for every moment to forget, there were moments to remember, wins to cherish, losses to learn from, and friendships that have stood the test of time. And God help the person who ever tries to take away my Captain's Mug.

You can call me corny or nostalgic or old-school, but it meant something to me to put on that Buckeyes uniform. I loved The Best Damn Band in the Land, the Captain's Breakfast, the Victory Bell, the Buckeye helmet decals, the Shoe, and the electric current created by that crowd. I loved the traditions and history of Ohio State football, and I was, and still am, honored to be a small part of that history.

Football isn't a compassionate game. There's a finality to every aspect of it. You either succeed or you fail. The standings, the statistics, the rankings, the depth chart, the game and practice film . . . they all determine your daily status. You become part of a football ledger sheet, and the only question that matters is this: Are you an asset or a liability?

My playing career frustrates me because I know what it could have been. Part of that is on me. Part of it was out of my control. I've kind of outgrown some of that pain and frustration, but not all of it. Even now I can remember every play of every game I played. I look back and wish I would have had more opportunities to show what I could do. But there aren't mulligans in football. I never sit around and bemoan what happened. It happened, and even though it didn't turn out the way I envisioned, it helped form who I am today.

I didn't know Cooper when I signed with Ohio State. Didn't know what kind of offense he ran. Didn't know which assistants he'd hire. Didn't know which players he'd recruit. Didn't care, either.

That was a mistake. I saw scarlet and gray instead of reality. I saw my dad in those old Ohio State photos. I saw those great Woody teams. I had a romantic view of college football. It was the view of a high school senior who was convinced that he could succeed in any situation, with any coach, in any offense. I was Kirk Herbstreit, master of my destiny. I would have the best work ethic. I would have the best attitude. I would be the best teammate and leader.

I believed in me. But some of my own coaches didn't share that same belief, and never would. Over time, I developed my own self-doubts. Like I said, football isn't interested in compassion.

Cooper and I weren't close during my time at Ohio State. There was no real bond there, mostly because I spent my first year as a redshirt and the next three years as a backup before getting my chance to start full-time in my fifth and final season. He and several of those assistant coaches didn't make an investment in me during those first four years, and there were times when I didn't make an investment in them.

Now Coop and I are, well, friends? Go figure.

By the time this book is published, Coop will be eighty-four years old. He married his high school sweetheart, Helen, sixty-three years ago on Christmas Eve. He still lives in Columbus, still is a welcome visitor at the football facility, still has a soft spot for Ohio State—even though Ohio State didn't always have a soft spot for him. Truth is, I get along better with him now than I ever did when he was my head coach. Time has a way of revealing these things.

Not long ago, he told a mutual friend of ours that had I played in this era of college football, of RPOs, zone reads, spread and hybrid option offenses, I would have been "one of the top quarterbacks in the country . . . goodness, it might have changed his life. In this spread offense, he would have been an All-American quarterback for us."

Now he tells me.

Instead, I started a grand total of 14 games, completed 197 passes in 349 attempts for 2,437 yards, five touchdowns, and 11 interceptions. Those are my career stats. In 2019, LSU's Joe Burrow matched my touchdown total in his *first* game. He ended up with 60 passing TDs in 15 games. He surpassed my yardage total after just seven games that season. He finished with 5,671 passing yards. I don't know if I threw for 5,671 yards during five years' worth of practices, off-season workouts, and games.

We didn't run that kind of offense at Ohio State. RPOs didn't really exist in that form. Nobody put up those kinds of numbers back then, though in the late 1980s and early 1990s Ty Detmer at BYU and Andre Ware and David Klingler at Houston were in the neighborhood.

But Coop is right. I would have loved running Chip Kelly's offense from his Oregon days, or what they're running at Oklahoma, Clemson, Alabama, LSU—and Ohio State—these days. The offense that Patrick Mahomes ran at Texas Tech and what he runs with the Kansas City Chiefs? That would have been right up my alley. I didn't have Mahomes's arm talent, but the offense would have fit.

Life is about timing, and it turns out I played about a decade or so too early. My game would have meshed perfectly with today's game.

I never had any bitterness of any kind toward Cooper. I didn't necessarily agree with his coaching style or his choice of offenses (especially with our 1991 team). He was a believer in hiring great assistant coaches. He trusted them. He would coach the assistants, and the assistants would coach the players. He was removed from a lot of the real-time decisions until game day on Saturday.

Regrets? Maybe a few. I wish I could have started one more year. I wish the coaches would have been more flexible and molded their offense to my talents rather than forcing me to reinvent myself as a player. I don't think those coaches ever fully grasped what I could bring to the table. To me, the most successful coaches are the ones who evolve and understand that an offensive scheme and system is only as good as the players in that system.

True story—and I'm glad I didn't know it at the time: My mom, who isn't afraid to speak her mind, once confronted Cooper.

"I can't understand why you're not playing Kirk," she said to him earlier in my career.

"He's a triple-option quarterback," he explained to my mom, "and that's not our offense."

My mom thought about it for a moment and said, "Then why did you recruit him?"

I wish we'd won more games, of course. Those 1988, 1989, 1990, 1991, and 1992 teams went through a lot of turmoil and tough times, but even though we didn't get over the hump, I think our 1992 team helped pave the way for a breakthrough during the next six seasons.

Once I left the program, and as the years passed, I became much closer with Coop. I was always a fan of his perseverance. I respect anyone who does everything they can not to be overpowered by adversity and negativity. He got crushed in the local newspapers and on TV and talk radio when he was at Ohio State. I'm not sure I know anybody who was vilified by the media and fans the way Cooper was in Columbus. That negativity is one of the reasons at least one of my teammates would never read the Sunday paper, win or lose. He said he only read the comics pages, because he knew that was the only section of the paper where we wouldn't get ripped.

Cooper was fired in January 2001. He left with more career wins at Ohio State than Urban Meyer, Jim Tressel, or Bruce. The only guy ahead of him on the win list is Woody. Cooper led OSU to 91 wins in the 1990s, including a Rose Bowl victory. He's in the College Football Hall of Fame.

But during his 13 seasons in Columbus he couldn't win enough bowl games (3–8) or beat Michigan (2–10–1) to satisfy the fans, boosters, and administration. And if you can't beat Michigan as the head coach at Ohio State, then you're going to be subjected to hell. People put FOR SALE signs in his front yard. He was not only criticized, he was ridiculed by the fans for those losses, for some of the recruiting misses, for the turnover on his staff. It was brutal and even cruel what they said and did to him.

Through it all, Cooper was never hesitant to describe the realities of the job—and the public criticism that came with it. A reporter from the *Los Angeles Times* asked him about the fan pressure. His response was spot-on: "That's Columbus. Ninety-five percent of the fans in Columbus, Ohio, are fantastic. They'll support you one hundred percent. But there's five percent of them that, hey, they don't like you. They didn't like Woody, didn't like Earle Bruce, and they don't like me."

If anybody had a reason to give a big scarlet and gray F-U to everyone in Columbus, it was John Cooper. It didn't matter that he won 111 of 148 games during his Ohio State career. His legacy, according to the fans, was largely defined by those ten losses to Michigan.

Like Bruce before him, Cooper stayed in Columbus after his dismissal. He became a grandfather. He loved taking his grand-kids for walks, and people in his Upper Arlington neighborhood would see him and wave, honk their horns. *There's ol' Coop with the grandkids.*

He always told me, "Kill 'em with kindness." And he did, and still does. Ohio State fans softened their views on him. They went from "John Cooper? I can't stand that SOB!" to "Good ol' Coop—there's our guy."

When I think of John Cooper, I don't think of football. I think of a loving husband, father, and grandfather. How can you not re-spect and appreciate that? That's who I see. I really love that guy.

Do I wish Coop had never hired Ron Hudson and Eliott Uzelac? Do I wish Kent Graham—with Coop's blessing—had never transferred from Notre Dame to Ohio State? Do I wish Joey Galloway hadn't torn up his knee in 1992? Do I wish I hadn't in-jured my ankle that same season? Do I wish had done a better job grasping the offense earlier in my career?

Yes, times five. But that's football. That's life.

Coop tells people who ask about my playing career, "Well, ev-erything turned out all right for him." And it did, better than I could ever have imagined. I'm a blessed man and humbled and thankful for my good fortune. Looking back on it, those experiences and struggles had an impact on how and where I aimed my life.

On January 1, 1993, I was a team captain and starting quar-terback in a New Year's Day bowl for one of the greatest pro-grams in the history of college football. On January 2, 1993, I was suddenly an afterthought, a memory, another name to be added to the agate pages near the back of the Ohio State football media guide. My locker was cleaned out, my name tag discarded. You exist, and then you don't.

Nothing prepares you for the moment you become *former* Ohio State quarterback Kirk Herbstreit. You know it's coming. The schedule says so. The scoreboard says so. There's always an expiration date on every player's career.

I was only twenty-three, but for the last nine years of my life, I had lived by a football calendar. I followed football's code: its demands, its rewards, its emphasis on team and sacrifice. It was all I knew.

Then it was gone. Suddenly I had no place to be, no place to go. No meetings to attend, no winter conditioning program to sweat through, no media obligations, no film sessions . . . no nothing. There was almost a sense of relief. I could finally exhale.

Now I was just a regular guy, one of 52,183 students at Ohio State that year in Columbus. I wasn't fighting for a starting job. I was beginning to look for a real job.

I had one more quarter of school to complete before I got my degree in business administration. My plan in 1993? I really didn't have one.

The NFL was a possibility, though I was probably a borderline prospect. Maybe I'd get drafted. Maybe I'd sign as a free agent. That's what I told myself as I began working out just enough to stay in shape.

You have to understand that I was never a kid who lived and died with the NFL. I liked the NFL, but I *loved* college football, and baseball, too. In fact, I went out for the Ohio State baseball team that spring. I hadn't seen a live pitch in more than four years, but head coach Bob Todd let me give it a shot.

Todd, who led OSU to seven Big Ten championships, retired in 2010 as the winningest coach in school history (901 victories). He knows a player when he sees one—and I wasn't one of them.

I had been an all-state third baseman in high school, but now I was trying to make a Buckeye baseball team that had won the Big Ten title in 1991 and would win it again in 1993. You can't go four years between at-bats and expect to be successful. And I wasn't. About a week into my tryout, we both realized it wasn't going to work. Coach Todd told me he appreciated my coming out, and I thanked him for the chance.

Meanwhile, I was also knocking around the idea of maybe getting into coaching (just like my dad had thirty-two years earlier), or possibly using my marketing major to get a job with a sports company such as Nike. I was all over the map when it came to my future. The same thing applied to my dating life.

My longtime girlfriend and I were still trying to figure things out. Were we done? Were we going to give it another go? We were stuck in neutral.

On April 3, I was at my place in Columbus waiting for the Kentucky-Michigan NCAA tournament semifinal to begin. Big Blue versus the Fab Five in the New Orleans Superdome. Mashburn, Brown, Ford, Prickett, and Dent against Webber (who wore my number—4), Rose, Howard, Jackson, and King. Steve Fisher versus Rick Pitino. It was hoops heaven.

A year earlier, the Fab Five—and they were all true freshmen during that 1991–92 season—beat Ohio State in overtime in the Elite Eight. In typical Fab Five fashion, they were obnoxious about it. Still, even though it was Michigan, I found myself pulling for the maize and blue instead of the Big Blue of Kentucky. At the end of the day, I'm always a Big Ten guy.

The phone rang. When I answered, there was so much background noise that I almost had to hold the phone away from my ear.

Above the noise, I heard a woman's voice.

"Is Kirk there?"

"This is him," I said.

Then I heard a muffled sound and the line went dead. She had hung up on me.

I put the phone back on the cradle and wondered, "What's going on here? Who was that?"

I settled back into my chair to watch the Wildcats and the Wolverines. The phone rang again a few minutes later.

"Hello," I said. Same restaurant/bar-type background noise.

"Is this Kirk? This is Allison Butler, Bryan's friend."

Bryan's friend? Wait . . . Bryan Niemeyer? Then it hit me. This was the cheerleader I had asked Bryan about on the team plane six months earlier.

I instantly could feel myself tense up. The super-shy version of me began to put up a protective shield.

"Yeah, hi," I said. "How are you?"

"Hey, a group of us are out," she said. "Would you like to meet us? Tonya is with Bryan. Why don't you come on over?"

Why don't I come on over? Because super-shy Kirk didn't do anything without a wingman. I still don't.

Every alarm in my head was ringing. Crowded bar . . . social setting . . . no wingman . . . discomfort level high . . . living room couch private and safe. Take a pass, Kirk.

Instead, I took a leap of faith.

"Okay, I'll stop by," I said.

Usually I would have taken one of my roommates with me. But they were out shopping. So for one of the first times in my life—and maybe one of the last—I went to a bar by myself.

As I walked toward the door, I kept telling myself, "Well, I guess I'm going to do this."

The place was packed. The Kentucky-Michigan game was on all the big screens. People were going crazy. I felt socially naked walking in by myself.

It took a few moments, but I found Bryan, Tonya, and Allison at a table. I was nervous, and Allison had that "Oh-my-god-I-can't-believe-I-called-him-and-he-showed-up" look.

Because of the noise in the bar and the intensity of the game (Michigan won in OT) we had to raise our voices to talk. For a first meeting (you couldn't classify it as a date), that made it a little awkward. Allison was incredibly nice, and it helped there was another couple there. We played pool and made small talk.

I knew I wanted to follow up and talk to her again. I was really attracted to her. She had such a positive energy and confidence. But I was still unsure of my own relationship status (Were my girlfriend and I done, or just regrouping?) and of my job status (Was pro football somehow in my future?). My life was a question mark. I wasn't in a hurry to complicate it.

Allison was four years younger than me, and was a sophomore at Ohio State at the time. She had a boyfriend in college, but the relationship had either just ended or was in the process of ending.

Her family was from Reynoldsburg, Ohio, which is a suburb just east of Columbus. Just like I wanted to play quarterback at Ohio State, Allison wanted to be a cheerleader there. She was a competitive gymnast for six years and then became a cheerleader in high school. One day she decided she was going to dedicate herself to becoming a college cheerleader. I respected that kind of commitment.

During Allison's freshman year in 1991, her mom saw a photo of me in the game program. She pointed me out to Allison. In 1992, Allison made the varsity cheerleading team as an alternate, and her first appearance was during that road game at Syracuse, where I first saw her during the timeout.

That spring I also played on a coed softball team with Bryan and Tonya. Allison would come to some of the games, but we still hadn't had an official date. Of course, that didn't stop my sister, Teri, from making a prediction. When she found out that I had gone alone to the bar to meet Allison that night in April, she told a friend, "Oh, he's marrying her. It's over."

Allison will tell you that she's the one who started the relationship—and she's right; I'm not sure I would have had the nerve to pick up the phone and call her. She'll also tell you that she liked the idea of dating someone taller than her. Funny, the things that matter at the beginning of the dating process.

Little by little, we began seeing each other. We were both go-getters and had similar interests. But the connection took a while to turn into something serious. We were still figuring out our own lives.

———

The NFL Draft was held in New York on April 25–26. There were 224 players chosen during those eight rounds, including four Ohio State players. I wasn't one of them.

Robert Smith was taken in the first round with the 21st overall pick. Roger Harper went in the second round, while my 1992 co-captain Steve Tovar went in the third round. My buddy Brian Stablein was selected in the eighth round.

I was a little disappointed not to be drafted, but I wasn't crushed. I'm not even sure I was surprised. I knew the NFL was a long shot. That's why I didn't bother to hire an agent.

There was talk that the Bengals might sign me as a free agent, or just bring me in for a tryout. Had I pushed the envelope, I probably could have worked my way into several other free agent opportunities. But I wasn't interested in pushing.

I have all the respect in the world for those players who want to pursue their dreams of playing pro football. But I knew I didn't want to be one of those guys from Ohio State who, if they failed to make the NFL, bounced around in the arena leagues or, at the time, the World League of American Football in Europe. For every Kurt Warner, there are one thousand other guys who don't come close to making the NFL.

Playing for Ohio State was my NFL. If you gave me the choice between playing for the Reds or playing in the NFL, I would have taken the Reds. Don't get me wrong: I would have happily played in the NFL had I been drafted, but that league, as great as it is, simply wasn't part of my football DNA.

Honestly, I had had enough. Once I didn't get drafted, I was good. It's as if the NFL helped me cut the cord to my playing career. I was ready to be a normal person. I was ready to compete in the next chapter of my life.

Even in the weeks leading up to the draft, I had already started focusing on that next phase. Larry Romanoff, an assistant athletic director at Ohio State, began connecting me with his wide network of business contacts. He gave me job leads and taught me how to put together my résumé and cover letter. I reached out to a handful of companies, including Whitby Pharmaceuticals, which manufactured medical supplies, and Worthington Industries, a worldwide steel and metals manufacturing company based in Columbus. Worthington Industries was founded by John McConnell, a World War II vet, Michigan State grad, and self-made billionaire who was instrumental in bringing an NHL franchise to Columbus (he was the founder and owner of the Columbus Blue Jackets). He was beloved in the city, and a lot of former Ohio State athletes worked at his companies.

Interviews were scheduled, and if all went well, I'd start my career in medical sales or as a steel rep as soon as Ohio State handed me a diploma in June. Real life, here I come.

But I also had one other idea . . .

I wanted to be a sports talk show host.

Chapter 9

The Decision

S ome kids grow up listening to rock stations. They can sing every song, name every band. I grew up listening to Reds baseball, Ohio State football, and sports talk radio. Even when I got to Ohio State, I listened to Cris Collinsworth on WLW-AM in Cincinnati. He became my Van Halen and Aerosmith. I was always intrigued by the job itself—you get to talk sports, bust chops, and get paid for it!—and thought it would be a cool way to make a living.

I was a marketing major, not a broadcast major. It never occurred to me to take any broadcast journalism classes at Ohio State. My whole academic curriculum had been built around getting into the business world. I knew a lot of the local TV and radio reporters, anchors, and producers, as well as the newspaper beat reporters and columnists, because of the constant coverage of Ohio State football. By then I had done hundreds of media interviews. A television camera, microphone, or notebook didn't intimidate me anymore.

With the exception of Cooper, I probably did more interviews in 1992 than anyone in our program. Everyone wants to talk to the starting quarterback, especially at Ohio State. Being the starting Buckeyes quarterback is the college football equivalent to being a pitcher for the New York Yankees.

During my final season at OSU, we were covered on a daily basis by twenty-four different Ohio newspapers and publications, two wire services, five local radio stations, and four local television stations. National writers from Chicago, New York, Boston, Los Angeles, Miami, Detroit, Philadelphia, Washington, etc., were no strangers to our football facility. Those numbers have only grown through the years.

When it came to public speaking, I had no choice but to take the plunge late in my career there. I went from being the kid who didn't want to give a speech in high school to doing weekly press conferences with thirty to forty reporters in a room, all of them pointing notepads, microphones, and cameras at me. It became part of my job at Ohio State. I did live shots on the local news. I did radio interviews. Through repetition, it almost became normal to me.

Just for the heck of it, I contacted two radio stations in Columbus: 610 WTVN and 1460 WBNS. After all, if you don't believe in yourself, who will?

WTVN told me its on-air roster was full. Sorry.

WBNS said it might be interested.

Every so often I would meet with Dwight "Ike" Kelley, a former two-time Ohio State All-American linebacker in the mid-1960s who played for the Philadelphia Eagles and later became a longtime executive at Worthington. It seemed as if Worthington was interested in hiring me. Even though I knew I had little or no chance at the radio job, I asked if the company could keep me in the Columbus area. I didn't explain why I was asking.

"No," Kelley said. "It doesn't work like that in steel plants. Wherever the sales job opens up, that's where we'll send you. You'll spend a year or so grinding, but then you'll have a chance to make six figures."

As the weeks and months passed, it seemed like I was destined to become a medical supplies rep. There was a preliminary Whitby job interview in Columbus, a follow-up interview with the regional sales guy in Louisville, and a follow-up to that interview with the national sales guy in Indianapolis. They asked me about my life goals. They asked me about my career goals. They asked me to take a urine test. Whenever a company asks you to pee in a cup, you know they're serious about hiring you.

About the same time that Whitby was moving me through its interview chain, WBNS Radio called and said it wanted to talk to me. I couldn't drive to their offices fast enough.

I didn't know it at the time, but I had an ally at WBNS 1460. His name was Terry Smith. Smith was the play-by-play announcer for Ohio State football and basketball, and also the station's sports director. Everybody in Columbus simply called him "The Voice." He just had a knack for describing the huge plays in such a perfect way. His play-by-play style was energetic and upbeat.

I had reached out to him earlier that spring. It was a cold call, really.

"Terry, just wanted to see if you guys might have any opportunities at the station," I said.

He said he would check, but the conversation didn't last much longer than a few minutes. He was polite but noncommittal. I thanked him for his time, and every so often I'd call him and ask, "Hey, anything going on?"

"Not right now," he'd say. "But keep calling me. Stay in touch."

What I didn't know is that after that very first phone call, Terry had gone immediately to his station manager and his operations manager.

"I just got off the phone with Kirk Herbstreit," he told them. "He's not sure what he's going to do, but he's interested in broadcasting."

WBNS 1460 was beginning to dip its toes into the sports talk radio format. It needed "talent" (that's what they call on-air people). And it needed talent with an Ohio State connection.

Station management was interested in Art Schlichter, a former Ohio State quarterback in the early 1980s who would later play in the NFL and ultimately become infamous because of his gambling issues. At the time, he had a high profile and was doing a call-in show in Cincinnati.

Another candidate was Tom Skladany, who was one of the greatest punters of all time. He was a three-time All-American in the mid-1970s at Ohio State and owned a printing business in Columbus. He was a good talker. He was funny and conversational. Management was high on Schlichter and Skladany.

But Terry kept pitching my name.

"What about Herbstreit?" he said.

"Why do you keep bringing him up?" said his bosses. "He's never done TV or radio."

"Because he just finished his career with this team," he said. "To me, this is an absolute no-brainer. If your argument is 'He has no broadcast experience,' I'm not buying it. This guy knows sports, no doubt in my mind."

Terry arranged for me to be a guest on several shows in different time slots. He wanted management to hear how I sounded on the air. Ohio State is king in Columbus, and he knew nobody would understand the current state of the Buckeyes program better than me. But in May, June, July—the dog days of the year when Ohio State football isn't much of a factor—you have to be able to talk about other things. I'm a huge baseball fan, so I could speak that language, too.

Terry won out. WBNS 1460 said it wanted to offer me a job as a cohost, with time slot and frequency of appearances to be determined. I'd also be the sideline reporter for Ohio State football games. The salary: $12,000, nonnegotiable. And by the way, no benefits.

Some people might have been insulted by the offer. I was thrilled.

Meanwhile, my negotiations with Whitby were in the homestretch. Several times I made sure to mention my situation with WBNS 1460. I asked them if they'd have any issues with my doing the radio gig. Their response: Shouldn't be a problem. We'll work it out.

Soon Whitby made me one of those offers you can't refuse: a salary and bonus package that put me near six figures, a company car, an attractive 401(k), and I could stay in Columbus. Perfect! Plus, this was just the entry-level number in 1993. The salary and bonuses would continue to climb each year.

It was more money than my dad ever made as a coach, or my mom made as a Cadillac salesperson—or even what they made combined. For a kid who had grown up under sometimes difficult financial circumstances, who got by on a few bucks each week as a college kid, this was more money than I could imagine.

Whitby had only one nonnegotiable condition: I couldn't do the radio show.

"Do you want to do radio, or work for us?" said the Whitby exec who offered me the job.

There, my friends, was my fork-in-the-road moment. My brain and wallet were telling me to take the medical sales job (by then I had eliminated Worthington from consideration). My heart was having a fistfight with my brain and wallet.

I called every person I trusted and loved and asked them for their opinion.

When I told my longtime girlfriend that I was wrestling with the decision, she said, "Well, obviously you're taking the sales rep job." When I said I was wavering, she said, "Are you out of your mind?"

Some of my former OSU teammates were equally blunt.

"You've got to let go of your playing days," said one of my teammates. "You need to get on with your life."

When I told other friends that I was considering the WBNS 1460 offer, they reacted as if I'd said I wanted to study yoga or move to Ann Arbor.

I understood their reactions. They certainly weren't alone. They thought they had my best interests in mind, and I don't doubt their sincerity. In a way, I knew they were right.

My dad, mom, and Teri said they were supportive of whatever I decided. If anything, they thought I should take the radio gig.

I wrote down the details of each offer:

Option 1: *WBNS 1460—$12,000, no benefits.*

Uh, okay, that's about it for that one.

Option 2: *Whitby—Almost $100,000 in salary and bonuses out of college, company car, 401(k), security, paid vacations, annual increases in salary and bonuses, stay in Columbus.*

I stared at that sheet of paper. Radio . . . medical sales. Medical sales . . . radio.

Finally, I picked up my pen and wrote down one more sentence: *Do something you love.*

That's when I knew. I knew the world could do without another sales rep. I called Whitby and refused the offer I couldn't refuse. I was going to be a sports talk radio host.

Even then, I realized it was more important to find a passion in your life than a paycheck. You can't regret what you never had. I never had money as a kid. I would collect Coke bottles, put them in my wagon, and take them to the grocery store for the recycling money. If I made two or three dollars, it was a great day. But I was never driven by money. Not then, not now.

Scared? Nope. I was excited. Pumped. Ready. And sure, a little bit clueless. I had no earthly idea where any of this would lead, but I knew the idea of it made me happy.

Once I made the decision, I never looked back. I got my diploma in June 1993 and showed up for my first day of work in August. I had never spent any real time in a studio. Now I had my own pair of professional-grade headphones and a microphone. I couldn't help myself: I pressed the green button in front of me and my mic went on. I pressed the red button and it went off. I was like a little kid. I don't think I ever quit smiling that day.

Terry was the cohost of the ninety-minute nightly show—or in radio speak, he would *drive* the show, meaning he got us in and out of commercial breaks, steered the conversations, took the calls from the listeners, dealt with the producer, tossed to the weather and traffic reporters. I was just the guy in the passenger seat. I was a sidekick . . . a guest, more than a cohost at first. I even waited for my cue to talk.

I'm forever grateful to Terry, who became my first mentor in the business. He was my mother hen. Others might take credit for giving me my start in broadcasting, but Terry is the guy I called first for help. I can remember sitting next to him in the studio, and it was like an out-of-body experience. I just couldn't believe this was my job. I was like a pig in mud. I couldn't get enough of it.

When I first started, paranoid me used to prepare a daily list of about a half-dozen potential topics, just in case nobody called in. It turned out to be a colossal waste of time. We never had a shortage of callers or conversation. I quickly learned that spontaneity is what made for good radio. You can't plan it; it just happens.

Our *SportsLine* show began at 5:30 each afternoon, and by the time we worked our way through the headlines of the day, took some calls, did some interviews, did the traffic, weather, and news updates, and talked about the Buckeyes, Reds, Indians, Browns, Bengals, Columbus Clippers, and whatever else, it was time to sign off at seven. Ninety minutes were gone in a blink of an eye.

WBNS was owned by the Wolfe family. The call letters stand for Wolfe Banks, News, and Shoes, which is how the family started building its fortune in the early 1900s. The Wolfes became incredibly powerful in Columbus. They owned everything: banks, television and radio stations, the *Dispatch*. They had huge interests in all types of real estate: commercial, industrial, even farmland. They were kingmakers. They could get candidates elected or voted out. They could get coaches hired or fired. People were terrified of the Wolfes. Feared them. That was the company I worked for.

Every week I'd go to my mailbox and get my WBNS Radio paycheck. After taxes, I earned about $175 per week. I thought I was rich. I had a couple of roommates and we were splitting utilities, rent, and beer. If you had said, "You can do exactly this for the rest of your life," I would have said, "Where do I sign?" For a guy just out of college, it was heaven.

I worked Monday–Friday at the station and on Saturdays worked the Ohio State sideline for its home and away games. For away games the Wolfe family spared no expense. We didn't fly commercial. Instead, the Wolfes arranged for the broadcast crew and other company media members to meet on Fridays at Lane Aviation in Columbus, where we would board a private prop plane and fly directly to our game-day sites.

Here I was, on the road for the first time as an employee. I had my own hotel room, rather than sharing it with an Ohio State teammate. Sometimes we'd go to the house of that school's athletic director for dinner and a couple of beers. Or maybe the school's sports information director would take us out to dinner. Sometimes our radio crew would find a nice steak house and Terry would pay with the company credit card. I couldn't believe it—he always picked up the tab.

The hardest part of covering the game was lugging around my radio equipment, which, counting the microphone, the cables, and the transmitter, weighed about ten to fifteen pounds. This was 1993; nothing was small. It was like walking with a Shop-Vac attached to your hip. Sometimes my buddy Craig Schmidt would carry the radio pack for me.

The sideline gig itself was comfortable for me. I knew the players, the coaches, the system, the support staff, the trainers. I knew my way around the stadiums. I knew the opposing players and coaches. I even knew one of the cheerleaders. (I saw Allison at the games. In the past, I had even told my family, "Watch for the cheerleader with the blond hair and the really long legs.") It was in my wheelhouse. I wasn't a trained sportscaster, but I could look at a formation and tell you what they were likely to run. I had a good feel for game plans, and there were those in the program who trusted me with background information that I could use on the broadcast. We broke a few stories for the flagship station. Also, I trusted my own instincts. It wasn't uncommon for me to say something like, "Hey, guys, don't be surprised if they open up the offense on this series." And they usually did.

I still had a tendency, both during the daily radio show and during the Ohio State broadcasts, to refer to the Buckeyes as "we" or "us." Some habits were hard to break.

For big games, the national networks would often send their top broadcast crews. Jack Arute, who worked for ESPN and ABC Sports, was considered one of the best sideline reporters in the business. I had watched him as a teenager and seen him on our sideline when I was an OSU player. He would wear Ray-Ban sunglasses, and even in the dead of winter, he'd always have a tan. He just looked cool.

I was a nobody in the broadcast business. And I definitely didn't look cool on the sideline. My microphone was the size of a metal detector. I carried around a backpack stuffed with a heavy battery and transmitter unit. I looked like a ham radio operator.

Meanwhile, Jack had one of those state-of-the-art, ultra-thin, wraparound-ear mics that Madonna used during concerts. He never looked stressed.

One time, Arute walked toward me and my metal detector, shook his head, and said, "Man, what are you doing? You've got to do some TV. Why don't you do some games on ESPN and ABC?"

I turned around to see if he was talking to someone else. No, it was me. He might as well have said, "Why don't you walk on the surface of Jupiter?" I was starstruck. I saw Terry Smith a day or two later and told him, almost in disbelief, "Jack Arute was talking to *me*."

Arute did several Ohio State games that season, and every time he would tell me the same thing. And every time I would smile nervously—*He can't be serious, can he?*—and then go about my business. The whole idea seemed so crazy that I couldn't even wrap my mind around it. The odds of my getting hired by ABC or ESPN were, what, a million to one? More? There were no TV minor leagues then. It's not like I could go to ESPNU and learn the craft, because ESPNU didn't exist back then. Nor did the SEC Network, the Longhorn Network, or the ACC Network. You were either at ABC and ESPN, or you weren't.

At the time, I didn't have a vision of what I was going to do next. There was no life coach telling me, "Okay, you're going to be in radio for X number of years, and then you'll go work for ESPN." I was living day to day and loving it.

In September 1994, WBNS 1460 made the switch from an elevator-music station to a full-time all-sports format. Management gave Terry his own show (*Talk to The Voice*) in the 2–4 p.m. time slot and I stayed on *SportsLine*, but now with an expanded time slot (three hours—from 4 to 7 p.m.) and a new cohost, longtime Big Ten broadcaster Eric Kaelin.

Meanwhile, I still did sideline work for the Buckeyes' football broadcasts. And every time I saw Arute on the sidelines, he would still pester me about TV.

"When are you going to put a tape together?" he said.

"Sure, a tape," I said. "That sounds cool. I'll do that."

Except I didn't know what he was talking about. *Put a tape together?* What does that even mean?

Turns out he was referring to an audition tape. On-air people will compile their best work and then send it along to a station in a bigger market or, if they're really ambitious, to a network. Problem was, I only did radio work. I literally had nothing to put on tape.

Plus, I was busy. At the time, no former Ohio State football player was doing what I was doing in 1994: a radio show five days a week, Ohio State games on Saturdays. Rinse and repeat. I was a creature of habit, and I liked it that way. Truth is, I sort of blew off Jack's suggestion.

As usual, there was plenty to talk about when it came to Ohio State football. And in 1994, Buckeyes fans were sharpening their knives for Cooper.

It didn't help that lower-ranked Washington beat Ohio State in the second game of the season, or that unranked Illinois later upset OSU to end a three-game Buckeyes win streak. When Ohio State got blown out at No. 1 Penn State, 63–14, to drop out of the national rankings and fall to 6-3 overall, the get-rid-of-Coop cries became loud and constant.

They beat Wisconsin and Indiana to give Cooper a little breathing room. They were out of the Big Ten and Rose Bowl race (nobody was going to beat Penn State that year), but all would be forgiven in 1994 if somehow Cooper could defeat Michigan. He had been at Ohio State for six-plus seasons and had never beaten the Wolverines. An 0-for-7 record would be fatal. He *had* to win this one, or else he was almost certainly going to be fired after the game.

When I covered a game for the Ohio State Sports Network, I didn't pretend I was 100 percent objective. I was objective about the news I reported, about the information I provided. If they were playing poorly, I said so. If I saw specific issues from my vantage point on the sidelines—injuries, arguments, bad attitudes, schemes that weren't working—I had an obligation to the listeners to say so. But I *wanted* Ohio State to win. I rooted for them to win. It was my school, my team, and, in a way, my life. That doesn't just go away when they hand you a microphone and a headset. I was always going to be the guy who cherished that Ohio State Captain's Mug.

On that day, November 19, 1994, about three hundred former Buckeye players formed a human tunnel at the Shoe for the team to run through. As former players, you knew what they felt as they ran out to face Michigan: the tension, the weight of the rivalry, and a sense of excitement that you can't measure. I don't know a way of fully describing that feeling to someone who has never put on that uniform. You have to be in that locker room, be on that field, play in that game to fully understand why it matters so much.

You can say it's just a football game, but that cheapens what we felt as players—and as former players, too. Ohio State–Michigan was never just a football game to me. And it never will be. It was everything I loved and craved about competition. It meant something. What made it so special is that it meant something not just that day but months, years . . . decades later. Even today, if I see a Michigan guy I played against, we can almost sort of nod at each other and transport ourselves back to our own memories of that rivalry. Nothing personal, but that doesn't happen when I see a former Syracuse player.

Imagine how Cooper felt that day. He walked onto that field with all those expectations and pressures on his shoulders. Rumors and speculation swirled about his job status. Every day of every year he had had to hear about his winless record against Michigan. It was his scarlet and gray letter.

The closest he had come to winning against Michigan was my final season, when we tied, 13–13. In 1993, Michigan had won 28–0. It was awful to watch.

This time, Michigan was ranked No. 15, Ohio State No. 22. In Vegas, The Game was a pick-'em. The crowd of 93,869 was so loud that you couldn't hear yourself scream. It was the kind of day that reminds you why college football is so spectacular.

There was nothing pretty about the game. It was physical. You could see the blood smears on the jerseys and pants. It was hyperintense—and that extended to halftime.

Ohio State led 12–3, but Cooper wasn't happy. When I played for him, he rarely raised his voice. But this time in the locker room, that soft Tennessee twang grew loud and angry. He worked himself into a rage, enough to throw a roundhouse punch at the locker room blackboard. For the players, it was a "Whoa!" moment. *Coop is fired up!*

Even when Michigan cut the lead to 12–6 in the third quarter, there was no here-we-go-again moment on the sideline. Something was different this time. Ohio State was different.

Instead of buckling under the pressure, Ohio State punched as hard as Cooper had punched against that defenseless blackboard. In the fourth quarter, OSU kicked a field goal and then used an Eddie George touchdown run to extend the lead to 22–6. The Buckeyes' defense did the rest.

The Shoe shook as the clock moved toward those zeroes. At last, a win against Michigan: the first one since 1987, and the first one at Ohio Stadium since 1981. If you were an Ohio State fan, it was the best three hours and thirteen minutes of your year.

The players hoisted Cooper on their shoulder pads and carried him across the field. His smile was almost as wide as an end zone.

Fans made a beeline for the goalposts, and none of the stadium security guards tried to stop them. It was as if the whole city, the whole state was going to celebrate this one, including the security guards.

As I waited along with the rest of the reporters in the stadium interview room for Cooper to arrive, I was overcome by the moment. This was personal for me. I had experienced the annual pain of losing to Michigan. I had seen an entire campus and town turn against Cooper because he couldn't beat Michigan. I had seen the faces of those players after those games.

As I stood in that room, I felt all those emotions well up in me. I couldn't control it. I started to cry. I was so happy. Happy to beat Michigan. Happy for Cooper, his staff and team. Just . . . happy.

Cooper walked in wearing a bandage on his right index finger. He didn't mention his fistfight with the blackboard, but the players did. When he was done talking with the media, he gave his daughter Cindy a hug. *Dispatch* sports editor George Strode was nearby and heard Cooper tell her, "I finally got it."

Then Cooper saw me.

"I finally got it for you guys," he said.

I almost started crying again. *"You guys"* . . . the players, past and present.

You could see the pride in his face. The relief. The joy. Just a game? Tell that to Cooper and that Ohio State team. Tell it to all those people in that stadium.

Cooper said it was the biggest win of his career—and this is a guy who won a Rose Bowl while coaching at Arizona State. "I didn't beat Michigan today," he said. "Just like in past years, I didn't think I lost to Michigan."

With that one win, Cooper saved his job. He not only saved it, he soon received a new five-year contract extension, which included an incentive clause for beating Michigan.

A few weeks after the win against Michigan, WBNS 1460 offered me my own radio show in the same 4–7 p.m. time slot. By
then, I was ready to fly solo. Nothing against Eric, who moved
to our morning lineup, but I wanted to control the direction and
shape of the show. After eighteen months of apprenticeship, I felt
comfortable with the idea of lining up my own guests, framing the
conversations, getting us in and out of the breaks, trading small talk
with the weather and traffic reporters, hitting the caller buttons.

Terry Smith suggested I talk to his attorney, Brian Chorpenning, who represented him in his contract negotiations (and still
does—Terry has been the radio voice of the Los Angeles Angels for
the last twenty years). Little did I know what a critical role Brian
would play in my life as my lawyer and friend.

With Brian's help, WBNS agreed to bump up my salary to
$25,000, and added medical benefits and access to its 401(k) plan.
At the time, that seemed like a monster deal to me.

In January 1995, I worked the sidelines for Ohio State's Citrus
Bowl loss to Alabama. In February I decided to take Jack Arute's
advice. I was going to put together an audition tape.

Problem was, I didn't know where to start.

The sports director at WBNS-TV was Paul Spohn. Everyone
called him "Moose." He was built like a linebacker and had started
at the station as a news photographer in 1974. He got his nickname
years earlier while covering a truckers' strike. One of the truckers
tried to punch him out, but Paul hit him first. As the trucker staggered to his feet, he pointed at Paul and said, "This damn moose
almost got me killed." The nickname stuck.

I first met Moose when I was still in high school. He and then–
Channel 10 anchor Mike Gleason came to my house shortly after I'd
officially committed to Ohio State. Mike ended up at ESPN. Moose
spent nearly forty-seven years at WBNS-TV before retiring in 2019.

Moose was a regular at Ohio State practices and games. Those were the days when the practices were open to the media, and reporters could talk to players before and after we got onto the field. Moose was always cordial to the players. We trusted him. By then he basically ran the station's sports department, and still worked as a photographer. In 1992 he became the sports director.

For whatever reason, Moose took me under his wing. He was kind enough to give me ideas for my audition tape. He even arranged for one of the station's cameramen, Mick Lewis, to work with me. The three of us brainstormed, but there was no getting around one glaring fact: it's hard to create a TV audition tape when you haven't done any actual TV work.

Mick and Moose came up with a plan. We would include the audio of some of my work from the daily radio show (there were no simulcasts back then). We would include the audio of some of my sideline work.

"And why don't you see if you can get a couple of Ohio State players to do something on camera with you?" they said.

The bigger the names, the better. So I reached out to my buddies and former teammates Joey Galloway and Eddie George. Joey had just completed his final season at Ohio State. In April, he would be selected by the Seattle Seahawks as the eighth overall pick in the NFL Draft. Eddie had just finished his junior season—his first as a starter—and rushed for more than 1,400 yards. He would go on to win the Heisman Trophy in 1995.

I convinced Joey and Eddie to come to WBNS-TV, where Moose and Mick had arranged for us to use a studio for the taping. I made up a TV show and called it *Buckeye Corner*. The idea was for me to shoot the breeze with Joey and Eddie on camera.

Mick counted me down, and then I saw the red camera light pop on.

"Welcome back to *Buckeye Corner*," I said. "I'd like to welcome our guests, . . ."

And off we went. Joey and Eddie were great: funny, conversational, opinionated. They probably performed better on camera than I did. Eddie, whose muscles had muscles, looked like an action movie star. Joey, even back then, had a playful, combative attitude. I interviewed them for about ten minutes, but I would end up owing them for years.

After we were done, Mick and I packed up the gear and drove to Ohio Stadium. Even though the audition tape was going to include examples of my sideline radio work, we decided to do something on camera, too.

The low temperature that day was zero degrees. When we got there, it was about 18 degrees. A warm front! The sky was dark gray; the freezing wind howled through the deserted old stadium. Mick set up his camera and I took my place on the field.

Usually when I did a game report, the place would be packed. I'd have to raise my voice to be heard over the crowd and the band. This time it was like doing a report from inside an empty meat locker.

I grew up in Ohio and was used to playing in cold weather. But standing in cold weather is different than playing in it. It said 18 degrees on the car dashboard, but with the windchill, it was a lot colder. I bounced around and tried to do anything to stay warm. My face was so cold that I was a little worried I wouldn't be able to talk naturally.

As Mick made his final adjustments on the camera, I thought through my fake report. If you're going to apply to a network, then you might as well pretend you work for the network, right? So I pretended that the legendary Brent Musburger was up in the Ohio Stadium broadcast booth.

Once again, Mick counted me down. Three, two, one . . . go.

In my head I heard the imaginary voice of the great Musburger telling his national TV audience, "Now let's go down to the field, where our Kirk Herbstreit has an update."

I took a deep breath. *Here we go, kid. It's only your future.*

"Thanks, Brent." And then I did a fake injury update on an Ohio State player who had been hurt earlier in the fake game. I taped another 30–40-second report on some other fake topic.

If you think about it, the whole thing was ridiculous. There was no crowd. There were no players or coaches. There was definitely no Brent. I had wind burn. My toes and face were numb. This had no chance of success.

Mick and Moose edited the material and made it look as professional as they could. They did two separate tapes. At the time, the World Wide Web was only a few years old. You couldn't just google the names and addresses of the people who made the on-air decisions at ABC Sports, ESPN, NBC Sports, or CBS Sports. Google didn't even exist. Back then, we still had phone books and yellow pages. You looked things up by hand. That must seem almost unimaginable to anybody younger than thirty years old today.

Because Arute worked for ABC Sports and ESPN, that's where I decided to first send my audition tapes. I called information in New York and asked for the phone number of ABC Sports. I knew ESPN was in Connecticut, but wasn't sure where. There is absolutely no chance I could have told you where Bristol, Connecticut, was on a map.

I talked to a receptionist at each network and asked who I should send my tape to. And, oh, can I get an address, too? I could almost see them rolling their eyes. How many aspiring broadcasters must have asked them those same questions over the years?

I got two names—and I had never heard of either one of them: Jack O'Hara at ABC Sports and Mo Davenport at ESPN. I didn't know their job titles or what they did. I just sent them the tapes and hoped for the best.

For weeks, there was no response. Then in April I got a letter from O'Hara. It was on ABC Sports letterhead. Turns out he was the executive producer in charge of all programming on ABC Sports. He was a heavy hitter in the business—a multiple Emmy Award winner, a guy who oversaw all the big events: *Monday Night Football*, the Kentucky Derby, college football, anything associated with the famed *Wide World of Sports* show. The list went on and on.

"Thank you for your note and tape," he wrote. "Unfortunately we don't have anything available right now. We'll keep your tape on file and keep you in mind for later."

It was so kind of him to take the time to write. I folded up the letter and placed it back in the envelope. Even though it was a semi-rejection letter, I was so impressed that O'Hara had personally responded. Very classy.

About a month or so later, ESPN called and asked if I could fly to its headquarters in Bristol for an audition. I couldn't believe it. Somehow me and my make-believe *Buckeye Corner* had made it into the hands of Davenport, the senior coordinating producer of college football. Davenport said later that the Arute connection probably got him to take a look at my tape before he considered the others stacked in his office.

Shortly after the call, I found Terry at the radio station.

"I've got something I want to tell you," I said. "I have an interview at ESPN."

"What? Really?" he said. He was as shocked as I was. "Man, that's fantastic. Don't get your hopes up too high. When you get there, I hope something good happens for you."

I was in a daze. I was also so naïve. I honestly thought I would have to pay for my own flight to ESPN. "No, no, no," they said. "We'll pay for your flight." I thought that was crazy.

I was an ESPN subscriber. Whatever it cost on my monthly cable bill, it was worth every penny to me. I lived for sports. I could hum ESPN's theme music for college football, bar for bar.

I could tell you every person shown during that pregame intro (Knute Rockne, Tony Dorsett, Bear Bryant, Doug Flutie, Desmond Howard, the USC drum major, the guys driving the Sooner Schooner, and Charlie Ward). I could name you ESPN's lineup of *SportsCenter* anchors. And now I had a chance to work at the same network? It didn't seem real.

As part of my visit, ESPN said I would spend time in one of their studios with a show host. They wanted to see how comfortable I was in front of a camera, and how I interacted with a studio host. Then, a few days before my trip, ESPN sent me the media guides and pregame notes from the 1994 Georgia-Alabama matchup in Tuscaloosa. I assumed that meant we would pretend the game was live and I would call part of it as if I were in the booth as a color analyst that night at Bryant-Denny Stadium.

Bama's Michael Proctor had kicked what turned out to be the game-winning field goal with 1:12 left to play. Quarterback Jay Barker had out-dueled Georgia's Heisman candidate Eric Zeier in the 29–28 win. And a Bama wide receiver named Toderick Malone had blown by a Georgia safety for a 49-yard touchdown reception. The safety was Will Muschamp, who went on to become the head coach at Florida and South Carolina. (Muschamp and Zeier had beaten my 1992 team in a bowl game.) The game was so good that it became part of the *ESPN Classics* rotation.

If I was going to call part of that game, I had to be prepared. You can't call a game without a board. A board is what play-by-play and analysts use to organize and identify the starting lineups, jersey numbers, the backups, the key special teams players. It includes highlighted notes and stats.

Terry was a master at putting together a board. He took a lot of pride in his Ohio State game-day charts. They were meticulous. I marveled at the detail and prep work that went into them. As a player,

I prided myself on total preparation for a game. Terry was the same way when it came to calling a game, and it rubbed off on me.

Terry gave me a copy of a chart he had done for an Ohio State–Purdue game. I used it as a model for my Georgia-Alabama game. On one side I had the Georgia offense and the Alabama defense. Flip it over and I had the Alabama offense and the Georgia defense.

My flight to ESPN was at 7 a.m. I stayed up until 3 a.m. the night before working on my chart. You would have thought I was making a project for the county science fair. I used a ruler to make sure every line was even and just so. I listed every starter, every backup on both sides of the ball. I searched through the Bama and Georgia media guides to jot down interesting tidbits and statistics about each player. *Larry's uncle played for the Dallas Cowboys . . . Bob's great-grandfather performed in the circus . . .* I had a highlighter, and by the time I was done with that board, there was no highlight, left.

That board was perfect. It was a work of football art. I carried it on the plane like it was a precious Van Gogh. The board was *not* going to be stored in the overhead compartment.

When I landed at Bradley International Airport, there was a car and driver waiting for me. For me! I didn't know what to do—sit in the front or back seat? It felt so weird having someone drive me and my game board.

About ten thousand thoughts were going through my mind as we made the forty-five-minute drive to Bristol. I was nervous, but prepared. I felt like I was getting ready to play a game.

I had never been to Connecticut. We drove through the heart of Hartford, then past a few smaller towns, then . . . nothing. This place was in the middle of nowhere. We were on I-84, took a right onto a rural road, and a few miles later there it was on the right: ESPN's worldwide headquarters. There were a series of low-slung buildings and huge satellite dishes everywhere.

The first stop was an interview with Davenport. He was gracious, but he had this little smirk on his face when he asked me, "What makes you think you have something to offer us? What do you bring to the table?"

So much for small talk.

It was a fair question. I had no on-air television experience. I wasn't a journalist. I worked in a medium-sized market as a sports talk show host. I did radio sideline reporting.

How many job applicants had sat in that same seat across from Davenport, all of them trying to make an impression? How many of them had been from the Columbus, Ohios, of the world, or even smaller?

What did I bring to ESPN's football table? I brought the experience of being a recent starting quarterback at one of college football's legacy programs. I brought my continuing connection with Ohio State and Big Ten football. I brought a new look and perspective—not of a big-time star but of someone who had had to work his way up the football and broadcast ladders rung by rung. I might have been the five-star high school recruit, but I was the zero-star broadcast recruit. I brought a work ethic, teamwork, and the constant need to get better.

Davenport's smirk began to disappear. I felt very comfortable talking to him. It started as a job interview and ended as a conversation.

"Let's go downstairs to the studio," he said. "Jack Edwards is going to do a few segments with you."

Edwards was a *SportsCenter* anchor. He must have drawn the short straw to have to work with a nobody who was in town for an audition. We shook hands and I took my place behind the studio desk.

There was no time to savor the moment, or to be terrified by it. The producer said we were ready to start, and suddenly Edwards turned to me and said, "Okay, Kirk, what do you think about the Colorado State–Colorado game?"

We went back and forth for about five minutes—just long

enough to start feeling a little bit comfortable—when the producer abruptly ended the segment.

"Okay, we're good there, thank you," he said. "Let's get that Georgia-Alabama game on the monitors. Jack, you'll do the play-by-play, and Kirk, you'll do color of the game."

All right, then, here we go, boys. I reached under the desk and pulled out the masterpiece of game boards. I had spent most of the flight from Columbus to Hartford studying and memorizing every detail of the board. I was ready.

Edwards leaned over to look at the board as I positioned it in front of me on the desk.

"Wow, you put some time into that," he said.

"Thank you," I said proudly. "I did."

A few moments later the producer counted us down.

Edwards did a quick setup, and then Bama kicked off to start the game. There was a touchback, and Georgia began its drive on the 20-yard line. There was a 10-yard run by Larry Bowie, followed by a 14-yard completion to Jeff Thomas, followed by a 1-yard run by Bowie.

I had barely looked at my board when the producer interrupted our broadcast.

"Okay, we're good," he said. "Thanks for everything."

Wait. What? I thought I was going to do the whole game, or at least the first half.

Edwards unclipped his microphone, stood up, shook my hand, wished me luck, and then took off. I sat there for a moment, just me and my magnificent board.

Davenport walked me out to the car, shook my hand, and said, "We'll be in touch. Appreciate you coming out."

And that was that. I flew back to Columbus and fell back into my routine of doing the 4–7 p.m. drive-time show. Nobody ever called in to talk about Colorado State–Colorado, but we did talk about the dreadful Ohio State basketball season (6–22 overall, 2–16 in the Big Ten), the arrival of spring training, and the start of the Indians' and Reds' seasons, as well as that of our Triple-A team, the Columbus Clippers, who were the International League affiliate of the New York Yankees.

The Columbus roster that season included a twenty-one-year-old shortstop who played 123 games for the Clippers: Derek Jeter. A twenty-five-year-old pitcher from Panama named Mariano Rivera started seven games for Columbus. Andy Pettitte, twenty-three, spent time in Columbus in 1995. So did twenty-four-year-old catcher Jorge Posada and even thirty-three-year-old former All-Star Darryl Strawberry.

At the time, we didn't know Jeter and Rivera were going to become Hall of Famers. They were just guys we watched during Dime-a-Dog nights at Clippers games.

May turned to June, June to July. I had never heard back from ESPN—so much for that dream—but there was one other TV possibility.

Weekend sports anchor Jay Crawford, who had been hired by WBNS-TV the same year I was hired for radio, had mentioned that he was going to be part of a new half-hour sports wrap-up show on Sunday nights.

I had met Jay at a local softball tournament and was impressed by his game. (Jay ended up playing a little minor-league ball as a pitcher, threw simulated games at spring training, and still pitches 80-plus innings in Over-40 leagues.) Those games were no joke. We worked for the same company, but WBNS-TV was a big competitor of WBNS-Radio on the softball field. We were playing for blood.

Jay was four years older than me, but we connected over baseball and formed a quick friendship. He had such an infectious personality. In fact, when Major League Baseball went on strike in mid-

August 1994, Jay and I began playing each other on a baseball video game. We even created our own World Series matchup on the video game: my Reds versus his Indians. I can't remember who won.

You know Jay, of course, from his long and successful career as an ESPN anchor and host. He's now an anchor at a Cleveland TV station.

But when we were both in Columbus, the idea of a local affiliate doing a late Sunday night highlights show was still a novelty. It was only after the local ABC affiliate did a half-hour wrap-up show that WBNS-TV decided to put together its own program.

Jay started to recruit me.

"Why are you in radio?" he said. "You're way too pretty to be on radio. You need to be in front of a TV camera."

Jay was kidding me about being way too pretty, but he was serious about the Sunday night show. He told me he thought I'd be the perfect cohost, that I would have credibility with the viewers because of my Ohio State career. And I think we shared sort of an energy, an enthusiasm about sports.

"I would love to do TV if I ever got the opportunity," I told him.

"I'd love to have you come in and help shoot the pilot," he said.

Behind the scenes, Moose had been pushing for me to become part of the show. I wasn't aware of his lobbying, but he told a reporter years later that he went to his bosses and said, "I think this kid can be a star. I'm not the brightest bulb in the pack, but I know how to hire."

They gave him the green light to offer me the job. His job pitch was short and sweet.

"Hey, look, we're starting a show on Sunday nights in September," he said. "We're calling it *Wall to Wall Sports*. How about doing it?"

I was twenty-five years old. I had never done live TV. I had never done live studio TV.

I said yes. In a heartbeat.

Chapter 10

The Sweat-Stained Miracle

I n early August of 1995, I was on a fishing trip with my dad, my grandpa, and my uncle Rick (my dad's younger brother) in the Upper Peninsula of Michigan. We returned from the lake one day and there was a message for me to call my roommate in Columbus. I didn't have a cell phone at the time, so I called back on a landline.

"Hey, I didn't know if this was important or not," he said, "but some guy named Mo Davenport called for you."

Hmmm. Mo? I didn't know a Mo. And then I remembered: Mo from ESPN. *That* Mo. It had been so long that I had almost forgotten who he was.

I immediately called Davenport. He had some news.

"We're getting ready to launch a new network called ESPN2," said Davenport. "There's going to be college football content, so we're looking for sideline reporters. We'd like to offer you a thirteen-game package. You'll be working some West Coast games and Big Ten games."

I couldn't speak at first. One minute I had been fishing for small-mouth bass and jumbo perch. And then, with a phone call to Bristol, Connecticut, my life changed.

Davenport continued.

"As for compensation, we're going to pay you $875 per game," he said.

As soon as he said that, I started doing the math in my head. *Let's see, $875 x 13 equals . . . $11,375!* That's almost what I made during my first year as a radio cohost at WBNS 1460. If I combined my WBNS salary with the ESPN2 offer, I was going to make nearly $40,000. I'd hit the jackpot. This was going to be the highlight of my career.

I tried to keep my voice even and professional.

"This sounds great," I said. "I'm in. Absolutely, count me in."

A week or two later, I was back in Bristol for ESPN's annual college football seminar. The entire network roster of college play-by-play announcers, analysts, producers, sideline reporters, directors, and executives were there, as well as the entire *College GameDay* cast, including Chris Fowler, Lee Corso, and Craig James. I couldn't believe I was sitting in the same room as them.

September 1995 was a month of firsts for me:

My first ESPN assignment.

My first trip to Hawaii.

My first time watching a running back who would later make history in both the college and pro game.

My first near-drowning.

ESPN sent me to Honolulu as the sideline reporter for the Texas versus Hawaii game. Once there, I reported to Roy Hamilton, a scary producer who didn't even try to hide his irritation with me. He was annoyed that ESPN had assigned him a rookie sideline reporter with no television experience. He resented the idea that he was somehow on baby-sitter duty.

Hamilton was a former big-time high school hoops player out of Los Angeles who ended up at UCLA and was chosen No. 10 overall in the 1979 NBA Draft by the Detroit Pistons, just nine spots after No. 1 pick Magic Johnson. He played one season for Detroit (Coach Dick Vitale was fired that season after just twelve games), and then one game for the Portland Trail Blazers in 1980 before he was out of the league. He transitioned to the production side of television in 1982.

I could sense Hamilton's frustration with me. He was right, I didn't know much about TV. But I knew how to work hard, and how to take coaching. Hamilton wasn't interested in that. So I went from the high of a pinch-yourself moment—"I'm doing my first game for ESPN!"—to the low of "Oh my god, I better not mess up."

During my short visit to Honolulu, I found time to head to the beach. I'm a Midwest guy: freshwater lakes, rivers, ponds. The Pacific Ocean was a beast.

I drove to a place called Sandy Beach, which is on the South Shore of Oahu. I was told Sandy's—as the locals called it—was *the* place to go for surfing, bodysurfing, and boogie boarding. They said the shore break there created perfect barrel waves.

What they didn't tell me was that the other nickname of Sandy Beach was "Break-neck Beach," because of all the broken bones and back and neck compressions caused by the waves. I also wasn't aware that those shore breaks also created powerful rip currents.

I should have known something was different when I saw some of the locals kneel on the sand, make the sign of the cross, and say a prayer before they entered the water. But hey, I was a former Ohio State quarterback, still in pretty good shape—how bad could it be?

Minutes after I swam out into the ocean, the water's edge dropped off. Then a wave appeared from nowhere and just crushed me. As I tried to swim to the surface, the undertow pulled me back. It was like somebody was trying to grab my legs.

I'm not the greatest swimmer, but I thought I was strong enough to work my way back to the shore. Instead, I kept being pulled by the riptides and pounded by the waves. I literally was fighting for my life. It was terrifying.

For ten or so minutes—it seemed like hours—I tried to break free. Somehow there was a moment when the waves and undertow subsided just long enough for me to break through and make it back. This time it was me who wanted to say a prayer.

My first ESPN game was a blowout. Texas won, 38–17. But how about being there the night a kid from Patrick Henry High School in San Diego made his Longhorn debut? His name was Ricky Williams, and he became the first true freshman running back to start a Texas season opener since Earl Campbell in 1974.

Texas was still in the Southwest Conference at the time, and Williams was in jersey No. 11, not what would become his signature No. 34. Didn't matter. He ran for 95 yards on just 10 carries. He scored twice. He caught a 48-yard pass.

Ricky would end the season as the conference freshman of the year, later become a two-time All-American, record two 300-yard rushing games and eleven 200-yard games, lead the nation in rushing as a junior and senior, and win the Heisman Trophy in 1998. The New Orleans Saints and Mike Ditka would trade away all their picks to get Ricky in the 1999 NFL Draft.

I can proudly say I was there on the field when he gained his first collegiate yard.

There was one more first for me in September: On September 17 at 11:35 p.m., *Wall to Wall Sports* made its live debut on WBNS-TV. Jay was the main host, along with me and Channel 10 sports reporter and anchor Dom Tiberi.

It's one thing to do a sideline report for an Ohio State football game. That was in my wheelhouse. But with the exception of my ESPN2 audition and my make-believe *Buckeyes Corner* bit for my audition tape, I had never spent any time in an actual television studio.

Making matters worse was the studio setup. Don't get me wrong, it looked impressive. We had a massive wall of TV monitors for the highlights, and we had a great production crew. But there was a piece of studio equipment that freaked me out.

The teleprompter.

I was used to holding a microphone and providing information. I just talked. Now I would be in a studio sitting in a director's chair, reading from a teleprompter, and then be expected to seamlessly talk to Jay and Dom, too. And did I mention the studio lights? Bright . . . hot.

The teleprompter was intimidating for someone who had no experience in TV multitasking. It would be like asking Jay to run the veer option. Jay knew how to read off a teleprompter and make it sound as if he weren't reading at all. He was just talking. Me? I sounded like I was reading a book report in front of my fourth-grade class:

Hi. I. Am. Kirk. Herb. Streit.

I tried to follow Jay's lead. He was so intense, so sure of what he was doing. We had to write our own lead-ins to each segment. I typed with two fingers and struggled to find the right words. Jay and Dom were always there to help in any way they could, but there was only so much they could do.

I was nervous and self-conscious. I was also sweating. I tend to do that.

For the first three or four weeks of the show, I was a mess. The studio crew actually placed a towel on my director's chair. They called it my "sweat towel."

Moose was there for each show and stood at the edge of the set, just outside the view of the cameras. When someone later asked him how I did during those early shows, Moose said, "He was shitting himself. You'd have to towel him down, wipe him off during every commercial break."

Yeah, that's about right.

At the time, I was the first former Ohio State football player to not only do radio but also TV. I was forging a broadcasting path that other OSU players would follow: Ryan Miller, Robert Smith, Eddie George, Joey Galloway, Stanley Jackson, Justin Zwick, Chris Spielman, and Joshua Perry, among others. There were growing pains, but after each show I would sit down with Moose and we would dissect the broadcast.

He would say, "I liked how you got in and out of that sound bite." . . . "Look into the camera. When you look into the camera, you're looking at the audience. They're watching you. They don't want to see the side of your face." . . . "It's okay to look at Jay once in a while, but remember to turn back to the camera."

Moose was always so positive and encouraging. He made suggestions, but in a way that made you feel good about yourself.

I soaked in all the advice. I wanted to get better. I would go home and watch other broadcasters on ESPN to see how they did it. That's what was so exciting for me: each week I could feel myself getting more comfortable in front of the camera. I was finding my rhythm. It was like learning a new offense. I went from "I'm not sure I can do this" to "Maybe I was made for this."

In late September, ESPN assigned me to the BYU–Colorado State game in Fort Collins. Sonny Lubick was the head coach, and on his staff was young, little-known assistant named Urban Meyer. Urban was a graduate assistant at Ohio State in 1986–87, and I remembered meeting him during a campus visit.

Week after week, I called Davenport for a critique of my work. I'd always end the conversation, "Hey, if there's a chance to do a game as an analyst, I'd love the opportunity." I was relentless.

"Listen, I'll do my best," he said, "but there's probably not going to be a game."

"Okay, all right, I hear you," I said.

And then the next week I'd ask him again.

Finally, in November, Davenport called with a game opportunity: Wisconsin at Minnesota. My play-by-play partner was Gary Thorne, a former-lawyer-turned-broadcaster whom I had heard countless times doing NHL and MLB games.

Neither team was very good (both would finish with losing records), but the game was so much fun to cover in a sold-out Metrodome. It was the first game I had done as an analyst in my life, but it felt so natural. There was a 100-yard kickoff return, a 60-yard field goal that might have been good from 70, and four touchdown passes of 51 yards or longer. Wisconsin won the game, and afterward, Badgers quarterback Darrell Bevell (now Meyer's offensive coordinator with the Jacksonville Jaguars) ran to the Minnesota sideline, grabbed the Paul Bunyan Axe, ran to the goalpost, and acted as if he were chopping it down.

They don't do that in the NFL.

In early spring of 1996, Davenport called and said ESPN wanted to tear up my existing contract, give me a raise to $90,000 a year, and add Arena Football League analyst duties to my schedule. I could stay in Columbus and continue doing my radio show and *Wall to Wall Sports*.

I nearly passed out.

"Yeah, man, let's do it," I told Davenport.

Once again, I turned to my lawyer, advisor, and friend Brian Chorpenning. To this day I have never signed any document unless it was first reviewed and approved by Brian.

At the time, Brian ran a local firm and was basically doing me a favor. We worked our way through the negotiations and trusted our instincts. Eventually, we agreed to a deal with ESPN, and soon enough, I was a color analyst for the Arena Football games.

Former Oakland Raider tight end Todd Christiansen was the veteran play-by-play man. Brian also improved my salaries for the radio show and the Sunday night TV show.

In June, Davenport called again.

"Hey, I wanted to let you know that Craig James left us for CBS," he said. "You're too young and you're not going to get the job, but we want you to come in and audition for the opening. We're going to fly Corso and Fowler in for the audition."

This was like a head coach saying, "Our star quarterback just declared for the NFL Draft. You're not good enough and you're never going to be the starter, but we'd like you to take a few snaps in a scrimmage."

Fowler, Coach Corso, and James had helped build *College GameDay* into a real force. But CBS had offered James a big-money deal and the opportunity to do college football, the Winter Olympics in 1998, college basketball, and tennis tournaments. James had been at ESPN since 1991 as an analyst and studio host.

"Craig is the best college football studio analyst out there, and now he's on our team," bragged CBS Sports executive Rick Gentile to reporters.

I was a huge fan of *GameDay*, and somewhere in the back of my mind I had it as a ten-year goal to be a part of that show. I didn't know it at the time, but Brian had reached out to ESPN when he first heard the rumors of James leaving for CBS.

"He's a fresh face, only twenty-six years old, good-looking kid," said Brian to his contacts at ESPN. "You know his work, he's a natural in front of the camera."

But Davenport made it clear that I wouldn't be a member of the show anytime soon. This was a courtesy audition, nothing more. In baseball terms, they were calling me up from the minors to pitch batting practice.

I learned later that they had already arranged for veteran sports-caster Mike Adamle to audition for the *GameDay* opening. I could see why. Adamle was an All-American at Northwestern, a Big Ten MVP, had played in the NFL, had worked for NBC Sports and ABC Sports, had anchored local sports at a large-market station in Chicago, and been a cohost of the popular *American Gladiators* show. He had a great voice and experience as a play-by-play guy, as an analyst, as a sideline reporter, and as a studio anchor. He had a national brand. I didn't. If you were handicapping it, Adamle would have been the even-money favorite, me the 1,000-1 long shot. In fact, when I told Terry Smith about my audition, his first reaction was disbelief.

"Oh my gosh, this is unbelievable," he said.

I flew into Hartford from Columbus the morning of the au-dition. I barely got any sleep the night before the flight. I had stared at the ceiling as I worried and wondered what they were going to ask me to do.

When I arrived at ESPN for the audition, I was as nervous as I've ever been for anything in my life, and that includes my first start as an Ohio State quarterback, my first audition at ESPN, getting married, having twins, and calling national championships. Coach Corso had flown up from his home in Orlando. Fowler had come from his place in Colorado, I think.

A producer stopped by and gave me my instructions.

"We're going to do a segment that includes some highlights," he said. "Familiarize yourself with the material and we'll get going in an hour or two."

He could see the nervousness on my face.

"Look, you've seen our show," he said. "We just want you to talk."

Sure, just talk. Except I was used to talking with my buddies at a bar. Or on *Wall to Wall Sports*. Or on my little radio show in Columbus. Or as a sideline reporter. Or in the relative obscurity of Arena Football League games. This wasn't just talking, this was *College GameDay*. This was Chris Fowler and Lee Corso. I knew I had no shot at getting the job, but I didn't want to embarrass myself.

I pored over the Nebraska highlights they had given me to study. I could feel my pulse beginning to settle down. The anxiety lessened as I did the prep work. This was football. I *knew* football. I'll just talk. Suddenly I had confidence that I could do this.

It was time to start the audition. I was fine until I walked into the studio and saw Fowler and Corso. The anxiety and nervousness returned. I suddenly had a case of the self-doubts. *What am I doing here? Can I actually pull this off?*

The studio itself was more like a garage setup. Whatever the opposite of state-of-the-art is, this was it. I think they used it for NASCAR and college basketball highlight shows back then. It definitely wasn't in the main building.

"Hey, nice meeting you," said Fowler, hand extended. I mumbled something back.

At the time, Chris knew a little bit about my work. But he also knew Adamle was the clear favorite for the job. *College GameDay* wasn't the mega-profile show it would later become, but it was important enough that the replacement hire for James could help determine its success or possible failure.

As I took my place behind the studio desk, I could feel myself starting to sweat. All I could think was, "I'm sitting next to Corso. *THE* Lee Corso."

This was 1996 Coach Corso. He was in his absolute prime, a force of TV nature. Edgy, funny, filled with attitude and conviction about anything he said on-air. He didn't say something just to say it. He believed in it, and it showed. I thought it then and I still think it now: he's the greatest entertainer in sports television history.

And he was sitting right next to me.

Coach could have big-timed me. I was a nobody compared to him. I was a nobody compared to his former studio partner, James. Coach could have said to himself, "Who's *this* guy? What are we doing here? I flew all the way up from Orlando for *him*?"

Instead, he leaned over and introduced himself—as if he needed an introduction. He couldn't have been nicer. Turns out that one of Coach's first broadcasting assignments at ESPN in 1987 was as a color analyst for . . . the Arena Football League. And as a former head coach at Indiana, he knew his Big Ten football history.

"Your dad coached and played at Ohio State, didn't he?"

"Yes, Coach, he did."

Fowler and Corso were as calm as could be. Meanwhile, my heart was beating out of my chest.

"Just relax," Corso said. "Let's have some fun."

Relax? I could barely breathe. My sweat was sweating, I was so nervous.

Corso told me years later that he treated me that day as if he were a coach and I were one of his players. To him, I was the nervous freshman quarterback making his first start. Like any good coach, his job was to inspire confidence. That's what he tried to do.

"Take it easy," he said. "You'll be just fine."

The *GameDay* theme music started. There were TV monitors on the floor, and I saw the *GameDay* logo appear on the screen. This was happening. This was really happening.

Chris jumped in and started to talk—and he sounded like just like the guy I had heard so many times on TV. It was surreal.

"Welcome back to *College GameDay*," he began. "Let's break down some football."

He turned to Lee. "Coach, what do you think about the Cornhuskers?"

Corso did an effortless twenty- to thirty-second analysis of Nebraska. And then he turned to me.

I don't even know what I said. I think I blacked out for most of the audition. In fact, I would be terrified to see that audition tape today.

I was sweating like Albert Brooks in that scene from *Broadcast News*. It was as if someone had opened a perspiration spigot. It was next-level sweating, epic and uncontrollable. It trickled down my face. It began to soak my dress shirt. I'm sure Fowler, Corso, and the people in the production room were looking at me and thinking, "Holy shit, what's going on with this guy?"

(Coach would later tell an interviewer: "On his audition . . . Holy mackerel. He was so nervous, sweating like a son of a gun. But I liked him. I wanted him to get the job.")

My body temperature has always run hot. My mom told me that even as a baby I would sweat. My head would stick to the pillow in my crib. I was a big, bald, overheated, reddish, sweaty baby.

With the exception of someone like George Clooney or Beyoncé, everybody has a physical feature they'd like to change. With me, I wish I could lower my body temperature. It can be the middle of winter and I'll still sleep with no blankets on the bed. In the summer I can crank the air-conditioning to 65 degrees, but still need a fan blowing on me.

Because I'm incredibly shy, I start to heat up when I'm forced out of my comfort zone. It's not necessarily a nerves thing, it's a discomfort thing. When I walked into that smallish studio for the audition, I instantly knew I was in trouble. Had the AC been lowered to, say, 58 degrees, I would have been like, "Boys, how you doing?" I would have known it was cold enough to keep me comfortable.

Instead, it was warm. Too warm. I started to worry that I was going to sweat, and that made me sweat even more.

Even now on *GameDay*, I have a fan that blows underneath the desk. There's even a vent that blows ice-cold air up the sleeve of my suit and dress shirt. During those August and September games, when it's still toasty in places like Baton Rouge, or Austin, or Miami, or Athens, or Clemson, I struggle to stay cool on the set. If they go to, say, a single shot of Des breaking down game film, I reach for the paper towels to pat down the perspiration on my forehead. When we get to late October, November, and December and the temperatures drop into the 20s and 10s in places such as State College, Ann Arbor, Pullman, and Minneapolis, I still have the air-conditioning cranked up on the set. Rece, Pollack, and Des crush me for that, but I don't care.

GameDay coordinating producer Steve Vecchione and *GameDay* producer Lisa Kraus were there that day of the audition. I don't know who else was watching. With the exception of Fowler, Corso, Vecchione, and Kraus, nobody really introduced themselves. After watching me get lathered up through the segment, they were probably counting the minutes until Adamle had his audition the same day.

I couldn't relax. Words were coming out, but I couldn't tell if they made sense. It wasn't a matter of being unprepared—I had studied the film of Nebraska long enough to feel good about my analysis. I didn't even write down any notes. I knew it cold. But then I had to articulate my analysis to that camera lens.

When it was done, I got the obligatory "Good job . . . We'll be in touch" line. I shook their hands as fast as I could, half-apologized for wasting their time, and then tried to find a napkin to discreetly towel down. The audition had meant so much to me, but all I could think was, "Man, I blew it."

I just wanted to go home. Enough's enough. I was sorry that I had even made the trip. Just get me to the airport and get me back to Columbus as fast as possible.

Once I got on the plane and had a chance to exhale, I realized that I had been too hard on myself. After all, I had taken on a very,

very intimidating, difficult, and challenging set of circumstances. Even though it hadn't gone perfectly, I had at least tried it and had lived to tell about it. That was worth something.

Davenport had said from the very beginning that I had no chance at the job. I had hoped to prove him wrong, but I was proud I had given it a shot. I could have said no to the audition request. I could have told ESPN, "You know what, I'm comfortable doing my radio show in Columbus, doing *Wall to Wall Sports*, doing the Arena League, and college sideline and analysis work for ESPN. I don't need *that*."

Me being wired the way I am—a creature of habit, of finding a comfort zone and sticking with it—it would have been the easy choice. But I took the chance. After all, who knew if I'd ever get another one? Plus, it was a cool experience to meet Chris and Coach.

After the audition, I resumed my usual weekly work schedule, which meant a lot of trips to Des Moines, Iowa. That's where quarterback Kurt Warner and his Iowa Barnstormers of the Arena Football League were based.

AFL scores were like the Big 12 Conference on steroids: 61–41, 62–55, 66–64 . . . Defense was always optional in that league. It was fun football, and the team names were fun, too: the Memphis Pharaohs, the Anaheim Piranhas, the Milwaukee Mustangs, the Minnesota Fighting Pike, and, of course, the Barnstormers, who were one of the best teams in the AFL.

I respected those Arena League players. A lot of them were former Division I players who were an inch or two too short, twenty pounds too light, a couple tenths of a second too slow. Some of them had knocked around in NFL training camps or played overseas.

The Iowa franchise played in the Veterans Memorial Auditorium, otherwise known as "the Barn." Capacity was 11,411 and, like all of the indoor arenas that the AFL played in, beer flowed freely in the stands. The fans were right on top of the field. It wasn't unusual to see fans toss beers at the players, or the players turn around and start arguing with the fans.

Warner was an AFL star. But did I think he'd go on to the NFL, become a Super Bowl MVP, and years later be inducted into the Pro Football Hall of Fame? No, I didn't see that coming.

During that 1996 season, Christiansen and I were assigned a July 6 Barnstormers game. I flew from Columbus to Des Moines the day before, with a connection in Detroit.

As I was walking through the terminal in Detroit to my connecting gate, my pager buzzed. (Yes, that's what we used back then.) It had a thin, tiny LCD screen, just wide enough to show about a dozen characters. I immediately recognized the number: Brian Chorpenning. I found a pay phone and called him back on his cell phone (he had one of the earliest models; it was the size of a brick). He was standing in a parking lot at his golf club in Columbus.

"Well, you got it," he said.

"Got what?" I said.

"You got *GameDay*."

Chapter 11

The Rookie

A t first, the words didn't register. And then, it hit me like Junior Seau. I could not believe what Brian had just told me. My life changed right then and there in the Detroit airport.

I stared at the terminal floor in shock. I started crying. I couldn't control myself. People walked by and looked at me as if I was having some sort of medical or emotional issue.

What I wouldn't learn until years later is that Al Jaffe, who oversaw ESPN's talent negotiations and recruitment (his nickname was "the Kingmaker"), had seen my audition tape. Jaffe prided himself in discovering and hiring new talent. Stuart Scott, Mike Tirico, Robin Roberts, Rece Davis, Kenny Mayne, Mike Greenberg, and Suzy Kolber, among many others, were all hired during Jaffe's twenty-eight-year ESPN watch.

Jaffe reported to Howard Katz, who was ESPN's executive vice president for production. Katz was in charge of what and who made it on the air at ESPN.

One day he walked into Katz's office and said, "I have a tape you should see."

It was my audition tape.

In a 2020 interview, Katz said that as he watched my tape he remembered something that his former colleague, famed producer Don Ohlmeyer, had told him.

"Don said, 'You can't make the camera like you. Either it likes you or it doesn't like you,'" recalled Katz in the interview. "The camera liked Kirk Herbstreit."

After he finished watching the tape, Katz turned to Jaffe and said, "Sign Kirk Herbstreit."

Brian told me that Jaffe had called him and said, "We like your guy. If you and I can work out a contract, he's got the job." Brian's knees buckled when Jaffe made the offer.

Brian had been with me from the very beginning. He had believed in me from the very beginning. This was the monumental break we had dared to dream about.

In that same 2020 interview, Katz said: "I have told people over the years that Kirk was the single-best hire I made. I got John Madden for *Monday Night Football*, which was an enormous achievement for us. But it didn't take a genius to know what John Madden could do in front of the camera.

"But Kirk is probably the hire I take the most pride in, taking a chance on someone who was a complete unknown. . . . I take tremendous pride in what he has accomplished in his career, and I know where he started. This one I got right."

I'm humbled and gratified by Katz's comments. He, Davenport (especially during my early years at ESPN), Jaffe . . . they all took a chance on me. The same goes for Terry, Moose (especially Moose), Mick, Dom, and Jay. I've never forgotten their kindnesses, their willingness to help me. During the course of my career, I've tried to follow their example and help others break into the business, or offer advice and guidance whenever I could. (By the way, Adamle also was hired after his audition to host ESPN2's weekly college football studio show.)

The headline in the July 9, 1996, *Columbus Dispatch* read:

"Herbstreit Lands TV Job With ESPN; Ex-Buckeye Will Be Analyst On Network Scoreboard Show."

In the sixth paragraph of the story, there was this:

"Some skeptics question whether Herbstreit, 26, with less than three years in a local radio market, is ready for network television. He has no doubts."

I didn't have any doubts about my passion for college football. Or my knowledge of the game. Or if it felt natural for me to talk about the game. But I knew there would be a learning curve and that it would take time to develop a working relationship with Chris and Coach. They had a four-year head start on me when it came to *GameDay*. There had been an on-air comfort with Craig James. Now here was a new guy.

Fowler once talked about it with a reporter:

"The show was just beginning to take off. Then Craig left for an opportunity at CBS. It was frustrating, because I thought the show was getting off the ground. The chemistry was great between Lee and Craig.

"Then Kirk came along. If you could see past the sweat, you knew this guy had the goods. There was an instant connection. He nailed the audition. He nailed it by being natural. He did not sound like a polished guy doing an impression of a TV guy. You knew it was going to be a very quick and strong connection with the viewer."

Fowler said one other thing that was absolutely true: "Kirk arrived at the perfect time. I don't think now with that profile you'd even get a chance to audition."

He's absolutely right. Today I would have had no shot at that audition. My career is such a one-in-a-million long shot. If you turn on the TV today, whether it's college or NFL, almost every single guy in every important analyst position had an illustrious playing career, won a Heisman, was a three-time All-America or All-Pro, won a Super Bowl, won a Super Bowl MVP. You knew them for their playing careers before they transitioned to TV.

I wasn't any of those things. The closest I got to a Heisman Trophy was when I walked by Archie Griffin's two Heismans at the Ohio State football facility, or saw Eddie George every so often. I played with All-Americas, but I wasn't one. I was an honorable-mention All–Big Ten. I never played in the NFL. I didn't even get drafted or signed as a free agent.

To go from local radio and TV in Columbus, to ESPN and *College GameDay* . . . zero chance these days. Less than zero, actually. Maybe I'd get a crack at the Big Ten Network or ESPNU—just to see if I had any talent.

Chris spoke the truth: I was in the right place at the right time. But it was up to me to take advantage of being in that right place. I think I'm the only guy on national TV who has risen through the ranks of sports broadcasting who had just an okay career in college. I'm not embarrassed about that at all. In fact, I'm kind of proud of it. I don't think you'll see it happen soon—not because there aren't talented people who deserve the same shot that I got, but because the system isn't set up for that anymore. It's harder to be a one-in-a-million like me.

———

A little more than a week after ESPN announced the *GameDay* news—Wednesday, July 17, to be exact—I was sitting at home watching TV, when there was a breaking news report. A plane had exploded and crashed just off the coast of New York. It was TWA Flight 800, bound from Kennedy International Airport to Rome, with a stopover in Paris. There were no survivors among the 230 crew and passengers.

A day or so later, as the passenger list was made public, I heard the news anchor mention a name that caused me to sit up in my chair in disbelief. Among those who had died in the crash was ABC Sports executive producer Jack O'Hara.

"Oh, my gosh!" I blurted out, almost involuntarily. "That's the guy I sent my audition tape to!"

On that same flight were his wife and his thirteen-year-old daughter. The family's twin boys had stayed back in suburban New York. O'Hara was only thirty-nine. I slumped in my chair when I heard the names. It was so incredibly sad.

O'Hara was going to Paris to coordinate ABC's coverage of the Tour de France bicycle race. Earlier in the week, he had been part of a management shakeup, so the Tour de France was going to be his last official assignment for ABC after fourteen years at the network, followed by a vacation with his wife and daughter. Before he left for the trip, he had written his colleagues a note thanking them for their talent and hard work.

It made me think of the kind note O'Hara had written me after he had received my audition tape months earlier. He probably had a thousand things to do that day, but he found a few moments to send along a handwritten letter of thanks and encouragement to a broadcasting nobody in Columbus, Ohio. It was a reminder of how a small gesture can mean so much. I'll always remember that kindness.

———

My personal and professional lives changed dramatically in 1996. My longtime girlfriend and I had officially called it quits, and I had started dating Allison on a semiregular basis. For months, Teri called her "Red Sweater," because of a photo I had of Alli wearing a red sweater. That's Teri.

Little by little I could feel myself drawn to Allison's kind spirit. She was loving and sweet, the kind of person who would do anything for anybody. She had a good soul. Yes, she was very pretty, but I was most attracted to her grace and unselfishness.

Meanwhile, I made my *GameDay* debut that fall. Back then, *GameDay* was just beginning to emerge as a weekly force. The show first aired—and was almost canceled—in 1990. Fowler was only twenty-seven years old when he got a job that nobody else at ESPN really wanted.

Year after year, it made more of an impact. There was the first road trip in 1993: No. 1 Florida State versus No. 2 Notre Dame at South Bend. Coach Corso put on an FSU ball cap when it came time to make the pick.

The show traveled to six games in 1994, and eleven games in 1995, including the national championship. People were beginning to take notice.

There were two rookies on the 1996 *GameDay* team: me and a $400-per-week (before taxes) researcher named Chris Fallica, a University of Miami graduate who had something I never came close to getting at Ohio State: a national championship ring—from the Canes' title run in 1991. Everyone affiliated with the UM football program, including the members of the football sports information department (Fallica was a student assistant), received one of those lug-nut-sized rings that featured Miami green stone and a diamond-encrusted UM logo. In fact, during his time at Miami, he never saw the Canes lose a home game in the Orange Bowl.

The show's season premiere—and my *GameDay* debut—came on August 31, but in the Bristol studio, not on the road. They cued the music, Fowler did his intro and set the table for the opening Saturday of the season, and then, just before they cut to all of us on the set, Chris surprised me with a 1992 highlight of a touchdown pass I threw in our upset of Syracuse.

"But it wasn't all good times for Herbstreit," said Fowler, as they rolled footage of me being sacked during a loss against Illinois—all the time showing my reaction in the studio.

"Oh, you slipped that in there," I said. "I like that."

"Welcome aboard—the new member of our College *GameDay* team," Fowler said. "You're in good hands, next to the veteran here, Lee Corso. That's 'Mr. Corso' to you. Stand up and sing your fight song like any true rookie."

There was no singing. In fact, moments later, we were talking about Nebraska's quest for a national championship three-peat. We ran footage of Cornhusker quarterback Scott Frost (now Cornhusker head coach Scott Frost) in the weight room doing dead lifts and power cleans.

I survived the studio show, but the following week we were in Boulder, Colorado, crammed into a little trailer on the University of Colorado campus. By the time I walked in for our Friday production meeting, Coach Corso already had his research and game notes arranged just so on the table, and his Sharpies lined up. He was ready to *go*.

Fowler, of course, just owned the room. He was young, but he had a seriousness about him that made him seem older. Vecchione was the coordinating producer and Kraus was the producer, but those were just titles. I had been around enough coaches and in enough team meetings to instantly recognize who had the goods, who commanded and deserved your attention. In our meeting room, that person was Fowler, who in many ways was not only the host of the show, but also a producer and director. He drove the bus.

Sitting in that first meeting, it was obvious that this guy was all business. He wasn't there to yuk it up. Back then our show was only an hour long. It was like running the 100-yard dash, and Fowler wanted us sprinting from start to finish, feet on fire. He demanded excellence, first from himself, and then from everyone else.

From my first day on *GameDay* in 1996 to Chris's last day on the show nineteen years later, I always appreciated how committed he was to the project, how much pride he took in developing the show's brand, how hard he worked to make that happen. He understood what *GameDay* was before it truly became *GameDay*.

It also was obvious in that meeting that there was turmoil and friction behind the scenes between Vecchione, Kraus, and Fowler. It wasn't like we showed up in Boulder that week and there was this feeling of "Hey, the band's all here! We're going to have a great two days!" Instead, there was this strange tension just below the surface. I recognized it immediately, probably because I had seen so much dysfunction in my own family.

I kept my mouth shut in that meeting. In fact, I never talked in those meetings, ever. The only exception was if someone asked me a direct question. I used to pray that nobody would ask me anything. I was in full Bill Belichick mode: do your job.

There was no talent office when I started at ESPN. There was nobody dedicated to coaching you up, to helping you get better on the air. My mom, and later Allison, were my talent coaches.

As I prepared for that first show, I decided I was going to succeed or fail on my own terms. I wasn't Craig James, and nothing personal, but I didn't want to be Craig James. From what I was told, James was an alpha personality on the show, a Texan who wouldn't back down to anybody or anything. I was the opposite. I didn't seek confrontation. I wasn't there to be an adversary. Creating friction was overrated to me.

A talent agent these days might tell a client: "Come out firing! Be a loud voice! Be the center of controversy! Have a hot take! Get people talking about *you*!" That wasn't me then, and that's not me now. Anybody can be shrill and go for the cheap take.

Rookie or not, I had my own *GameDay* mission statement. I was determined to make it about the sport itself, about the traditions, about the coaches, the players, the fans, the atmosphere, the games. I never wanted it to be about me. I wanted it to be about them, about what the audience wanted. I wanted to be true to college football and to myself. I wanted the viewer to feel that same sense of awe that I felt watching Ohio State games as a kid.

There was only one way to do that: I vowed to become the most-prepared, hardest-working analyst in television. They might not know my name or who I was, but they were going to know that nobody would outwork me, out-prepare me, or care more about the sport than me. I wanted Chris, Lee, and the viewers to be able to depend on me. Rookie or not, I was going to hold up my end of the bargain on that side of the *GameDay* set.

It was no secret that I was the upset winner of the *GameDay* bake-off competition. I was a virtual unknown. But early in my career at ESPN I had set a huge goal for myself: I wanted to be the Dick Vitale of college football.

Vitale was a force of nature. As soon as I saw his face or heard his voice on ESPN, I instantly thought of college hoops. The man was invested in all things college basketball. His enthusiasm and passion for the game was infectious—and it still is. His style wasn't my style—loud, filled with all those great catchphrases ("PTP'er" . . . "Diaper Dandy" . . . "Awesome, baby!") in that New Jersey accent of his. But in many ways, I could relate to Vitale. He had come from humble beginnings, worked his way up through the coaching ranks, had a forgettable and brief career as an NBA head coach, and had gotten into broadcasting by accident and with no formal training or experience. He just jumped into the deep end of the pool and learned how to swim. I admired that. I had jumped into that same deep end.

Above all else, I loved the way he loved college hoops. It was what he lived for. That's who I wanted to be. I wanted to build my image and brand totally around college football, around the sport I lived for.

Even in that first production meeting, I gravitated toward the football coach in the room. That's what I knew from years of playing the game. Chris, Steve, and Lisa were TV people. Lee was a *coach*. I could relate to that.

I watched how Coach prepared for the show. For starters, he had a binder and three different-colored Sharpies: black, blue, and red. He had a copy of the rundown, which is a minute-by-minute, segment-by-segment breakdown of the show. It is our version of a game plan.

If the rundown called for Coach to discuss a game or, say, break down a pass play or a blitz package—and we wouldn't see him on camera during his analysis—he would jot down a few notes in black. Black was for his regular comments. If he was on camera, and he wanted to make a special point or had a really strong stat, he'd write those notes in blue. He called those his "blue liners." The red Sharpie, he said, was for his "throw line."

I nodded my head as if I understood, but the whole time I was thinking, "What the hell is a 'throw line'?" (I later would learn that a throw line is a designated word or sentence said on the air that lets the producer know when to roll the tape.)

I was always amazed that Coach's notes on Friday were recited word for word on Saturday. I thought he had a photographic memory. When he was on a single shot (meaning, the viewer would only see him), oh, my god—boom!—he'd say his opening line spot-on. Then he'd do his video lines—boom!—perfect. Then he'd hit his throw line—boom!—another perfect delivery. It was incredible to watch.

It wasn't until years later that I learned that son of a buck would go back to his hotel and spend the entire Friday night practicing his lines over and over again. That's right, sweetheart: Those "notes" weren't notes; those were his script. He was doing what he knew best: preparing like a coach, using repetition to eliminate mistakes.

Early on, I didn't know about Coach memorizing his lines on Friday nights. I just saw his prep work at the production meetings. So I figured if it worked for Coach, it would work for me. I got a binder. I got three different pens. Holy cow, did it stress me out. I would have sleepless nights on Friday just thinking about all my notes. I'd lie in bed mumbling things to myself, trying to keep the pen colors straight in my head. It was nerve-racking.

There were probably about two hundred people surrounding our set for that show at Colorado. CU was Fowler's alma mater, and I fell in love with the campus, the city of Boulder and the Flatirons and Rockies. If you're the Colorado coaching staff and get a recruit on that campus, I don't know how the kid doesn't sign then and there. It's gorgeous.

As we neared the final segment of the show, Coach asked one of the crew members on the set for some help.

"See that guy's hat over there?" he said. "Can you go get that hat for me? I want to borrow it."

The crew member ran down into the crowd and brought back the hat. And that's what Coach wore when it came time to pick the winner of the game.

I had a blast on that first road show. I kept saying to myself, "This is a pretty good gig." I was twenty-seven and having the time of my life. I did the show and then got to stand on the sideline of Folsom Field and watch the game—and they were paying me! I was working with two guys I admired and I got to talk about football, which I would do for free. Other than playing shortstop for the Reds, or playing in a Rose Bowl, this was the greatest gig you could ever have.

But it got better. The following week I was introduced to the Southeastern Conference.

I grew up on Big Ten football. My football geographical map featured the Midwest: Columbus, Ann Arbor, East Lansing, West Lafayette, Minneapolis, Madison, Evanston, Iowa City, Bloomington, Champaign. It was the land of changing leaves, of sleet, of gray, of seeing your breath through your face mask, of snow, of looking into the stands and seeing fans bundled in puffy coats, ski caps, scarves, and gloves. They were incredibly devoted fans (I was one of them as a kid), but the SEC had its own vibe. Its fans weren't better or more devoted, just different.

My first-ever visit to Knoxville for the Florida versus Tennessee game was jaw-dropping. In fact, it was my first-ever SEC game. It was a world outside of what I knew. It was like taking a space shuttle to a different planet. (And here's another reason why I'm crazy about Fallica: he skipped a close friend's wedding to be at the game. Devotion, man.)

Tennessee was ranked No. 2. It had the great Peyton Manning. It had Neyland Stadium, which is one of the cathedrals of college football.

Florida was ranked No. 4. It had the great Steve Spurrier and quarterback Danny Wuerffel, who would go on to win a Heisman. It had a new defensive coordinator named Bob Stoops.

The Gators had beaten Tennessee three in a row and eight of the last ten. The Vols were sick of losing to Florida. Sick of Spurrier's swagger and little digs at Tennessee. There was such a buildup and vibe to the game.

I had experienced the Ohio State–Michigan rivalry, both as a fan and a player. This had that same type of football passion. I wanted to inject it into my veins. I loved it all: "Rocky Top." The Pride of the Southland Band. The Power T. The Tennessee

Judy and Jim Herbstreit on their December 28, 1958, wedding day. My dad had just finished his sophomore season at Ohio State.

My dad shortly before the beginning of the 1959 season. At 5-foot-8, about 160 pounds, he started at both defensive back and running back.

The 1961 Ohio State coaching staff. At twenty-two, my dad (front row, second from right) was one of the youngest full-time assistants in major college football. That's head coach Woody Hayes (front row, middle) and close friend and future Michigan coach Bo Schembechler (front row, far left).

All dressed up for a photo shoot at age three.

Me (far right, third from front) and our Trotwood neighborhood gang of kids. If there was a game, I wanted to play it.

Me and my dad walking to the car after one of my Centerville High School football games. He and my mom never missed a game.

Ohio State football uniforms in the early 1990s: arm pads, hip pads, thick thigh and knee pads. Loved to spat the cleats, too.

Since Ohio State began playing football in 1890, there have only been three father-son team captain combinations. I'm proud to be part of that history. This is me and my dad at OSU's 1992 Photo Day.

Posing with the family at Ohio Stadium in 1992. (From left to right: my dad; my sister, Teri; me; my mom; and my brother, John.)

As keepsakes go, this is one of my favorites. My Ohio State Captain's Mug.

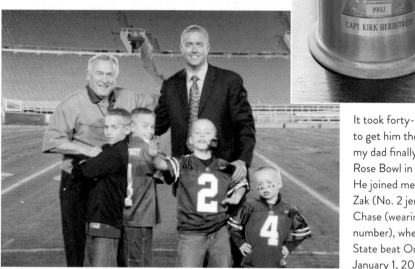

It took forty-nine years to get him there, but my dad finally saw a Rose Bowl in person. He joined me, the twins, Zak (No. 2 jersey) and Chase (wearing my old number), when Ohio State beat Oregon on January 1, 2010.

From my *GameDay* audition in 1996 to now, Chris Fowler has always been there for me. Chris and me in the Rose Bowl booth, January 1, 2020.

Everyone ducks for cover as a half-blinded Coach fires off his personalized OU Ruf/Neks shotgun at the 2018 Oklahoma–Texas game. (Seated from left to right: Desmond Howard, Rece Davis, guest picker Toby Keith, Lee Corso, and me.)

Putting some eyeblack on the Sunshine Scooter for a 2013 appearance at his alma mater, Florida State.

This is from my fiftieth birthday party in 2019. (Back row, left to right: Jake; my mom; Teri; my uncle, Rick; Tye; Teri's son, Noah. Front row, left to right: Chase and Zak.)

My wife, Allison, has always been the rock of our family. (From left to right: Jake, Alli, Chase, me, Tye, and Zak.)

River just across the street. The Vol Navy. A then-NCAA-record crowd of 107,608. Spurrier's confidence. Deafening noise. A steady rain. It was incredible.

Then the game started.

On its first drive, Florida drove to the plus-side of the field, but then faced a fourth-and-11. Instead of attempting a 52-yard field goal, Spurrier kept Wuerffel out there.

What? Nobody did that back then. They do it now (the analytics say it's the smart play, depending on field position and first-down distance), but not in 1996, they didn't.

Spurrier didn't care that it was pouring rain. Or that the crowd noise was deafening. Or that Manning was waiting on the sideline to take over if the gamble failed.

I was standing in the end zone. I couldn't believe Spurrier was going for it. Are you kidding me?

Then Wuerffel dropped back, threw the ball with that compact delivery of his, and found wide receiver Reidel Anthony open in the checkerboard end zone for the 35-yard touchdown catch. The Florida band sprang to life, but the 100,000-plus Tennessee fans switched to silent. You could almost hear them saying to themselves: "Here we go again. Florida is going to beat us." It reminded me so much of those days during Coop's tenure when Ohio State struggled to beat Michigan. There was an instant sense of dread and resignation whenever something went wrong.

Florida scored 35 points in 21 minutes. The game was basically done at halftime, though Manning did what he could. He threw for 492 yards and four touchdowns, but Stoops's defense also had four interceptions. Florida won, 35–29, and it wasn't that close. Manning would never beat Spurrier and the Gators during his UT career.

I left Knoxville amazed and impressed by the passion and energy of the SEC. It was just so cool to see it all in person.

As the season moved forward, I quickly learned to sit next to Coach Corso during the weekly production meetings. He said nothing. He prided himself (and still does) on saying nothing during those meetings. He was there to go through the rundown and spend the rest of the day preparing on his own for the show. He listened—Coach hears all—but he stayed out of the politics and inner workings of the show.

I did the same. During my early years on *GameDay*, I concentrated on being prepared and delivering my comments. That was it. I was concerned about me.

When you're doing live TV, you're so focused on your assignment and role. Just do your job. I was like the rookie quarterback just trying to comprehend the playbook and not make any mistakes. You were sort of on your own. Nobody said, "Hey, you got this, kid! You'll crush it."

I didn't think in broader terms: how can the show be better? Fowler thought that way, though. Chris cared soooo much about *GameDay*. He was like the father of the show. He has such good television instincts that if he saw something he thought would make the show better, he fought for it. That would create some very tense moments in those production meetings. In fact, it wasn't a matter of if he, Vecchione, and Kraus were going to disagree, but when the eruption would happen. It was a volatile situation at times. I would sit quietly near Corso and wait until the three of them finished battling it out.

For the September 28 show we went to Notre Dame, another first for me. The No. 5 Irish were playing No. 4 Ohio State. I picked Ohio State, and heard some of the Notre Dame fans in the *GameDay* crowd yell, "Homer!" But I would have picked the Buckeyes even if I had a Notre Dame degree.

That Ohio State roster had all sorts of NFL talent on it and the defense—the "Silver Bullets"—included two future head coaches,

Mike Vrabel and Luke Fickell, as well as Shawn Springs, Greg Bellisari, Antoine Winfield, and Andy Katzenmoyer. The Buckeyes won, 29–16.

On October 5, 1996, *GameDay* history was made—and Allison was in the middle of it.

By then, Allison and I had begun dating on a regular basis. She had graduated with a communications degree in the fall of 1995 and was working at a local radio station in the sales department. *GameDay* was in Columbus for the big Penn State versus Ohio State game. The Buckeyes were ranked No. 3 in the country, Penn State No. 4.

Coach Corso wanted to try something different for this match-up. Usually he'd pick a winner at the very end of the show and put on a ball cap of that school. This time, he wanted to think big.

He asked me if Allison would contact the Ohio State cheerleading coach about the possibility of borrowing the Brutus Buckeye mascot head.

"What are you talking about?" I said.

"I need Brutus," he said. "I want to make my pick by putting on the mascot's head."

I asked Allison to ask her former cheerleading coach, Judy Bunting, about Coach's idea. Bunting quickly said no. This was unheard-of, she said. Nobody but the person playing Brutus (a closely guarded secret, by the way) got to wear the mascot head.

But Coach was persistent.

"C'mon, try again," he said.

So Allison made another run at it. This time the request began to move up the Ohio State chain of command. It made its way to the desk of then–athletic director Andy Geiger. Geiger was understandably protective of the way Brutus Buckeye was portrayed. Brutus is a big deal to Ohio State fans.

Geiger gave the thumbs-up, and a tradition was born.

Near the very end of the show, Fowler asked me for my pick. I turned to the camera and listed a series of reasons why I thought the Buckeyes were likely to win the game. I was like a lawyer providing a final summation to the court: calm and logical.

"I like Ohio State, 24–13," I said.

Then the showman went to work. He didn't care about calm and logical. He knew his audience, and his audience was wearing scarlet and gray.

"All right, good pick," said Corso, barely acknowledging my list of reasons. "I'll tell you one thing—"

And then he leaned down under our desk, picked up the Brutus head, and plopped it over his own head.

"Buckeyes! Ohio State No. 1!" he yelled through the mesh mouth opening of Brutus.

Our set was located not far from the famous Ohio Stadium rotunda on the north end of the building. By then, there were thousands of fans in the area, and they went crazy when Coach put on the very first headgear of his *GameDay* career.

The usually straight-faced Fowler burst out in laughter. I sat there almost stunned by the sight of it all. It was the weirdest thing to be sitting next to someone wearing a Brutus head on top of a coat-and-tie body. Years later, Fowler put it perfectly when he said it was appropriate that Coach put on a headgear that represented an actual nut, which is what a Buckeye is.

When the show was done, we congratulated Corso on his brilliant theatrics. It had been a huge hit, but I thought it was a one-and-done thing. It was a funny and awesome and, sure, maybe he'd do it again when we came back to Columbus for another game. Nobody on the set or in the production truck thought this was an actual *thing*. It was a one-off.

Instead, Coach found his end-of-show niche, and *GameDay* stumbled into an iconic, attention-grabbing pick-'em device. It was accidental genius. And to this day, Coach always says, "Make sure you give Allison credit for that."

So, Alli, thank you.

GameDay lasted an hour, but the *GameDay* set—and it wasn't much more than an oversized desk back then—stayed open until midnight. We did the show, and then spent the rest of the day and night doing segments leading into the afternoon games and the 7 p.m. kickoffs. Then we'd do postgame segments for *SportsCenter* and the college football wrap-up show. Long days, but I loved every minute of it.

My weekly schedule was action packed. On Sundays I'd fly back to Columbus and do *Wall to Wall Sports* that night. I had my radio show. I had my prep work for *GameDay*. I'd fly to Bristol on Wednesday nights or first thing Thursday mornings for planning and story-line meetings, and then do a thirty-minute pregame studio show with Chris and Lee, and a halftime show for the Thursday night games. Then, depending on the week, we'd either do *GameDay* at ESPN's studios or take the show on the road. I traveled so much that my car could drive itself to the airport.

Fallica, the new statistics and research guy, was fast becoming a favorite of mine. He had replaced someone in the statistics and information department at ESPN, and there was pressure on him to uphold the standard set by the previous guy. In a way, he had to fill that guy's shoes much like I had to fill Craig James's shoes.

I'm drawn to people who love college football, who love the competitive nature of the sport. I appreciated how much Fallica loved football. He had played it at Westhampton Beach High School on eastern Long Island, but also had written about it for the school newspaper and talked about it on a student-run TV show. Even then, Fallica knew sports was his passion.

I also appreciated his self-drive. When he was in high school, he wrote a letter to the legendary Chris Berman and requested an interview. Berman agreed.

He worked in Miami's sports information department and also freelanced as a sports research guy. During his sophomore year in 1991, he saw the Hurricanes go undefeated and win the national championship. That was the season of Wide Right I (versus Florida State) and shutting out Tom Osborne's Nebraska team in the Orange Bowl. I watched that title game and remember that loaded Miami roster: Gino Torretta, Lamar Thomas, Kevin Williams, Horace Copeland, Michael Barrow, Jessie Armstead, Darrin Smith, Rusty Medaris, Carlos Huerta, and an offensive tackle who would go on to be a big-time head coach: Mario Cristobal.

During Fallica's junior year, he saw Torretta win the Heisman Trophy and the No. 1–ranked Hurricanes reach another national championship game before losing to Alabama in the Sugar Bowl. That same junior year, WFAN Radio in New York hired him to do stats work for a New York Knicks–Miami Heat game. Fallica later asked WFAN's Mike Breen about internship possibilities—and later got one. And when ESPN offered him the *GameDay* research job in 1996, Fallica didn't bother asking about the salary. He wasn't in it for the money. *That's* why we connected. We simply couldn't believe we got paid to do something we loved.

From the earliest days of our professional relationship, I regarded him as one of the offensive linemen of our show. First, he was built like one. Second, he was a grinder, a blue-collar guy who was all about supporting his teammates. Third, he wasn't interested in getting any credit. Do your job, right? I recognized instantly that I wanted to take this guy under my wing. This was a guy I wanted to be buddies with, hang with before and after the show. We just became friends in a very natural way.

Fowler leaned on Fallica more than I did. I wasn't a big stats guy. But I learned that Fallica didn't just give you numbers, he gave the reasons behind the numbers. That was valuable information. I also learned to stay away from him if the Canes lost a game. Or in the case of 1996, two games in a row: UM lost at home against FSU, and then the following week against East Carolina. When it came to Miami football, that was sacred to him. He was a passionate New York Jets fan, New York Yankees fans, New York Islanders fan, but his love of UM was at a different level. If the Canes dropped a ball game, he got incredibly mad. The dude had a serious temper.

If Miami was playing a huge game that week, Fallica would take his national championship ring out for a walk. It was a big piece of jewelry, and Fallica wore it proudly. But it only made an appearance if he really meant business.

Fallica became my lovable buddy, the kind of guy you'd punch in the arm in a loving way. That's how I'd treat my Ohio State offensive linemen. Fallica became my center, which is the best compliment I can give a guy. I depended on him.

We had our routines during the week, especially on Thursday night. That's when I found out the big fella had a soft spot for . . . *Friends*.

We would do the pregame show and then quietly make our way up the stairs to a work area above the studio. There was a bank of telephones where several young production assistants would call the stadiums where the Thursday night games were being played. This was before the internet was part of our daily lives, so the PAs would call the press boxes and constantly update the stats from the games.

There also were TVs on that mezzazine level. Fallica and I would grab our dinners at the catering area, find a couple of empty seats, and switch the channel from the Thursday night game (those games weren't always the most interesting match-ups) to *Friends*. We had to have our weekly fix of Rachel, Monica, Chandler, Phoebe, Joey, and Ross. Even Fowler would sneak up there, too.

We took *GameDay* on the road to Iowa for the Ohio State game on October 26, and then to Baton Rouge on November 9 for the Bama-LSU game. I had heard about the legendary tailgating at LSU, but until you see it in person, you can't appreciate their devotion to football, food, and drink.

We got into town on Thursday night. By then, there were campers, RVs, and tents set up everywhere. The grills and smokers were already fired up. You could see the charcoal smoke rising up, and smell the food in the air. The campus, the atmosphere? Forget about it. It was fantastic.

For the fans, it was a seventy-two-hour football Mardi Gras. Touch football, cold beers, brisket, gumbo, crawfish—you name it, it was there. It was like a giant five-star restaurant. Even now, if you had me close my eyes and took me to an undisclosed campus the morning of a game, I could pick out LSU just based on the food smells. And maybe the smell of bourbon, too.

Months earlier, LSU had reached the College World Series championship game and trailed Miami 8–7 with a man on base and two outs in the bottom of the ninth. An infielder named Warren Morris, who didn't have much power and had been injured for much of the season, stepped to the plate and hit a walk-off home run—his only dinger of the season—for LSU.

We had Morris near the *GameDay* set, showed him on camera, and then showed the highlight of him hitting the dramatic home run in June. The LSU fans went crazy.

When it came time to make our picks, Coach did what he did best. He entertained.

"I LOVE this town!" he said.

The crowd roared.

"I LOVE Warren Morris!"

The crowd roared louder.

"But I've got to go with Alabama."

Then he put on the Big Al elephant head, waved a huge Alabama flag, and yelled, "Rolllllll Tide!"

I turned to look at the crowd and that's when I saw this golf ball flying toward us on a line. It hit the pole that Coach was waving and bounced into my hands. Coach just kept on yelling, "Rolllll Tide."

By the way, Coach was right: Bama won, 26–0.

Later that season, we went to Tallahassee for the epic No. 1 Florida versus No. 2 Florida State match-up on Nov. 30. Victorious FSU fans got pepper sprayed as they tore down the uprights, which was another in-person football first for me.

It was around that time that one of the show's assistant producers pulled me aside. He produced a lot of the show's big feature stories. He was a big-time guy on the show.

"Can I give you some advice?" he said.

"Sure," I said. I've never been afraid of constructive criticism. In fact, I seek it out.

"What you're doing is not going to work with Corso."

And then he explained that I was too passive, that I needed to challenge Corso, to get in his face. I needed to assert myself.

"Craig James wouldn't be this way," he said. "You can't sit there and take it."

Maybe he had read the story in a St. Petersburg, Florida, newspaper that said, "the chemistry between [me and Coach] hardly sizzled. [Herbstreit's] biggest crime is simply not disagreeing with Corso and providing fun debate."

The producer was right about James. James would tell Coach, "You're crazy, old man! Let me tell you why you're wrong!" They argued. They were loud. They were cocky, confident, combative.

Meanwhile, I would call him "Coach." I would agree with Corso. I would defer to him.

As the producer made his case, I thought to myself, "Well, then I'm going to get fired."

There was no way that I was going to call Coach "an old man." I couldn't do that to a coach, to an older guy I respected. That wasn't who I was. I couldn't turn myself into a character.

I listened to the producer's advice, but I wasn't going to follow it. I'd rather lose the *GameDay* gig than pretend to be someone I wasn't. Corso and I disagreed on topics, but in a respectful way. He literally was my coach on the show, so I owed him that kind of respect. I owed it to myself to follow my own instincts. So I did, and I never heard a peep from that producer again.

My first season on *GameDay* ended at the Sugar Bowl for a rematch between UF and FSU, this time for the national championship. The Gators, who switched to a shotgun formation to protect Wuerffel in the title game, crushed the Noles.

On January 3, 1997, the day after the championship, I exhaled for the first time since April 25, 1996, dating back to working those Arena Football League games. I also tried to self-scout myself: what had I done well, what could I improve upon? Of course, it was impossible not to see or hear about the reviews from the national media critics. One media writer who had had his doubts about me now put me in his "most improved" category.

I looked at it as a competition. The media evaluations convinced me to follow my own instincts, but they also motivated me to constantly try to improve. Do the research. Make the phone calls to coaches. Talk to players. Watch lots of film. Take lots of notes. If I kept doing that, I didn't need a schtick. I didn't need to argue with Coach for argument's sake. I wasn't good enough to be a performer. My schtick was that I didn't have a schtick. I wanted to be the same person before, during, and after the red light on the camera went on.

My goal then, and my goal now, is to have the lowest-man-on-the-totem-pole mentality. They could have told me to clean up the set after the show, take a Greyhound bus back to Columbus, and I would have said, "Yes, sir, no problem." I wanted to be that second-stringer willing to do whatever it took to become a starter. I feel the same way today. I never want to settle, to say, "Well, I know everything there is to know about that."

I returned to Columbus to what suddenly seemed like an easy work schedule: the radio show and *Wall to Wall Sports*, with an occasional ESPN request, such as being part of the network's coverage of the NFL Draft in April. (I was with Sterling Sharpe and Tom Jackson, and the reporters on the coverage team included Chris Myers, Chris Mortensen, Andrea Kremer, and Gary Danielson). A week after the draft, I was at Ohio State's spring game, where I agreed to take part in a halftime skills competition against other former Buckeye quarterbacks. I finished third, ahead of Greg Frey, Cornelius Greene, and Mike Tomczak, and behind Kent Graham and winner Jim Karsatos.

I did one other thing that off-season. I got serious with Allison.

Chapter 12

A Father's Day to Remember

knew I always wanted to get married and have a family. I also knew that I had scar tissue from my own experiences growing up in a broken family. I'm not complaining about what happened; everyone coped with it as best as they could. But our home wasn't like that 1970s sitcom *Happy Days*, where Mr. Cunningham came home from work at 6 p.m., and his wife, Marion, had dinner waiting, and the kids, Richie and Joanie, were all smiles, and the Fonz stopped by to say hello. That wasn't our reality.

I was in love with Allison for lots of reasons. Most of all, I just knew I wanted to raise a family with her. She was just old-school to me, and I liked that about her. Whatever concerns or hesitation I had about marriage in general—and it was all based on what I had witnessed as a kid, teenager, and young adult—was outweighed by the thought of a future with Allison.

In the summer of 1997, Brian Chorpenning let me use his place in Hilton Head, South Carolina. I took Allison down there. My high school center and college buddy, Craig Schmidt, and his girlfriend met us down there, too.

Craig knew Alli from our Ohio State days. She was in Russian Literature 101 with him. In fact, he came back from class one day and said, "Have you seen the blond cheerleader?"

Make no mistake, I had seen her. Schmidt said I threw the "baby blues" at her back then, but I would have been too nervous to try something like that.

Schmidt was in on the plan. He knew I was going to pop the question to Allison in Hilton Head. Allison's dad knew, too. I had asked him for permission to marry his daughter.

We all went out to dinner and got back to Brian's place at about 10 p.m. I asked Alli if she wanted to take a walk on the beach. I had the ring in my pocket.

I was trying to be so clever, but it was obvious that I was nervous. Finally, I pulled the ring from my pocket—she instantly saw it—dropped to one knee in the sand, and asked if she would marry me. The proposal was a total surprise to her. I was just hoping she'd say yes.

She did, and then she started crying. I started crying because she was crying. We couldn't get married that fall, so we scheduled the ceremony for the following summer.

I was no longer a *GameDay* rookie in 1997, but I'm not sure I completely understood the impact of the show on fans. It wasn't until I had a home game in early October (we did the show in Columbus for the Iowa-OSU match-up) that it hit me—literally.

Somebody in the crowd threw a piece of pumpkin that landed on the set. Then I got hit in the face with a loaded marshmallow. It was like playing at Wisconsin again, but this time without a helmet.

The following Friday at LSU, when we were taping a segment for another show, someone flung a can of Budweiser that almost hit Coach. That was it. The next day, there was a protective netting at our backs.

Even with the netting, it could be dangerous out there. We were in Ann Arbor for The Game late that November. Michigan was

No. 1 in the AP poll and undefeated, while Ohio State was 10–1 and ranked No. 4. The winner would go to the Rose Bowl. It was a match-up with huge national championship implications, and with all sorts of national hype and buildup.

My mom and Alli were with me that day. They hung out in the production truck and spent some time at the back of the set during *GameDay*. They were having a blast.

I have a pretty good track record of being respectful and fair to Michigan on the air. I've always been able to separate Ohio State Kirk from ESPN/ABC Kirk. Part of that comes from my relationship with Bo and from my respect for that program and the rivalry with Ohio State. The other part comes from my responsibility to the viewer.

We were down on the field, and Michigan dominated the game in the first half. It led, 13–0, at halftime, thanks to a 78-yard punt return by cornerback Charles Woodson. Coach and I were standing close enough to the sideline to reach out and touch him as he ran past us for the touchdown. It reminded me of standing on that same sideline in 1991 when Des flew past me.

A few minutes before the end of the second quarter, Coach and I hustled up the stadium tunnel, where someone was waiting in a golf cart to take us to our set to do a hit for the halftime scoreboard show. By then, Michigan fans were beginning to fill the concourse and it was hard to maneuver the golf cart.

Our driver honked the horn every so often, just to give the fans a little bit of a heads-up—"Watch out, cart behind you"—that sort of thing. Every time he honked the horn, though, the Michigan fans would turn around, recognize me, and start letting me have it.

"Ohio State sucks! . . . You're a joke, Herbstreit!" This went on for the better part of five to ten minutes as we worked our way through the crowd and to the set. I was used to the ribbing, but there was part of me that wanted to say, "Hey, you're up at halftime. Be happy about your team. Why are giving me a hard time?" After all, Michigan had upset Ohio State most recently in 1996, in 1995, and in 1993. In each of those three years, the Buckeyes were undefeated and ranked No. 2, No. 2, and No. 5, respectively, while the Wolverines were No. 21 in 1996, No. 18 in 1995, and unranked in 1993.

My mom and Alli found a place off to the side of the set to watch the halftime show. Then, just as I settled into my seat, I was rocked by something that slammed against my chest. It was a snowball—more like an iceball—and whoever threw it must have been a helluva pitcher. There only was about a ten-inch opening in the protective netting, but this guy was able to thread it through and hit me flush in the sternum.

It scared me more than anything. I looked around to see where it came from. Standing behind the netting were about fifteen Michigan fans. They were laughing, pointing at me, yelling something, but because I was wearing two earpieces, I couldn't hear what they were saying.

When I got done with the hit, I took my earpieces out and the Michigan fans, who must have forgotten that we never beat the Wolverines during my time at Ohio State, yelled, "F—- you, Herbstreit!"

My mom and Alli were nearby. I had been hit with a snowball. And, yeah, the Ohio State in me bubbled to the top as I listened to those idiots. For one of the few times in my entire career, I let my emotions get the best of me.

"F—- me?" I said to them. "F—- you! F—- you!"

I said it slowly so they'd understand.

Older me would have ignored them, would have never stooped down to their level. Younger me got caught up in the competitive nature of the rivalry. I was impressed with the snowball throw, though.

That also was the season that ABC Sports, ESPN, and *GameDay* were accused by angry Tennessee fans of costing Manning the

Heisman Trophy. It didn't matter that Fowler and Corso had voted for Manning, and not the eventual winner, Woodson (I didn't have a vote). It also didn't matter to them that as the anchor of the show, Fowler had never campaigned for Woodson. All he had ever said was that the Heisman race was still fluid, that Manning wasn't a lock to win the award. Just to show you how the narrative has changed over the years, ESPN was accused of being biased toward the Big Ten. These days we're accused of being pro-SEC.

The whole thing was ridiculous. We didn't have an agenda. We didn't get paid more if Woodson won and Manning didn't. Our ratings didn't spike if a Big Ten player held the trophy. In Fowler's case, he stated the obvious, that momentum appeared to be building for Woodson. Woodson was such a unique player—cornerback, wide receiver, returner—and so instrumental in Michigan's success. Manning was the best quarterback in the country, but voters seemed conflicted by Tennessee's loss to Florida earlier in the season. If it had beaten Florida, Manning would have been a Heisman lock.

In mid-December, when Woodson did win the Heisman, we got crushed by some Tennessee fans. Fowler received a lot of hate mail from them, some of it very scary. Someone sent a box of manure to him.

They also were upset that Fowler referred to the reaction of those extreme fans as "trailer park frenzy." They thought there was an ESPN conspiracy against Tennessee, especially when an ESPN.com investigative reporter later dug into the school's tutoring system for football players.

When bowl season arrived, I got the best news possible: we were going to do *GameDay* from the Rose Bowl, where No. 1 Michigan would play Washington State on New Year's Day. It should have been the highlight of my season, of my professional career at that point, but it turned into something painful.

I'd never played in a Rose Bowl, covered a Rose Bowl, or attended a Rose Bowl as a fan. But I loved everything about the Rose Bowl.

Growing up in Ohio, it's usually freezing cold and dark and dreary by late afternoon on January 1. Then you'd turn on the TV at five o'clock for the Rose Bowl and suddenly the screen was filled with sunshine, green grass, the mountains, a beautiful rose logo in the middle of the field, a packed house of more than 100,000 fans, the cheerleaders, the voices of Dick Enberg and Merlin Olsen, the Big Ten versus the Pac-10. You'd look at it in wonderment and ask, "Where is this magical place that looks like heaven?"

I couldn't believe I was actually there. We arrived the day before and when I saw it in person, I was stunned by its beauty. TV didn't do it justice. The grass was like the fairways of Augusta National. You almost didn't want anyone to play on the field because it was so perfect.

Washington State had quarterback Ryan Leaf, who would be selected No. 2 overall in the 1998 NFL Draft, just behind Manning. Michigan had Woodson, quarterback Brian Griese, and a redshirt sophomore backup quarterback named Tom Brady. This was pre–Bowl Championship Series, so the polls still determined the national champion. If Michigan won, it would finish undefeated and earn at least a part of the national title. If it lost, then all the attention would turn to the Orange Bowl on Jan. 2, where No. 2 Nebraska would play No. 3 Tennessee and Manning.

I had a problem, though: I couldn't feel the lower part of my right jaw.

It was only my second year on *GameDay*, and my first time at the Rose Bowl. I didn't want to complain, but the pain in my jaw was increasing by the minute. I made it through the pregame show, but I needed help, and I needed it fast.

I was so desperate that after the show I went to the Michigan sideline in search of its team doctor. He looked at my jaw and told me I needed to immediately get to a doctor's office. That wasn't going to happen. It was New Year's Day, it would be difficult to find an available specialist, and I had work to do.

The Michigan doctor gave me a couple of pain pills so I could get through the next three hours or so. I watched the field from the sideline, took notes for our next show, and then headed to LAX after the Michigan win for a red-eye to Miami. At that point, my pain was still manageable.

When we landed the next morning, I went straight to a local hospital emergency room. I sat there for hours in the waiting room. The pain got worse and I soon noticed a growth beginning to protrude from underneath my jaw. It was grotesque. By the third hour, the growth was the size of a golf ball.

My cell phone rang. It was one of the senior production managers telling me they needed me at the set—right now—to tape the Orange Bowl pregame show. They sent a runner to pick me up, who took me to my hotel so I could change quickly into a suit and tie, and then brought me to the stadium. You should have seen the reaction of the ESPN producers and makeup artist when I showed up. Even with a collared shirt, you could see the lump on my neck. I was miserable.

As we walked out to the set at the then Pro Player Stadium, the Tennessee fans were waiting for us. It was one of the wildest scenes I've witnessed in my twenty-five years of doing *GameDay*.

Before every show started, Fowler would have our audio folks open up the mic to the crowd. Fowler would thank them for coming, tell them what a huge role they played in the success of the show, and wish each of the fan bases good luck in that day's game. He meant it, too.

This time when Chris turned to address the crowd, the Tennessee fans began screaming obscenities and booing him. He tried to calm them. He told them that he had nothing but respect for the Vols football team, apologized for the trailer trash comment, wished them the best against Nebraska. It was a classy gesture.

The Tennessee fans didn't see it that way. If anything, they got more fired up. So now we had these angry fans, and I had a painful jaw with a growth underneath it.

With Michigan having won the Rose Bowl, we talked about what a Nebraska win might mean to the voters in the AP and Coaches polls. Could there be a split national championship? We talked about it being Tom Osborne's final game as head coach at Nebraska. And we talked about the battle of the quarterbacks: Manning versus Frost.

We got through the show, and nobody threw anything at us, which is good. If there was one group you didn't want to have your back to that day, it was those folks.

This was Peyton's last college game, too. Of course, it was a coincidence, but every time *GameDay* showed up for a Manning game against Florida, Tennessee would lose. It happened in 1996 and 1997. It also happened that night against Nebraska.

People forget how good those Tennessee teams were in the 1990s. They were loaded with talent. But Nebraska was loaded, too, and the Cornhuskers put it on Tennessee, 42–17. Afterward, around midnight, our producers told us the AP poll had just been released—Michigan had been declared its national champion. But our bosses back in Bristol wanted us to stick around until the Coaches poll came out.

By then, I was really worried about my jaw. If you've ever had an agonizing toothache, where it felt like every nerve is throbbing, that's what I felt . . . times 100. Tylenols didn't make a difference. Plus, counting the Rose Bowl show, the Rose Bowl game, the red-eye to Miami, the emergency room wait, the Orange Bowl show and game, and now the postgame wait, I had been up for two days. I was on fumes.

Under normal circumstances, I would have been pumped about the intrigue and controversy of a possible split national championship. But now all I wanted to do was go home, go to a doctor, and then go to sleep.

I couldn't believe how long it was taking for the Coaches poll to be released. What, were they driving the results by car to New York? C'mon, already.

The pain in my jaw got so bad that I had to leave the set area and go crash in a rental car used by one of our runners. I tilted the seat back and somehow fell asleep. An hour later someone tapped on the window to wake me up. The Coaches poll was in—Nebraska was its No. 1.

All right, here we go, boys—let's ramp up the energy and break down these polls at 3 a.m. Let's talk about who's better, Nebraska or Michigan? And that's what we did, though I didn't have much energy.

When we got done, I went back to the hotel, threw my clothes into my bag, and caught the first flight to Columbus. I went directly to Riverside Hospital, where the specialist, after examining my jaw and the X-rays, said I needed to get into surgery. I had an abscess under one of my lower teeth. Had the abscess burst, he said, I could have died. I spent six days in the hospital and never felt so lucky to be stuck there.

Despite the medical emergency, it had been a successful season. Our *GameDay* ratings were up 25 percent from the previous year. I was gaining confidence in my own work. I even received my first-ever Sports Emmy nomination in the Studio Analyst category. Me nominated for an Emmy? That didn't seem possible.

I didn't win (Cris Collinsworth, my teenage sports-talk radio idol, received the statuette), but it was an incredible honor to be a finalist. At the awards ceremony in New York, Alli sought out ESPN's Mo Davenport in the crowd.

"Thank you for giving him a chance," she said to Mo.

Thank you, Mo, a thousand times over.

I still did the daily radio show. One of my cohosts had bad breath, slobbered, and took naps during the show. Her name was Megan, my golden retriever.

I got Megan as a puppy when I was in high school. She actually lived with me at my Ohio State dorm for a quarter. Dogs weren't allowed, so everyone on the dorm floor helped conceal the secret from the resident assistant. I lived at the end of a hallway, so I would sneak Megan down the stairs to take her out for walks.

I'm an animal lover, and I'm crazy about dogs, especially goldens. Megan is the reason why we have three goldens in our house today.

She was incredible. I had seen something on David Letterman's show where a guy taught his dog how to "talk." If he said, "Speak," the dog would start a series of different barks. If he said, "Whisper," the dog would do a low, "Grrrr."

I taught Megan how to do that. I taught her all sorts of silly things. I'd point a forefinger and thumb at her and pull an imaginary trigger. She would fall on her side. I taught her to flop on her back. She would bring me things. I swear, she was half-human.

Some days I would bring her into the studio with me. If I was talking about Ohio State football—which we often did, even during the off-season—I would pull the microphone toward Megan and say, "Let's bark for the Buckeyes." And she'd bark her approval. If someone called in to rip on Ohio State, I'd tell Megan, "Whisper for the Buckeyes," and she'd do the growl.

I know—it was silly, but we had so much fun together on that show. The listeners got a kick out of it, too.

Later that summer—June 13, 1998, to be exact—Alli and I got married. I was twenty-eight, she was twenty-five. Schmidt was my best man.

I remember two things specifically about the ceremony: I had requested that the air-conditioning in the church be lowered to the coldest temperature possible; I did not want to sweat that day. The second thing—one that I'll never forget—is the sight of her walking down the aisle, her arm hooked around her dad's arm. She looked like an angel walking toward the altar. I had to fight back the tears.

———

It wasn't an accident that *GameDay* took a pass on visiting Knoxville during the 1998 season. We were in Athens when the Vols lost to Georgia. We were also in Tempe, Arizona, months later when they beat Florida State in the first-ever BCS National Championship.

In 1999, I got another career break: ESPN asked me and Coach to do the Thursday night college football package with Mike Tirico and producer Tim Corrigan. I'm not an actor, but this would been like being told you were going to get acting lessons from Meryl Streep, or have someone say, "Kirk, I want to meet your guitar teacher, Eric Clapton."

Not counting my one game in 1995, my college football broadcast booth experience could fit into a thimble. I had done Arena Football, but that was so different from college ball. Now I was in the same booth as Tirico and Coach, and had one of the best leaders in television in Corrigan, and one of the best production trucks and crews in the business. How lucky was I?

Three-man crews often don't work, because they don't operate as teams. There's too much talking. Or one person dominates the broadcast.

Mike was so good as a play-by-play guy, it was almost like stealing when you were on his crew as an analyst. He taught Coach and me how to be successful as a three-man team. He had a way of putting the ball on the tee so we could drive it down the middle of the fairway.

For instance, Mike would ask me a question about a certain play or situation, and even though he already knew the answer, he wanted it to come from the analyst. He was so unselfish. He and Corrigan always put us in the best position to be successful.

I had my *GameDay* family. And now I had my Thursday night family. We were always on the road on Thanksgiving, so we would have a Turkey Bowl touch-football game on Wednesday. Every year, Mike would stand up and give these beautiful, heartfelt toasts to the entire crew, and we'd all be crying.

We spent our share of Thanksgivings doing Egg Bowl games at Ole Miss and Mississippi State. One year we stayed at one of those old-time motels, the kind where you park your car a few feet from your room window. It had those noisy, rickety AC/heating floor units. Coach came back to his room and somehow the heating unit—and part of his room—was on fire (the fire was extinguished before there was major damage).

On Thursday mornings during the season, Mike, Coach, and I would find a local restaurant and have these epic football breakfast sessions. We stuffed ourselves with food and with information. We talked about everything related to that night's game. We traded our research, our interviews, our stats, our opinions. As a young guy learning the profession, it was so cool to be with a play-by-play person who was all about one thing: what's best for the broadcast. Mike would let me make a copy of his spotting board for the game, and then I'd add my own notes to it.

I was a sponge. Whatever suggestions Mike, Tim, and Coach gave me, I tried to put them into practice.

At the time, I was in my formative stages at ESPN and so was the Thursday night package. We were trying to convince these major conferences to move one of their Saturday games to Thursday. One of the first programs to take the plunge with us was Virginia Tech. Frank Beamer and the Hokies were trying to grow their brand, and we were trying to grow our audience.

Like me, Tim was a coach's son. His dad was the late Gene Corrigan, who was a basketball, soccer, and lacrosse coach in college, and later became an athletic director at Virginia and Notre Dame before eventually being named the commissioner of the ACC. Gene was a legend.

Tim, Mike, and I were all about the same age, give or take a few years. They taught me how to take whatever studio skills I had and translate them to calling a game. I had to find the rhythm of the game. I needed to learn how to let it breathe, that I didn't have to say something after every play. Or as Mike once told me: "You're not taking over somebody's couch. You're talking to somebody *on* the couch."

Coach was a natural about injecting his personality into a game. I was more Xs and Os, but between the four of us (I always include Tim in the equation), we developed a great on-air and off-air relationship.

Mike has said watching me and Coach work together was like watching a father/son team. I could say the same thing about watching Mike and Coach work together. In fact, Mike put it perfectly: "Lee was the perfect person at the perfect time in our lives. I got him two days a week and Kirk got him for four."

I was a Midwest guy. Mike was from New York and went to school at Syracuse. But we shared a common pain and experience: our fathers weren't consistent presences in our lives. Mike especially grew up without a dad's influence. We talked about that, and it was one of the reasons we bonded.

You remember the little moments: the late-night drive-thru at the Wendy's in Blacksburg, the Starbucks stop in Morgantown, the car rides from a regional airport to a campus—me in the front seat, cell phone pinned to my ear, legal pad out, scribbling notes with my fat-point black Sharpie in the world's worst handwriting as I talked to an offensive coordinator or a quarterbacks coach on a Wednesday. Even today, I don't go to any meeting without my fat-point black Sharpie. And you could always depend on Coach for a pregame scouting report on where the press box restroom was located. We could be in, say, Fort Collins for a Colorado State game at old Hughes Stadium, and Coach would approach you with a dead-serious expression and say, "Go down one flight of stairs, turn left, take twenty-nine steps and that's where the closest bathroom is." Only him . . .

We all became lifelong friends. In fact, it was Coach who told us that if we kept working hard, he thought we could make something of ourselves in the industry. It's been so cool to watch Mike's career unfold at ESPN and now at NBC. I root for Mike, and I know Mike roots for me.

————

That 1999 season was the beginning of a nonstop, pedal-to-the-metal weekly schedule: the local TV show on Sunday night, the radio show early in the week, the prep work and Thursday night game, the pivot to *GameDay* on Saturday.

Some people want to get to the end of the race instead of enjoying the race itself. They keep track of their days worked, of how much time they're owed for vacation, of how many nights they spend in hotels. I didn't want to be that person. My motto was "Anyplace, anytime." I was Kevin Bacon in *Animal House:* "Thank you, sir, may I have another?"

I was on the road four to five days a week. I slept in rental cars. I slept on the floors of rental car offices. I used my carry-on bag as a pillow and slept at departure gates. I was with my guy Lee Corso, who was thirty-four years older than me. He didn't complain about the travel, so why would I?

We would do a game at, say, BYU or Utah on a Thursday night, then sprint through the Salt Lake City airport trying to make a red-eye to Atlanta. We'd get to Atlanta and walk to the Delta Crown Room, where Coach had membership status, but I didn't. He would sweet-talk the receptionist and ask if he could bring me in as a guest. I would give her sort of a sad look, as if I had nowhere else to go (which I didn't, by the way).

"Okay, Mr. Corso," the receptionist would say sympathetically, "he can come in with you."

I'd find a corner in the room, puff up my carry-on, and then crash until we had to catch our connection to, say, Tallahassee. I loved every second of the travel madness.

In late December 1999, our Thursday night crew was assigned the Holiday Bowl in San Diego. Allison was with me on the trip.

Since our marriage, we had been trying to have a child, but with no success. But during our Holiday Bowl trip, Alli had a feeling she was pregnant. She kept it to herself, and didn't even tell me that her pregnancy test came up negative.

From San Diego, we flew to New Orleans for the BCS National Championship at the Sugar Bowl—redshirt freshman Michael Vick and No. 2 Virginia Tech versus No. 1 Florida State. Again, without me knowing, Alli tried another one of those pee-on-a-stick pregnancy tests. This one came up positive, but she didn't say a word.

On New Year's Eve, Alli and I joined Fowler and his then-girlfriend (now wife) Jennifer, Fallica and his wife, Molly, and Coach Corso at Jackson Square, where everyone was gathered to watch the lowering of the ball for the new millennium. The count-down toward midnight began: ten, nine, eight, seven, six—the ball was dropping—five, four, three, two, one . . . Happy New Year! And that's when Allison turned to me and said, "We did it! We scored a touchdown! We're pregnant!"

I burst into tears and hugged her. I hugged Fowler. There were handshakes and congratulations. It was great to share that moment and that news with trusted friends.

There would be more news. During one of the earliest ultra-sounds, the doctor let us listen to sound of the heartbeat. When we returned for the next regularly scheduled ultrasound, he began listening again and then suddenly did a double take.

"What was that?" he said.

Allison and I were on instant alert.

"You know what it is?" he said, listening again.

We didn't.

"You're going to have twins."

It took a few seconds for the news to register.

"What?" I said. "Get out of here. I can't believe this."

We were excited. Twins! How great is that?

As the months passed, the doctors assured us that everything was going well. At week 20, we arrived at Riverside Methodist Hospital for our scheduled ultrasound, this time using the latest diagnostics technology: 3-D imagery.

Shortly after the ultrasound began, the doctor detected a problem.

"You're funneling," he said.

I didn't know what that meant, but I learned fast. Cervical funneling means an increased risk for an early—much too early—delivery. The cause, said the doctor, was the result of an "incom-petent cervix"—the weight of the twins, combined with weak cervical tissue, was causing the birth canal to begin to open prematurely. Alli's body was trying to go into labor in week 20, not the usual week 37–42.

This was a major problem. The doctor immediately sent her to the OB-GYN floor, confined her to bed rest, had her feet raised to counteract gravity. As it was, they could feel one of the twins' heads against the cervix.

If they couldn't stop the dilation, then there could be a miscarriage or a dangerously early birth. According to the statistics, incompetent cervix condition happens once every 100 pregnancies. We were the one of this 100.

We went from a routine checkup at week 20 to having to worry what might happen next. The doctors told us it was a matter of math. Every hour, every day, every week, and every month the pregnancy continued, the twins had a higher chance of survival and a lower risk of long-term health issues such as cerebral palsy, vision, hearing, and dental problems, and learning impairment.

I was so naïve. I just assumed everything was going to be okay. I knew the risks, but I didn't fully realize that the odds weren't necessarily in our favor.

We needed Allison to hang on for as long as she could. The longer we could delay delivery, the more time the twins' lungs, brains, hearts, eyes, immune systems, etc., could develop and mature.

Every day that passed was a victory. The 20th week turned to 21, 22, 23. . . .

Meanwhile, Allison had a Navy SEAL mentality. She was *tough*. I think back to some of my football injuries, and they were nothing compared to what Alli was going through. At 24 weeks or so, the doctors wanted to show her photos of what a baby would look like at that delivery age. She didn't want to see them.

She wanted to concentrate on making it another day, giving the twins the best possible chance.

At week 28, a full 9–12 weeks before the original due date, Allison underwent a C-section to deliver the twins. We wondered what all parents might have wondered in that situation: Would they breathe? Would they have brain damage? Would they survive?

They were born Jake and Tye Herbstreit. They weighed 2 pounds and 5 ounces, nearly 3 pounds less than a normal-sized twin baby. And they were born on June 18—Father's Day.

There is nothing that prepares you for that moment. Nothing. Allison had been through hell, but she was okay. Like I said, Navy SEAL–tough.

Under normal circumstances, there would have flowers and balloons in the room. Photos would be taken with the newborns and the exhausted mom and the proud dad. Everyone would be excited.

We didn't experience that. We didn't know whether to be happy or scared, so we settled on grateful. We were grateful Alli had survived the ordeal, and that the twins were stable.

The twins were taken to the NICU—the neonatal intensive care unit. They looked like baby robins, they were so tiny. They were placed in an incubator and connected to an EKG monitor.

We invited a select few family and friends to see the twins. Craig Schmidt and his wife, Sarah, who had spent nearly thirty days in a row visiting Allison during her bed rest at the hospital, were two of the first to arrive. We put on surgical gowns to visit the twins.

Craig called the twins "JT." They instinctively grasped his pinkie. I turned to Craig and said, "Oh, my god, I'm so scared. I'm a new father."

Teri was there, of course. She had worked at a Columbus hospital in labor and delivery, so she had been around a lot of preemies. She had also spent time with Alli during her bed rest.

My dad also made the drive from Cleveland to see the twins.

"Do they have a chance?" he asked Teri after seeing the boys. "They don't look like they're going to make it."

Teri reassured him, but she knew—we all did—that the twins had been born at the very edge of viability.

Allison and I would go to the NICU every day. We'd feed them breast milk through a tiny tube through their noses and the back of their throats. Their bodies were so underdeveloped, their skin so translucent that you could see completely through their arms and legs.

One time I was with them and their hearts flatlined on the EKG monitor. *Oh, my gosh, they're dead!*

A nurse appeared, gently shook their legs, and their heartbeats began bouncing up and down on the monitor again. I felt like my own heart had stopped.

I could take the wedding band off my finger and run it up and over their toes, feet, ankles, legs, past their knees, and to their hip bones. Their legs were as thin as one of Coach Corso's No. 2 Ticonderoga pencils. I would stare in wonderment as these two tiny boys lay next to each other in the incubator, many times holding each other's hands. It was as if God was helping them get through it together.

I'm not saying Allison and I didn't have moments of fear, but we never let our minds wander to the worst places. It was never "What if?" It was always "What's next? What can we do to help the twins?" It was all about being positive.

Every day there was a new goal. We just wanted to see some sign of improvement in them, however modest it might be. Just keep jumping over a hurdle.

Talk about tough? Those little guys were tough. The nurses were running out of places on their bodies to take blood. They had little puncture marks on their arms, feet, heels, even their toes.

Allison was with them almost all the time. We would take turns holding the twins near our shoulders, rocking them in a rocking chair after the nurses taped their oxygen tubes to the side of the chair. I would talk to the twins as I rocked them, tell them how much I loved them, how they were going to be okay, what great fighters they were. They were a combined five pounds, but you couldn't measure their strength and courage.

It was a traumatic experience for Allison and me, and for our families. The true heroes of that entire experience were those Riverside NICU doctors, nurses, and staff members. They not only pulled Tye and Jake through, but they pulled Allison and me through, too. We are forever in their debt.

Eight weeks after they were born, we were allowed to bring the twins home. The key was the development of their lungs. Once they were able to get off the oxygen machine and breathe on their own, the doctors felt better about discharging them.

Waiting for them at home was our golden retriever, Megan. In the previous weeks and months, Megan had fallen ill. But it was as if she had willed herself to hold on long enough to meet the twins. She had been such a loving dog to Allison and me, and she was no less loving and protective of the babies. About a month or so after we brought the twins home, Megan died. I hope to see her again one day.

As the weeks and months passed, the twins got stronger and slightly bigger. Allison was incredible. She dedicated every waking moment to taking care of those twins. They were still in the lowest percentiles when it came to relative height and weight, but at least they were out of the danger zone. For that, we were incredibly grateful.

———

The years passed and our family grew, but the pregnancies were always difficult for Alli. We were blessed with Zak on December 9, 2002, which was about three weeks before Ohio State beat Miami for the national championship at the Fiesta Bowl. Compared to the size of the twins, Zak was a monster. Alli spent three and a half months on bed rest before he was born, and then only after undergoing a cervical cerclage to help prevent a premature delivery, and then a C-section. Even then, Zak was born about four weeks early.

During that 2002 season, I brought the twins on the *GameDay* set when the show was in Columbus for the Washington State–Ohio State game in September. They sat with me as I picked the Buckeyes. Ohio State won, which means the twins are 1-0 as guest pickers.

Thank goodness I didn't bring them with me for our *GameDay* visit at the Air Force Academy about a month later. They would have seen their dad make a huge mistake in judgment.

On the day before the show, Air Force officials invited me and Des to take rides in F-15 fighter jets. I thought they'd hand us a couple of flight suits, give us a thirty-second safety talk, and off we'd go into the wild, blue yonder, climbing high into the sun. Instead, there was a briefing that seemed to last nearly two hours, including twenty to thirty minutes of instruction on how to properly eject from the aircraft. I looked over at Des and gave him a look, as if to say, "We're not really going to do the parachute thing, are we?"

Des's brother was career Air Force, so he knew some of the language. All I remember is the instructor telling us, "Keep your eyes on the horizon."

I have occasional bouts of motion sickness. Getting into a fighter jet that can fly faster than Mach 2—twice the speed of sound—was a big, big mistake. I don't know what the g-forces were, but they were enough to cause my g-suit to tighten around my legs and stomach area. The suits are designed to prevent you from blacking out from the g-forces.

They don't, however, prevent you from throwing up or having the dry heaves, I can tell you that. I did both, repeatedly. I started sweating, and at one point had to take off my oxygen mask. The ride was exhilarating, and the pilot was outstanding, but I've never been happier to get out of a plane.

We did *GameDay* on Saturday morning and were there that night for the battle of unbeatens: Notre Dame versus Air Force. It was the featured game on ESPN that night, with Dave Barnett, Bill Curry, and Mike Golic in the booth. By the time the game ended, it was late, especially for those of us on Eastern Standard Time.

The Air Force Academy is an amazing place, but there are only a few roads in and out. When Fallica and I got in the rental car to the leave Falcon Stadium, all we saw were thousands of red brake lights. Nobody was moving.

Fallica gets grouchy when he gets tired, and he doesn't hide it, either—especially in bumper-to-bumper traffic. We had arrived at the AFA about 6 a.m. and parked in a lot close to our set. Unfortunately, when it came time to leave (and this is years before we were lucky enough to get police escorts or have detailed getaway plans), we were at the back of the line.

It had been a long day for both of us, and we were on fumes. Fallica growled about the traffic but eventually nodded off. I did my best to hang on as we inched forward, but I couldn't keep my eyes open any longer. During one of the many standstills, I took a quick glance at the dashboard clock—it was 1 a.m.—leaned back on the headrest, and fell sound asleep. The next thing I heard was Fallica yelling, "Kirk!" I looked at the clock; I had been asleep for twenty minutes, my foot still pressed hard against the brake.

It took us three hours to get out of that parking lot, which has to be a *GameDay* record.

Chase was born on August 7, 2006, the same date as Coach Corso. No wonder he's Lee's favorite. But once again, Alli required bed rest and a cerclage before delivering Chase.

There was joy with each arrival. But there also was heartache and devastation. In 2004, we had had a baby who was a stillborn.

You move forward, and that's what we've always done as a family. We prayed. We considered ourselves blessed to have our boys.

Each year we would take the twins to see the doctor for their annual checkups. Alli was so proud of their progress. Then, almost out of nowhere, the doctor said matter-of-factly, "You know, they're never going to play football."

Alli began to cry. It wasn't so much that he said they couldn't play football, as much as it was the suggestion that their lives were going to be different from other kids their age. We knew they were small—we saw the growth charts compared to other little kids—but to try to take away that *hope* of them playing was something you don't forget.

After I became a father, I constantly assessed and questioned the job I was doing. Was I there for the twins, and when Zak and Chase came along, was I there for them, too? Was I raising them the right way?

I had a lot of doubts about how to be a dad. It wasn't insecurity, but more like, do I have every base covered? Am I totally prepared? It was almost as if I were prepping for a game. This isn't a criticism of my own parents, but because of their difficulties I didn't really have examples of that kind of stability in my own life.

As the boys got older, I even called Archie Manning and asked him for parenting advice. After all, he and his wife, Olivia, had done a remarkable job raising their three boys: Cooper, Peyton, and Eli. I called Coach. I called Brian Chorpenning. I had long conversations with Galloway about raising kids. Joey's dad had worked two jobs, including as a custodian at the public library. His mom had worked at a grocery store for thirty years. He wore the hand-me-downs of his two older brothers. Joey came from a grounded family. Ask my mom to list her favorite people, and Joey is on the short list.

I called David Pollack and Tom Rinaldi. I talked to Kinely Williams, a longtime member of our security detail. Des has three children, including twin boys. We came from humble beginnings, but are trying to raise children and instill our values into kids who have the benefit of a privileged setting.

I've never been afraid of asking others for advice, especially if it helped me become a better father.

My parents were part of our lives, but it was getting more difficult with my dad. He was a kind, nice guy, and I wanted to stay connected with him, and him with us. Through all of the dysfunction in our family when I was a kid, I never lost my affection or love for him.

I can't even begin to count how many newspaper stories there were over the years about me following in his footsteps at Ohio State. It was the perfect football fairy tale. But it was always a little more complicated than that, like life always is.

As sweet a man as my dad was, he had a blind spot when it came to our relationship: he didn't listen. Ever.

I was at a point in my career where I had begun to build strong professional relationships with lots of college coaches. I prided myself on keeping a trust. If they told me something off the record or on background, it stayed that way. Because of that earned trust over the years, I've been given access to meetings and practices, been told about injuries and suspensions, been privy to insights and information that aren't shared publicly—all as a way to provide me with context and perspective when doing *GameDay* or even more important, when calling a game as an analyst. With that context and knowledge, I could reference a situation during the show without burning a coach. Even today, if Jim Harbaugh handed me the Michigan playbook and game plan for the Ohio State game, it would go to the grave with me.

When I got back to Columbus each week, there was only one guy I wanted to share those experiences with: my dad.

I'm not talking about sharing information regarding suspensions, or injuries, or staff unrest, or any of that. I'm talking about the on-field football part of it, the film room part of it, the personalities part of it, the schemes, formations, and coaching part of it.

My dad was so removed from the game by then, that I thought as a former college player and defensive coordinator he would want to hear about what coaches were saying about the zone read, how defenses were attacking certain offenses, etc. My dad was such an Xs-and-Os guy that I was sure this would be a way to connect with him.

Instead, the conversation would go something like this:

"Dad, I got a chance to talk to Pete Carroll when we were at USC and he drew up on the board how they run the zone blitz. He said they run a concept where—"

And then he would interrupt me.

"You know, that reminds me of the time I told the Old Man that we needed to play our safeties deep against Purdue . . ." Or, "I remember when Bo asked me what I thought about switching up our practice schedule. . . ." And the story would go on for fifteen minutes.

Or even worse, he would give me a halfhearted "Is that right? Oh, okay." And his voice would trail off—just like his interest level—and he'd return to reading the newspaper or watching TV. It was as if I didn't exist.

He would listen to me, but he wasn't hearing what I had to say. Time and time again I came back from a road trip with a half-dozen stories to tell him about Nick Saban, Dabo Swinney, Urban

Meyer, Chip Kelly, Vince Young, Tim Tebow, Marcus Mariota, etc. I couldn't wait to see him. And time and time again, he'd interrupt me three sentences into my story and steer the conversation back to his playing or coaching career.

Just once I wanted to actually finish a story, and just once I wanted him to say, "Kirk, that's wonderful. I'm glad you're having so much fun. You're doing great. What else have you seen?"

What should have been a neat father-son moment became another example of the growing distance between us. Every time he interrupted me or lost interest in my stories, it was like shooting an arrow into my heart. I felt anger and pain at his indifference.

I didn't know this until years later, but my sister Teri had confronted my dad about those failed conversations.

"You're losing Kirk," she told him. "You're losing him. You need to shut your mouth and listen to him."

"I know, I know," he said. "I just get to talking."

"Dad, give the gift of listening."

I appreciated her doing that, but it didn't work. For several years I tried to connect with him through those stories. It came to a point, though, where I quit trying. I either wouldn't bother telling him any of the stories, or if he interrupted me, I would get so mad I'd just shut down completely and let him drone on about the 1961 team for the millionth time of my life. When he was done talking, I would say, "Okay, Dad, see you later. Good talking to you."

There's no other way to say it than it sucked.

When I was growing up, our family didn't always communicate well with each other. There were layers and layers of silence—not all the time, but enough to matter over time. I learned how to interpret our family's language of dysfunction. I became the fixer. I always wanted to help, and it remains that way today.

If you and I were standing in a room with thirty people of friends and family, I would be constantly assessing the situation. Does somebody feel left out? Is somebody not involved in the conversation? If they were, my alarms would go off: "Man down! Man down!" I would try to rescue the situation. I would try to pull them into the conversation. I would make sure they didn't feel left out. That's how I am by nature. The only problem is that sometimes I see ghosts—situations that aren't real yet because you assume the worst. You brace for the stress and hope for the best.

The only good that came out of my dad's unwillingness to listen is this: I make it a priority to hear what my kids have to say. I try to do the same with Alli, my mom and siblings, my friends, colleagues, coaches, players, and even perfect strangers. In his own way, my dad taught me that lesson. I try to remember it every day.

Chapter 13

Transition

In the early 2000s, my role on *GameDay* began to evolve, mostly because I was beginning to evolve as an analyst. When I first started on the show, Chris was a mentor (and still is). He was the guy you watched and listened to. He set the tone in the production meetings. He controlled the set. He knew how to steer the show from fun to serious and back to fun. So much of what we did was spontaneous, and Chris always put us in a position to react to what was being said.

That role requires a really good point guard who can go hard and then pull back at the right time. It's such a unique leadership opportunity. In those early years, I learned about the show, my craft, and my role from Fowler.

As time went on and I started calling games with Mike and Lee, I became more polished. More reps meant more confidence. My relationship with Fowler went from teacher-student to more of an equal. I think he started to respect me as a broadcaster.

GameDay doesn't use teleprompters. We have notes, but the show is 100 percent live. You don't get do-overs. When I first started, I was a Belichick do-your-job believer. But I learned I could do my job better if I understood the jobs of others. It was like being a quarterback again, where I knew what route each receiver was running, what each running back was doing, what pass protection the offensive line was using.

I started asking more questions. I wore out the producer and director. I wanted to understand the structure of the rundown (each show has a minute-by-minute, segment-by-segment breakdown). I wanted to know about the graphics packages, the features, the elements we used to make *GameDay*, well, *GameDay*. I wanted to have a true understanding of the entire show.

There came a point where Chris could shoot me a quick glance while he shuffled his note cards as we ran a graphic or B-roll (video of something), and I knew he needed a few moments to get his bearings. I would give him a little nod back to let him know I would cover for him. I couldn't have done that in 1996.

In 2003, we were in New Orleans for the BCS National Championship. In 1998, the BCS "system" had replaced the Bowl Alliance, which had replaced the Bowl Coalition, which had replaced the practice of bowls locking up games months and months in advance. The whole purpose was to create a match-up between the two best teams in the country. The BCS was based on computer formulas and the polls.

That was the year six teams finished the regular season with one loss, but the BCS ranking determined that Oklahoma and LSU would play in the title game, even though USC was No. 1 in the AP and Coaches poll. It was a huge controversy and gave us plenty to discuss on the show.

Fallica and I were at our hotel restaurant, chowing down on a meal, when Coach Corso spotted us. Fallica loved food and talking football. I loved food and talking football. We spent a lot of time together.

Coach wore his usual uniform: white sneaks, light-blue jeans, silk shirt, gold chains. He had the perfect Florida tan.

"Hey, look at you guys!" he said. "You eating again?"

Guilty. Plates of food covered our table.

"And you, Fallica," he said. "You're like a big bear. You eat, you take a nap, you take a shit, and then you come back down and do it all over again. You're like a bear."

From that moment on, I called Fallica "the Bear."

Fallica didn't know what to make of the nickname. But now I can't imagine him without it. He is and always will be "the Bear."

The following season, Lee Fitting was named the producer of *GameDay*. He was a brash, in-your-face Long Island guy who had incredible ideas and instincts. He was like a good coach who could fire you up to play. He had an energy that I responded to.

Fowler was the pilot, but Fitting became the copilot. The show could be five minutes heavy, which is a lot in TV time, and Fitting would somehow figure out a way to toss parts of the show overboard to make up for those minutes and then safely land the wobbly *GameDay* plane on a bobbing aircraft carrier in the middle of the stormy Pacific. He was a savant in the front row of that production truck, and in 2008 he was named coordinating producer of the show. His last season with the show was 2016, and he's now a senior vice president at ESPN. Fowler is responsible for much of *GameDay*'s DNA, but Fitting helped elevate the show to new levels.

———

Eventually, my ESPN schedule forced me to give up the radio show and *Wall to Wall Sports*. It was like saying goodbye to old friends. Those shows—and the people who worked with me in Columbus—are partly responsible for whatever success I've had.

The Sunday night highlight show was like my TV training wheels. They were so patient with me as I sweated through show after show. As for the radio show, I still can't believe they paid me $12,000 to do what I would have done for free.

My cohost for nearly four years on the radio show was Ian Fitzsimmons, who had come to Columbus from a station in Birmingham, Alabama. Ian now works for ESPN as a radio host and college football sideline reporter and analyst.

I loved working with Ian, and he was great at getting guests for the show. One day I walked into the studio and he told me he had arranged for Pete Carroll to call in at such-and-such time, followed later by Oklahoma head coach Bob Stoops, followed later by Cincinnati Bengals starting linebacker Takeo Spikes. It was a great lineup.

"Cancel all the guests today," I told him. "I'm talking about Taco Bell instead."

Ian's face dropped.

"Herbie, these guys are locked in," he said.

"Don't care," I said. "We're talking Taco Bell."

I was big into Taco Bell. I probably kept Taco Bell in business for twelve years. I ate there all the time. I would even call the company's hotline number to brag on one of their restaurants if the service was good, if the tables and floor were clean, even if the tortilla shells were super fresh. I'd get the restaurant number, the name of the manager, and call in the compliment.

But on this day, I had pulled into one of my go-to Taco Bells in Columbus, and as I was waiting in line at the drive-thru, I saw one of its workers taking out the trash and scratching his rear end. I eventually ordered my food, and when I got to the pickup window, I saw that same dude making my taco! For the sake of us who love Taco Bell, that was not going to stand.

We did a whole show about that particular restaurant and then opened up the phones so callers could give us their fast-food horror stories. Then we did an entire segment about the best and cleanest fast-food restaurants in town.

Taco Bell handled the situation with a sense of humor and a sense of urgency. In an effort to prove that this was a onetime incident, they invited Ian and me to visit the restaurant. I ended up working the drive-thru window for an hour and Ian worked the front counter. Then we did the radio show. In fact, Taco Bell became a sponsor on our show.

We were a sports talk show, but during the football off-season we would have a segment devoted to what Ian called "the purple section," a reference to the Life section of *USA Today*, which had a purple logo on that front page. Those topics were about everyday things: parenting, food and dining, great little human interest stories, etc.

Ian also helped book our guests. He acted as if we were a drive-time show in New York City, not Columbus, Ohio. He tried for all the big names, and got a lot of them. If, say, something big had happened with the New York Yankees a day earlier in Seattle (the Yankees' Triple-A team was based in Columbus), Ian would try to track down the manager by calling every luxury hotel in the city. He called it "hotel bingo." He might get seven nos, but it was worth it if he got one yes. It was a competition to him.

We got Bob Knight on the show when he was coaching at Texas Tech. He asked Ian how he was doing, and Ian said, "Striving for mediocrity."

"Then what the hell am I doing here?" growled Knight. "I want to talk to Kirk. I'm done talking to you."

Bo Schembechler would do the show. All the top football coaches would come on.

There only was one guest who intimidated me: Marty Bren-naman, the Hall of Fame play-by-play announcer for my *Cincinnata* (I got that from my great-uncle Fritz) Reds. I would get so nervous every time he came on the show. He was bigger than life to me.

The Reds are still my team. Every Opening Day I say the same thing: "This is our year." In fact, if the game started at 12:35, Ian and I would drive down to Cincinnati, watch as many innings as we could, and then head back to Columbus in time for our 4 p.m. show. While we were there, I'd find the Skyline Chili stand at the stadium and get a cheese coney dog, maybe even a 3-Way too (spaghetti covered with chili and cheddar cheese). On the one-hour-and-forty-minute drive home we'd stop at Dairy Queen or LaRosa's Pizza. Back then, I worked out to eat. My metabolism ran a little faster in those days.

During the springs and summers, we talked a lot of baseball on the show. I could name every lineup and every starting rotation in the big leagues. Ian would say, "'86 Mets, go . . ." And I would re-cite the infield, outfield, and pitchers with no problem.

One time, on a drive back to Columbus, Ian asked me to name the best third basemen who played for the Cubs over the years (this was before Aramis Ramirez and Kris Bryant). I spit out the names—Ron Santo, Stan Hack, Bill Madlock, Ron Cey, a few others. But there was one name that slipped my mind. For the life of me, I couldn't remember it.

Months later, after football season had begun, I called Ian's cell phone late one morning. When he answered, I simply said, "Steve Buechele."

"You bastard," Ian said.

Buechele was the missing Cubs third baseman.

I did have to miss one of our radio shows in 2004. I had a good excuse, though: my induction into the Centerville High School Athletic Hall of Fame.

After the awards ceremony (I was inducted into the same HOF class as Coach Gregg and Coach Engleka), a woman in maybe her mid to late forties approached me. She looked vaguely familiar.

"I don't know if you remember me," she said, "but my name is Jeri Neidhard. You were in my English class."

Yes! Ms. Neidhard! Now I recognized her.

"You've come a long way from refusing to give speeches in English class," she said. "Now you're talking to millions of people on TV. And you're on the radio, too."

She was right. Then she suggested that I tell people of my fear of public speaking—and how I overcame it.

"That could help somebody," she said.

So, Ms. Neidhard, I'm seventeen years late, but I told the story.

Those years doing the show with Ian were the most fun I had in radio. What I loved about it was the local connection. Columbus was my home. I had played college ball there. I had built my first house there in 1996. Gotten married there in 1998. Beginning in 1999, had my kids there. Built my dream house there in 2005.

When Alli and I decided to build that dream house in Upper Arlington (which is just northwest of the Ohio State campus), it was going to be our forever house, where our kids would eventually bring their kids to visit. We would grow old in that house.

By then, my career had reached a point where I wanted to concentrate only on football. In the past, ESPN had asked me to appear on other shows (a hunting and fishing show, a panel debate show), but in those cases, I went against my "Any place, any time" motto. It just didn't feel right. I would make an exception for Jay Crawford's ESPN morning show, *Cold Pizza*, but that was about it. The producers of the prime-time hit show *Dancing with the Stars* contacted me to gauge my level of interest about being a contestant. I not only told them no, but *hell* no. There is not enough money in the world to make me do that. I did say that Allison could take my place and represent the Herbstreit name. She would have been great.

I wanted to be identified with football in general, and college football in particular. (Two seasons as a cohost of *Battle of the Gridiron Stars* barely qualifies.) If you saw me on TV, I was going to be on a college campus or in a football stadium. That's it.

In 2006, I was promoted from the Thursday night game to the brand-new ABC *Saturday Night Football* broadcast. Mike had received a promotion too: to the *Monday Night Football* telecast. For me, that meant doing *GameDay* in the morning and a prime-time game at night. Brent Musburger was the play-by-play announcer, former Notre Dame coach Bob Davie and I were the analysts, and Lisa Salters was the sideline reporter that first year.

Think about it: I was going to share a booth with one of the greatest sportscasters of all time. I had been watching Musburger since I was eight or nine years old. On Sundays, the TV in our house was always tuned to CBS's *NFL Today*, where Musburger would open the pregame show with his signature phrase: "You are looking *live* at . . ." Then he'd welcome in Irv Cross, Jimmy "the Greek" Snyder, and Phyllis George. Jayne Kennedy later replaced George.

We watched that show every week. I had a Sunday schedule: watch *NFL Today*, watch the Dallas Cowboys (my favorite NFL team), watch *60 Minutes*, and then go to bed.

I had watched him through the years call or host the biggest sporting events in the world: the NBA Finals, March Madness, the World Cup, the Masters, U.S. Open tennis, and the biggest games in college football (I can still remember exactly where I was [our living room couch] when Brent called the 1984 Doug Flutie's Hail Mary to beat Miami). I would get goose bumps as a kid when he did an Ohio State game.

"You are looking live at Ohio Stadium along the banks of the Olentangy."

It made you feel like you were going to run out of the tunnel with the players. And years later, when I was playing at Ohio State, Brent would come to our practices and I would ask him questions about broadcasting.

Holy cow, there were times during that 2006 season that I couldn't believe I was in the same booth with him. It was such an honor. How did I get from a 1995 audition tape where I pretended I was taking a toss from Musburger, to actually doing a game with him eleven years later? I was in awe of him.

But as much as I loved working with him, I could sense early on a chilliness when it came to my presence in the booth. It didn't happen all the time—in fact, there were many times when Brent was very warm and welcoming, and always professional—but it happened often enough that I could feel it.

Put yourself in Brent's place. He was a legend who, after his dismissal from CBS, joined ABC Sports in 1990. He had been the centerpiece of every big sports broadcast for years. But the broadcast world was changing. In 2005, ESPN basically took over everything associated with ABC Sports: programming, sports rights negotiations, marketing, finance . . . it was all moved under the ESPN umbrella.

To the longtime veterans at ABC Sports, ESPN was like the kids' table on Thanksgiving Day. The adults ate at the ABC Sports table, and the ESPN folks and their cable network were seated at a folding table in the corner with the other children. Now the kids' table was in charge, and the change didn't go over well with some of the old-guard ABC Sports people. In fact, I can remember sitting at our company college football seminar in 2005 as a very high-ranking ESPN executive began explaining to the great play-by-play man Keith Jackson how to get to commercial break during a broadcast. Do you know how many times Jackson must have gone to commercial break during the course of his legendary ABC Sports career? I'm sure he couldn't believe what he was hearing from the ESPN executive.

Then there was the *GameDay* part of the equation. For years and years, it was a huge deal if Keith Jackson and Brent Musburger came to your campus to do a game on ABC Sports and network television. But as *GameDay* began to gain in popularity on ESPN, there was more of a buzz on the campuses for the show in the late 1990s and 2000s. Not only that, but now Brent had this young *GameDay* guy—someone who had come from the kids' table—as a partner. I just got this vibe from Brent that was like, "Maybe you guys on *GameDay* have a lot of fun putting on mascot heads, making some game picks, but now you're coming into *my* booth. We don't do that headgear stuff here."

The irony is that Brent had been a major part of such a groundbreaking studio show as *NFL Today*. *GameDay* stood on the shoulders of studio shows like that. But despite us sharing that sort of background, I thought Brent's general attitude toward me was, "Well, I guess I have to work this *GameDay* guy."

Urban Meyer's Gators beat Ohio State for the championship in 2006, and I would find out later that I had played a minor—and unwanted—role in the Florida national title.

Florida had lost earlier in the season at No. 11 Auburn. They hadn't looked dominant during their November schedule, either. So when No. 2 Michigan lost by just three points at No. 1 Ohio State in late November, but would eventually finish behind one-loss Florida in the final BCS ranking, I said on-air that I didn't agree with the Wolverines' drop. I didn't understand why Michigan should be penalized so harshly for losing a close game on the road to the top-ranked team in the country. If anything, I thought there should be a rematch.

I later learned that Urban took my comments, twisted them or made up new ones, attributed them to me, and had the quotes taped to the walls of their meeting rooms at the team hotel during the national championship week. Urban is all about getting his team motivated and angry.

It wasn't just me. He put up a quote on the wall saying that Florida didn't have enough speed at wide receiver, and attributed it to another broadcaster or sportswriter.

He used me in a big way, and I didn't appreciate it. I understand what he did, and I tried to laugh it off when I eventually found out. I have no problem defending what I actually say on the air. But I shouldn't have to defend something that a head coach makes up on his own.

I've known or known of Urban since 1987, when he was on Bruce's staff at Ohio State and they were recruiting me. When he was an assistant at Notre Dame, I came to a pep rally before a game against Michigan (he still refers to the Wolverines as "That Team Up North"). Years later, after he left Bowling Green to become the head coach at Utah, Coach Corso and I spent time with him talking about the concepts of his read option offense. When he went to Florida, we did our share of *GameDay* and Saturday night games there. When he walked away from coaching after the 2010 season and came to ESPN as an analyst, we hung out at the annual seminar and talked on a regular basis. We had become friends by then, and like everyone at the time, I wondered how he would manage his stress and health concerns when he took the Ohio State job in late 2011.

He won a national championship and three Big Ten titles during his seven seasons in Columbus. His first team went undefeated.

Urban has said that it's unhealthy to live a life of fear. Ironically, he feared that happening to him—coaching for his job, coaching scared—every day during those seven seasons at Ohio State. It didn't happen because Urban won 83 of the 92 games he coached there (a mind-boggling 90.2 winning percentage). He went 7-0 against Michigan.

Even then, the demands of the job and the effects on his health caused him to retire from coaching after the 2018 season. Still, I wondered if he was really done. Could he stay away from the sidelines?

He lasted two years before taking the leap from TV studio work to the NFL and the Jacksonville Jaguars in January 2021. I know there are questions, all legitimate, about his ability to manage his health. But from a football standpoint, I can tell you this about Urban: he is very, very smart about analyzing every facet of a job before he signs on. He had been studying the ways of the NFL for more than a year. He had talked to owners, team presidents, general managers, coaches, and players about the league.

The outside world might think the Jaguars are a train wreck. They finished a league-worst 1-15. But Urban is looking at the No. 1 pick in the draft, the cap space, the roster flexibility, the freedom to shape this team from scratch. One thing about Urban: I've never seen him put himself in a position where he didn't have a chance to be successful.

We were both born and raised in Ohio. We both played college football in Ohio. We both played baseball in Ohio (he was drafted and played briefly in the minors). We both have a history at Ohio State. We both have an appreciation for the purity of the game, and the discipline required to play it well.

I'm rooting for him in Jacksonville. He loves challenges and he'll get one there. If his health holds up, he'll be successful there.

Chapter 14

My Second Dad

My cell phone rang on May 16, 2009. I looked at the caller ID: it was *GameDay* producer Lee Fitting. Knowing Fitting, he probably just wanted to catch up, maybe give me a hard time about something. That's Fitting.

Instead, his voice was solemn and softer than usual. He said that Coach Corso had suffered a significant stroke that morning. He would survive, said Fitting, but he was having issues with paralysis on the entire right side of his body.

I was devastated by the news. Coach was seventy-three at the time, but he had the energy of someone half his age. How was this possible? The Lee Corso I knew was invincible.

I had seen Coach and Fowler only a few weeks earlier. Each year in Centerville, there is an awards banquet to honor the memory of Sonny Unger, a 1963 Centerville High School graduate and football player who was killed while serving his second tour of duty in the Vietnam War. Coach and Chris had been kind enough to travel to Ohio for the fund-raiser. They were a huge hit that night.

Details emerged about the stroke. When Coach awoke that morning, he did what he had done every day of his life: he recited the "Lord's Prayer." On that morning, though, he couldn't remember the words—not even the first two, "Our Father . . ."

At about 8:30 a.m., Coach had walked to the driveway of his Orlando-area home, bent down to pick up the morning newspaper, felt an odd sensation, walked back into the house, sat down to read the sports section, started to ask his wife if she wanted some orange juice . . . and then the stroke struck in full force.

His mouth wouldn't work. When his wife saw him, the right side of face had drooped and was nonfunctioning. He was taken to the hospital, where doctors asked him to say something, anything. He couldn't speak. They asked him to swallow. He tried, but his mouth and throat were ignoring his brain.

The man known best for his ability to talk on TV—and talk loud—now couldn't utter a word. He would later tell a reporter that he cried like a baby at the hospital that day.

I was concerned and worried about Coach. I began leaving messages for him.

"Coach, you got this. You'll be okay. Nobody tougher than you. I'm here for you. Whatever you need."

I called almost every day. I knew he couldn't talk to me, but he could hear my voice. He could hear the love and encouragement.

Coach was old enough to be my father, and in more ways than he'll ever realize, he is a father to me. I first remember him from his days coaching at Indiana. He had that jet-black hair and he constantly paced the sidelines as if he would give anything to run out there and play. Even as a coach, he had a brash, entertaining personality.

I would come to know the other side of Coach. The one who never misses Catholic Mass. The one who has a kind word for everyone, who will stop and pose for every photo. The one who will outwork anybody and never say a peep about the long hours and the unrelenting travel. The one who cries at old footage of him coaching at the Naval Academy. The one who, when he visits a school's football facility, asks to watch film with the graduate assistants rather than the head coach or the defensive coordinator because he doesn't want to big-time the GAs. I know this because GAs have mentioned to me how much it meant to them.

He won't offer many details about his past. You have to ask him, and even then he will never brag about his accomplishments. I read a story about him years ago in *Orlando* magazine. He was the only child of Alessandro and Irma Corso, who came to America as immigrants from rural northern Italy. Of his two parents, Irma had the education; she had made it through fifth grade, his dad, second grade.

They moved from Chicago to Miami when Coach was ten, and he saw his dad earn seventy-five cents an hour laying floor tile, while Coach's mom worked in a school cafeteria. The proudest and happiest day of their lives was when Coach reported to Florida State for his first day of college.

You might know the rest: the high school star became a college star in football and baseball, and earned a nickname that we repeat on *GameDay* today—the "Sunshine Scooter." His roommate at FSU for a year was Burt Reynolds, then known as Buddy Reynolds.

He became an assistant coach at Maryland and Navy, and a head coach at Louisville, Indiana, Northern Illinois, and finally, at the Orlando franchise of the late, great USFL. He auditioned for a college color analyst job at ESPN in 1987. The other finalist was former Georgia Tech coach Pepper Rodgers.

The story goes that during the ESPN interview process, Rodgers insisted that he travel first-class and not work more than two games per month. When Rodgers told Coach of the demands, Corso said, "I might not get this job, but I *know* you're not getting it."

Coach, who only asked ESPN for a chance, nothing else, got the job. Then he became a sportscasting revelation. Best of all, he became my mentor, my friend, my second father.

When I auditioned for *GameDay* in 1996, Coach was there to help me through my sweat-a-thon. He would say later that he remembered watching some of my game film when I was at Ohio State. He said I could throw the ball well (tell it to the OSU coaches), and recalled that I wore No. 4—the same number he wore when he played high school football for the Miami Jackson Generals.

Coach turned out to be a tremendous teacher. He helped me with my career without even knowing he was doing it. He taught by example.

When I was hired, I thought I was going to be Mr. Serious Football Guy. Football, football, football, and more football. Thank God I sat next to Lee Corso.

If you saw the video of those early shows, you'd see me staring at Coach in amazement. I would do Serious Football Breakdown, and then Coach would call me "Sweetheart," or say, "Not so fast, my friend," and then follow with a series of crazy one-liners. I'm thinking, "What the hell is this guy talking about?"

In late 1998, I was doing my research for the upcoming bowl games, including the match-up between Arkansas and Michigan in the Citrus Bowl. As always, I wanted to be the most prepared analyst, so I dove deep into the prep work.

When it came to that Citrus Bowl, I broke it down as if I were a graduate assistant fighting for a job on the Michigan or Arkansas coaching staffs. It was exhaustive next-level research. My notes included every match-up—offensive lines versus defensive lines, secondary versus receivers, kicking games, etc.—and detailed analysis of the two-deep depth chart. I was humming.

When it came time for our bowl show, I delivered a thorough Xs-and-Os analysis. Lloyd Carr would have been impressed.

Out of the corner of my eye, I could see Coach looking at me. He was growing impatient with my minute-long breakdown of the difference between the football DNA of the SEC and the Big Ten, and these two teams.

"Are you done yet, sweetheart?" he said. He was looking at me like I was from Mars.

I smiled nervously. I was done now.

"Geesh," said Coach, glancing at me, "all I know is that it's the Cadillacs versus the pickup trucks, and I'm going with the pickup trucks."

Just like that, Coach had analyzed the match-up in a way that everyone could understand. Arkansas was the pickup truck built for power, and Michigan was the fancy Cadillac.

He got the pick wrong (Michigan won, 45–31), but the way he set up the pick was perfect. It was Coach personified: simple, direct, entertaining. Always entertaining. Meanwhile, I was talking about the two-deep.

Lesson learned.

It didn't take long for the light to come on. This dude knew how to entertain people. He was witty, opinionated, a genuine showman. He—no one else—taught me the value of not taking yourself too seriously. He has told me a thousand times, "We're in the entertainment business, sweetheart, and football is our vehicle."

Because of his influence, I've learned that I can be a football guy, an Xs-and-Os guy, but when the time is right, when it happens spontaneously and naturally, that I also can have some fun and be a little silly.

When you watch *GameDay*, you're going to get serious football talk, you're going to laugh, you're sometimes going to cry when you watch the features, you're going to get Xs and Os. What Coach taught me is the difference between being funny and trying to be funny. I'm not a professional comedian. My job is to talk about football, but Coach's style gave me permission to talk football in a way that was conversational, that allowed for a one-liner here and there.

In 1997, we were at Michigan State to do *GameDay*. During our Friday production meeting, LC carefully wrote down all his notes and comments with a black Sharpie. Coach doesn't go anywhere without a Sharpie, always black.

Coach always has an opening line ready to go for the start of the show. He calls it his "Hello" comment: Something like: "Hey, it's great to be here in East Lansing, but let me tell you . . ." And then he'll deliver a one-liner to get the crowd riled up.

At Michigan State, he was scheduled to do a *SportsCenter* hit early that Saturday morning before *GameDay* began. When I asked him what he was going to talk about, he waved it off.

"Pffft, are you kidding?" he said. "Not even my own mother watches that show. I'm saving my best stuff for the big show."

For *GameDay*.

The only show that Coach's mom watched on ESPN was *GameDay*. If the other shows weren't good enough for Irma Corso, then they weren't good enough for her son.

To this day, in honor of Coach's mom, we refer to the opening segment of our show as "Irma." When we discuss the rundown during our production meeting, the producer will say something like, "Okay, Des, you start Irma, then let's go Kirk, then Coach, then back to Rece."

During our first four or five years together, Coach and I were more colleagues than friends. Our relationship began to change when we started shooting commercials in Los Angeles during the off-seasons.

A car would pick us up at the scheduled time of 6 a.m., but Coach would be in the hotel lobby at 5:45, pacing near the front door, calling me up, asking, "Where are you?" As long as I've known him, there's Actual Time and then there's Coach Time. Coach Time is fifteen minutes before Actual Time. Lord help you if you're late and he has to wait.

During those car rides in the morning LA traffic and later in the early evening traffic, we got to know each other on a more personal level. I floated a question out there about being a parent—just to see if he wanted to talk about it—and he told me about raising his own kids. Little by little, I asked for more of his advice: about my contract situation, about my mom and dad, about marriage. If there was something that bothered me, I could run it past him.

Sometimes you got Yoda. Sometimes you got Don Corleone. He would listen. Nod. Maybe offer a "Wow. Woo. That's terrible. That's crazy." And then he would pause for a moment, raise his right finger, and say, "Okay, this is what you do."

One time I said, "Coach, they're asking me to do these ABC games, but I still want to do *GameDay,* too."

Pause . . . right finger, and then he said, "Sweetheart, sweetheart, sweetheart—don't ever get away from the camera. You stay in front of the camera, people know who are. If you do games, they'll never see you. It could be anybody talking during a game broadcast. When you're on *GameDay*, it's your face and your voice."

When I got married, Coach told me, "You're going to get a house, right? And when you do, when your wife says, 'What do you think of the purple pillow?' you say, 'I love the purple pillow.' If she says, 'What do you think of the paisley wallpaper?' you say, 'I love the paisley wallpaper.' Happiness in a marriage is you nodding your head and saying, 'Yes.'"

That was his advice, and he was right. Conflict is overrated.

Another time, we were at an ESPN function and an on-air talent told us a long story about his contract situation with ESPN. This person was upset about his negotiations and the role someone in management was playing in them.

As the story dragged on, Coach acted as if he were sympathetic to the person's situation. He would say, "Oh, my gosh, I can't believe that." . . . "Woo. Wow. Really?" . . . "That's terrible."

Finally, I interrupted the on-air person and said, "Let's hear what Coach has to say about this."

LC leaned forward and told a story about coaching at the Naval Academy. He said he was walking the grounds at the Academy, when he walked past a Navy captain.

"Morning, sir," said Coach as he breezed by.

"Get back here," demanded the captain. "You see these stripes?" The captain pointed to the four gold stripes on his uniform sleeve. "You walk by me, you salute me."

"Yes, sir," said Coach.

The story complete, Coach lowered his voice to a half whisper and said to the person who was complaining about the ESPN executive, "I learned a valuable lesson that day. You don't have to respect the man, but you had better respect the position,"

The story was Coach's way of telling the on-air talent that you might not like your boss, but the boss is the boss.

Because of all the time we spent together (at those commercial shoots, traveling together for the Thursday night games, at *GameDay*), he became one of the few people with whom I could discuss the most sensitive things in my life. I can tell Coach anything. The successes. The heartaches. I can show him highlights from, say, Zak's high school game and my pride suddenly becomes his pride. I can ask him about a contract negotiation, an Italian recipe, his thoughts on whether to trust a certain coach. He has said that he treats me like a son, which is an incredible honor, given my respect for him.

And like a father, he can gently put me in my place. If I get irritable on the set or in the booth, he leans over, puts his hand on my forearm, and says, "Sweetheart, they're paying us to do this job."

If you ask him his secret to success in business, he says, "Never prostitute your integrity to get a job or to keep one. If you try for a job, and they want you to compromise your integrity, leave— leave right away."

When he's on a roll picking winner after winner each week, he'll say, "When you lose, you say little. When you win, you say less."

During the last month of the 2019 season, Coach worked despite having pneumonia. He wasn't feeling well at the national championship game, but there was no way he was calling in sick. That was the Alessandro and Irma in him.

There were times when I asked him to get his rest, to take care of himself. I worried about him. But Coach could break his arm and if you asked him how he was doing, he'd say, "I like when my is arm broken. It's betta' this way." That's one of his words: "Betta'." He'll never give in.

Coach is the same tough guy who was confronted by angry Miami fans after we did a show there in 2000. It was serious; they were trying to get at Corso. Security officials created a human wall for us, but as we tried to squeeze through, someone reached over and grazed Coach.

Coach stopped and glared at the Miami fans. He immediately assumed an old-time boxing stance, like he was world heavyweight champion Jack Dempsey from the 1920s.

"Which one of you sons of bitches touched me?!" he said defiantly, ready to rumble. "Which one?!"

That's the football player in him talking. The coach in him talking. The son of hardworking Italian immigrants talking.

Coach picks his moments to give you a hard time. During Rinaldi's first season with the show in 2003, Tom did a heartfelt piece on a player whose team was an underdog in one of the featured games that day. It was the kind of lovingly told piece that Tom would become famous for.

When the feature was finished, Tom added a few comments and then tossed it back to the set. Fowler complimented Tom on the piece and then Coach chimed in.

"That was a nice story by Timmy, but they're still going to get crushed," he said.

"Did you just call Tom Rinaldi 'Timmy'?" Fowler said.

From that point on, we called Tom "Timmy."

At a bowl game we covered one year, Rinaldi wandered into a room at the stadium marked "Talent Lounge." When Tom walked in, Coach said, "Timmy, this is the Talent Lounge. You don't belong in here. I'm sorry."

I think I snorted on that one. It was rare when you could leave Rinaldi speechless.

Coach had his stroke on May 16. Our first *GameDay* show was less than four months away, September 5 in Atlanta, Alabama versus Virginia Tech. After Coach finished crying that day in the hospital, he made a promise to himself. One way or another, he was going to be in Atlanta for that show.

There were people who thought he was crazy. They told him so, too.

"You can't do it, Lee," they said. "It's too soon."

In his mind, there was no debate. "I have to do it," he told himself.

I thought he would come back. I didn't know at what level of capacity, but I knew he would be there. I kept calling. So did Fowler, Fitting, and others.

He began intensive physical and speech therapy sessions. He had to teach his facial muscles to work again. He had to relearn phrases and words. His brain itself had to heal from the stroke. This took time.

Coach could read a calendar. We all could. September 5 wasn't far away.

You know what he did? He worked harder. He began to recover. The words came slower than before, but nobody was going to stop the talker from talking.

He said later that he had great people helping him, and that the Lord was helping him, too. Makes sense, since he began slowly reciting "The Lord's Prayer" again.

I first saw him that summer at a few photo shoots, and then at our annual college football seminar. It was very emotional to see him again.

When you potentially lose someone—and while we were told that Coach would survive the stroke, we didn't know for sure if or when he would return to the show—it makes you appreciate what you have. And we had a national treasure.

You could tell something was a little bit different with him. I didn't care. I was overjoyed to see him again. I also was in awe of his courage.

Television can be merciless. There is no place to hide, especially on live television. You can see a droplet of sweat (me). A fly on a vice president's head. You can hear a bungled word, a botched phrase. It's hard enough to do well under the best of circumstances, but how about the courage to go on live national television, without a teleprompter, and do it less than four months after suffering a stroke? That was Coach.

He was on that set in Atlanta on September 5. He's been there every football Saturday since then. The man is fearless and tough.

He stumbles over a few words here and there. People say, "What's wrong with Corso?" What's wrong? How about, what's right? He overcame a stroke. He still has forgotten more about football than I'll ever know. He still is the consummate showman.

He has slowed down a little bit. He would be the first to admit it. He was a pitcher with a 97 mph fastball and now he's learned to succeed with an 83 mph curveball. He has adapted.

I look out for him in these later years, just as he looked out for me in my early years. I'm not the only one; all of us on the show are protective of Coach.

When we talk on the phone, I end every conversation by telling him I love him. I didn't used to say that, and he's never said it back to me. Lee is one of those guys from a generation who doesn't want to go there. But though he doesn't say it, I feel it from him.

On *GameDay*, I have always sat to his left. He is my security net, and I'm his. When he returned from his stroke, I told myself, "I got him, I have his back." He didn't have his fastball, but he was still Lee Corso. I didn't want him to have any fear, to worry about making a mistake and feeling isolated on that set. I would do whatever I could—we all would—to sand over the rough spots. If I see him struggling for a word, or searching for the name of a player or coach, or needing an assist during his headgear segment, I'm there for him. We all are—me, Rece Davis, Chris before Rece, Des, David. We would run through not one, but two walls for Coach.

He had done the same for all of us over the years. He has never looked at me as a threat, never said in those early days, "Who's this young guy? Is he going to take over the show?" He looked at me as someone who could help the show get better. And if the show succeeded, then everyone succeeded.

The comment I hear from people the most about my work on television has nothing to do with calling a game or talking about football. Instead, I can't tell you how many times people have said, "Thank you for the way you treat Lee." My own mom says she's most proud of me because of that.

I appreciate the kind words, but how else would I treat him? It's not a burden, it's an honor. It seems, at times, that we live in a society that doesn't value a life lived well and in full. I think it's important for people to appreciate and celebrate those who have been through both the good and difficult experiences in life.

My respect and love for Coach is genuine. People are kind to thank me for the way I treat him, but the truth is, he helps me as much as I help him. He doesn't need many assists.

At the end of the 2010 season, Coach was honored by the National College Football Awards Association for a lifetime's worth of contributions to the sport. About a minute into his acceptance speech, Coach thanked Chris, me, and Desmond for our support and help, "especially the last two years, when I really . . ."

Then Coach broke down. I had never seen him do that. And then I nearly broke down with him. As tears streamed down my face, Coach composed himself after a brief hug from Chris. He turned to the audience and said, "Especially in the last two years, when I really needed you guys, boy."

How can you not respect that vulnerability? How can you not admire that honesty?

Some of his best moments on the show have come since his return from the stroke. In 2011, we took *GameDay* to Houston in mid-November. There weren't a lot of big games that Saturday, Houston was 10-0 and favored big over SMU, and we figured it was a good way to introduce America to the Cougars' program.

We went down there and it was a great show. Huge crowd. Olympian and Houston alum Carl Lewis was our guest picker. Lots of energy.

When it came to make the final pick of the day, I took Houston. No-brainer—they were huge favorites that day. Lewis did the same, and even predicted they'd go undefeated. The crowd roared.

Coach milked the moment and then turned on Lewis.

"Holy cow, how can you pick against SMU?" said Coach, apparently not aware that the Mustangs were 6-4 at the time. But that's Coach—you zig, he zags.

Then he reached down and picked up an SMU cheerleading megaphone. It was painted red, with S-M-U in white and a thin blue border around each letter.

"Look at that one there," he said, raising the megaphone to the crowd. "Red, white, and blue."

Then he started chanting, "U-S-A," and pulled the megaphone toward his mouth.

The crowd had no reaction. Coach was trying to get them fired up by picking SMU. Then he tried the U-S-A thing. Still nothing. Worse yet, the director in the production truck wasn't keeping up with Coach for the crowd shots he wanted, *and* we were about to blow past the noon handoff to the Nebraska-Michigan game.

Just as I was wondering how he was going to salvage the moment, he tossed the megaphone toward the set and said, "Aw, f—- it!" Then he grabbed the Cougar mascot head, put it on, and did the Corso Miss America wave to the crowd and the cameras.

I was in shock. Fowler dropped his head in disbelief. Bear, who had been packing his work bag off to the side, looked at me and mouthed, "Did he just say that?" I nodded yes.

The crowd reacted this time. Meanwhile, Lewis laughed and said, "Glad there's a delay."

But there wasn't a delay! It was live, and it was spectacular. Through my earpiece, I could hear Fitting and the rest of the truck explode into laughter.

When we were clear and off the air, Coach removed the mascot head and started telling us how much he enjoyed the show.

I said, "Coach, you said 'F—-' on the air."

"So what?" he said.

Within thirty seconds of the end of the show, all three phones in the production truck began to light up. It was upper management calling from ESPN headquarters in Bristol. They wanted Corso to issue an on-air apology on all four ESPN networks by the bottom of the hour.

Fitting had to stifle his laughter as he got the order. After all, it was just Coach being Coach.

Fitting walked out to the set and found Corso sitting off to the side. Fitting shook his head and Coach said, "Did it make it on air?"

"Yeah, Coach, it did," Fitting said.

"Good," said Coach.

"Coach, we're going to need you to read this little script here— Card 99—and offer an apology for what you said."

"I'll be happy to. I understand. I'll make good for what I did."

Coach took his seat behind the desk and the camera light turned red. Coach read Card 99.

"Earlier today on *College GameDay*, while picking the SMU-Houston game, I got a bit excited and used an expletive I shouldn't have used. I apologize and I can promise it won't happen again."

It was perfect, except for the part where Coach read the whole thing, but ended it with a big Lee Corso smile on his face. Fitting made him do it again. This time, Coach left out the smile, and the apology was aired midway through the first quarter of the noon games.

Right after the show, me, Bear, and Deron Brown (my spotter on the Saturday night broadcasts) flew to Eugene, Oregon, for the USC-Oregon game. When we landed, I ducked into the small private terminal for a few minutes before we headed to the stadium.

While I was in there, a guy introduced himself and said he was Phil Knight's driver. Knight was the cofounder and chairman of Nike, and a proud Oregon alum.

"He just wants to say a quick hello, if you have time," said the driver.

I followed the driver outside, where Knight had a luxury RV parked. Knight bounced down the steps of the RV with a grin and high-fived me.

"F——-ing Corso," he said. "He's absolutely crazy. How about that. What happened?"

So I told him the story of the f-bomb.

Then I got to the stadium and walked down to the field. Oregon coach Chip Kelly and USC coach Lane Kiffin were already there as their teams warmed up.

I was at the twenty-yard line and Kelly was at the opposite twenty. He waved and then sprinted sixty yards to me.

"Dude," said Kelly, "he's my hero. What was he thinking? He's nuts."

He was talking about Corso.

Kiffin came over to chat.

"What's up with Corso?" he said. "I can't believe he did that."

I was worried that Coach might be in trouble. But Coach wasn't your normal ESPN on-air personality. Nothing happened to him, except Card 99. He's the only guy who can drop an f-bomb and people think it's the greatest thing in the world.

It wouldn't be the last time he said something he shouldn't. We were at UCF in 2018 and there was a panel discussion on whether the undefeated Knights belonged in the playoff mix. Coach raised his left hand to make a point, waited patiently, and then said, "Let me tell you something. These people don't give a shit about that."

The crowd applauded and I said, "You did it again. You did it again."

Rece Davis, who had replaced Fowler in 2015, handed Coach a note card.

"Here's Card 99 for later," he said.

Coach has dressed as the Statue of Liberty. Been thrown to the ground by Bill Murray. Danced in a leprechaun outfit at Notre Dame. Worn a purple cow head. Addressed the crowd as James Madison. The list is endless.

When Murray threw him down on the set at Clemson, Coach was dressed as Florida State mascot Chief Osceola. He was also carrying a spear, which Murray threw toward the crowd.

Afterward, I asked Coach when he and Murray had time to rehearse their headgear act.

"We didn't rehearse it!" he said. "I had no idea he was going to do it!"

He loved it, though. Entertainment, sweetheart.

Coach doesn't have a laptop. He doesn't do social media. He has never been on the internet. He didn't even have a fax when people used faxes. If you don't have his private number (which he rarely answers), you have to leave a message at the pencil company (Dixon Ticonderoga) he works at two days a week. You'll get his voice message, and at the end of it, he says, "And remember, life is gooood."

He is a creature of habit. Concerns about Covid-19 prevented Coach from traveling with the show in 2020, but during a normal season and a normal *GameDay* week, he shows up at our Friday morning production meeting fifteen minutes early. He has all his clippings—forget the internet, he clips out stories with scissors from the *Orlando Sentinel.*

These days I usually sit next to Bear at our production meetings, but Coach is close by. He rarely says a word in those meetings. He wants to get out of there as fast as possible. Before he heads back to his hotel, he'll make a loop around the food table and stuff his black satchel with candy bars, pieces of other candy, potato chips, Cokes, Sprites, Dr Peppers, root beers, Cheetos.

When he orders his lunch, he doesn't want anything from a national chain but from the best local deli in town.

Once he gets into his room, he lines up his drinks over there, and his snacks over here. He puts on his blue pajamas, his white footies, his white T-shirt, and then he spends the next three or four hours going over his notes, practicing his delivery, and eating his food.

On Saturday morning, he is always one of the first ones in the production room. He gets his makeup done and then finds an empty room or a hallway to work through the vocal exercises his speech therapist taught him. Then it's showtime.

After *GameDay* is done, he'll go back to the hotel, rest for a little while, and then return to the stadium to watch the game in person. I love that he stays for the game. He's down there on the sidelines, arms on his knees, just like he's coaching again. He reminds me of when my dad would watch my high school or Ohio State games from the sideline. Same stance, same intensity.

Wherever Coach goes on the road, our security team arranges for a local police officer or state trooper to be with him on campus and at the stadium. For those of us who know Coach, we almost feel sorry for those law enforcement folks. They have no idea what they've gotten themselves into.

Coach doesn't *watch* a game. He lives it. First of all, he only stays on the sideline of the team he picked that morning on *GameDay*. And once the game begins, he's speed-walking from one end of the field to the other end. It's almost comical to watch a state trooper, who has to wear all of that heavy equipment, try to keep up with Coach. If there's a punt or a kickoff, Coach is gone. By the time the ball drops into the arms of the return specialist, Coach is halfway down the sideline—the officer jogging behind him, trying to keep up. And you should see him if the refs make a call against "his" team. He'll wave his arms in the air in disgust. He'll pace back and forth. He's so into the game that you'd think they'd hand him a headset. It's a treat to watch.

Coach turned eighty-six in August 2020. Has he mellowed? Not a bit.

In 2012, I was prepping for the national championship game between No. 1 Notre Dame and No. 2 Alabama. As I studied film of the two teams, I zeroed in on Bama All-American guard Chance Womack. I did a deep dive on the effect Womack could have if he got to the second level and was able to block Notre Dame star linebacker Manti Te'o.

During the pregame show, I broke it all down for the viewers. Womack. Te'o. Second level. Serious football.

Coach had heard enough.

"What the hell are you talking about?" he said.

To this day, Coach says that was one of his favorite moments with me. He loved giving me a hard time. He loved telling me to make people smile, make them laugh, have some fun. And to this day, if I start to talk about Xs and Os, Coach will tell me, "Uh, oh, we're going to talk serious football. Chance Womack time."

It has been more than twelve years since Coach had his stroke. When I had first heard the news, I thought, "What would we do if we didn't have Lee? What would *I* do if I didn't have Lee?"

It was a sobering moment, and ever since then I've tried not to think about it. I'm going to ride this thing out as long as I can with him.

Lee Corso is a made man. If he wants to be at ESPN, he'll be at ESPN. That's the way it should be. He's earned that. I hope I'm there with him for as long as he wants to stay.

Chapter 15

The Diagnosis

"**W**here's Jim?"

Those two words marked the exact moment that a near-perfect day became a terrifying night.

We began the 2009 *GameDay* season in Atlanta for the Alabama–Virginia Tech match-up. But it was the September 12 location and game—No. 3 USC at No. 8 Ohio State—that had me so excited. Great game. Great stadium. *GameDay* in the morning, the prime-time broadcast that night. The best part: my family, my mom, my dad, and my friends could all come to the show, stay for the game, and then we could hang out afterward. Perfect.

My dad had married for a third time, but I still wanted him in our lives. I would talk to him every so often, but there was always that disconnect when it came to him listening to me. We had a relationship, but it had faded partly because I had devoted all my energies into my marriage, my own family, and my job. Still, it was important to me and Alli that our boys spent time with their grandfather. And it was important to me, too, that I spent time with him.

He had come to *GameDay* shows in the past. I loved having him there. I would glance at him during a commercial break, maybe nod at him. He would smile back, and I could tell he was proud of his seeing his son on that set. He always tried to stay in the background and off to the side. He didn't want to get in anybody's way.

In recent years, my dad had become more uncomfortable going to games and being around large crowds. He preferred watching the games from his couch. A year earlier, he had come with us to the Kentucky Derby, but had disappeared at the racetrack for three hours that day. We didn't think anything of it. He liked doing things on his own. He could be a bit of a loner, but he always came back.

I got him a pass for the USC–Ohio State match-up. It was a tight, entertaining game, and played in front of a then Ohio Stadium record crowd of 106,033 fans. USC scored the winning touchdown with 1:05 left to play.

Afterward, I met our whole group at the *GameDay* bus, which was parked down the street near St. John Arena. We were laughing, talking about the game, and breaking down the key moments. Fans from both programs stopped by and said hello. It was about midnight.

And then someone said, "Where's Jim?"

My dad wasn't there.

We looked inside and outside the bus. We took turns calling his cell phone. Maybe he had stopped by the Ohio State locker room to say hello to someone he knew. Maybe an old friend was bending his ear on the field.

No answer.

We looked in St. John Arena. No sign of him. We walked around the entire lot. Nothing.

This was serious now. My dad had a habit of doing things by himself, but when he didn't answer his phone, we got worried.

We got in our cars and each of us picked a different road to follow out of the stadium. If he was walking somewhere after the game, maybe we'd spot him.

About five miles from the Shoe—and only a mile from my house—we found him. He was walking along Lane Avenue by himself.

"Dad, what happened?" I said. "What's going on?"

"I don't know," he said.

And then he started making excuses about why he had left.

We knew something was seriously wrong. He went to a specialist a week or so later. The diagnosis: middle-stage Alzheimer's disease.

It made sense now. The wandering off at the Kentucky Derby . . . the disappearance at the Ohio State game . . . the desire to be more withdrawn than usual. More than five million people in the United States had Alzheimer's in 2009, and my dad was now one of them.

What a year it had been so far. My dad diagnosed with Alzheimer's, and my second dad, Coach Corso, challenged by the effects of a stroke.

My dad's condition wasn't dire. He could function day to day. But he had moments where his memory simply didn't work. For the most part, he was Dad, but the doctor warned him—and us—that the condition was likely to worsen over time.

Even though my mom and dad had been divorced for years, my mom was worried about him. She wanted to help take care of him, but the relationship between her and my dad's wife was not good.

As usual, Teri helped monitor the situation. I kept in touch, too. My dad was adamant about one thing: he wanted to continue living in his own house. Whenever he referred to his condition, he would say, "I've got this damn Alzheimer's." Of course, that didn't stop him from getting in the car, pulling out his old AAA paper maps, all folded like an accordion, and driving the back roads of Ohio as part of his appraiser job.

In the office at my house, I have dozens of photos on the walls, shelves, and desk: family vacation photos, family portraits, the boys doing the O-H-I-O cheer, dog photos, a photo of me moments after throwing the game-tying touchdown pass to Greg Beatty against Michigan, a photo of Woody wearing his signature ball cap, glasses, and short-sleeve white shirt—in a snowstorm, a photo of my mom, a photo of me and the *GameDay* crew, a photo of my dad, former Ohio State teammate and NFL star Tom Matte, and Woody, a photo of Kenny Chesney, Urban, Deron, and a few other buddies from a concert in Columbus, a photo of me icing Zak's head after he took a spill on the concrete. On and on it goes.

But one of my favorite and most meaningful photos is of my dad and the boys at the Rose Bowl after the 2009 season. He was seventy at the time, only seventeen years younger than the Rose Bowl stadium itself.

In 1957, Ohio State won the Big Ten, beat Oregon in the Rose Bowl on New Year's Day, and won the national championship. But freshmen were ineligible to play back then, so my dad didn't make the trip west for the game.

Ohio State didn't reach the Rose Bowl during his remaining three years as a player, but they did win the Big Ten in 1961, when he was an assistant coach. But the school's faculty committee voted against the Rose Bowl bid. My dad essentially boycotted the game from that day forward.

Fast-forward to 2009.

After my dad's Alzheimer's diagnosis, I decided his Rose Bowl boycott was going to end. Like it or not, my dad was coming with me and the family to Pasadena. It was time to quit talking about these things, and actually start *doing* them.

In a cool bit of serendipity, Ohio State and Oregon faced each other in the Rose Bowl for the first time since the 1958 game. I was in the broadcast booth with Musburger, and my dad was in the stands with his grandsons—and he had the biggest grandpa happy face you ever saw.

He also liked the final score: Ohio State 26, Oregon 17.

Chapter 16

Moving On

Doing *GameDay* and calling a big game of the week on network TV took me to a different stratosphere as far as the public eye. Going back to my high school days, I had always been uncomfortable with being the center of attention. Fame wasn't a priority of mine. I just wanted to do my job, and do it well.

But as the popularity of *GameDay* and the prime-time telecast grew, it created some unsettling situations. I began to notice that cars would pull up in front of our house at all hours of the day. Sometimes I'd wake up at midnight and there would be someone parked out front. On occasion, total strangers would come to our front door.

I love talking to people about football, but not at my house with random strangers. What worried me most was that I was on the road for three to four days a week. I had a wife and young boys.

As the boys got older, they became huge Ohio State fans. Like grandfather, like father, like sons. They also began to play football, including the twins, who had slowly caught up in size with kids their age. When I would come home from a *GameDay* and game-of-the-week trip, I'd sometimes bring home a jersey from the campuses I had been at. Depending on the situation, a player or coach might sign the jersey, and write something like, "Hey, Tye, keep working hard." That sort of thing.

The boys would wear them to school or around the neighborhood. To them, they were just cool jerseys, nothing more.

But grown adults actually confronted them and said, "You're a Herbstreit. Why are you wearing an Oregon jersey?"

They were just little kids, innocents. They'd say, "We're Buckeyes! We're Buckeyes!"

If I questioned or criticized Ohio State on the air, or said anything positive about Michigan, there was a small, but incredibly vocal percentage of Buckeye fans, especially in Columbus, who accused me of being a football traitor. If one of those fans saw you (or you and your family in public), they didn't hesitate to make some sort of crack. There was even a situation where my mom overheard an opposing Pee Wee football coach tell one of his players, "See that Herbstreit kid? Hit him hard. Go hit him hard." Alli heard a parent tell his son, "Go kill that kid, he's a Herbstreit."

When you live in the public eye, there is no handbook on how to handle that sort of thing. What do you do when a coach or a parent instructs a player to try to hurt your child? How do you explain to your own sons that people don't like them because of their last name, because of their dad?

Our boys were blessed and, through no fault of their own, they were cursed. The blessings are many: their health, the fact that Alli and I can provide a comfortable and stable life for them, they have access to moments, places, players, and coaches not available to other kids. My boys have played football on the Rose Bowl field after the real game was done. They've been in locker rooms, film rooms, and coaches' offices with me. Chase is so used to being on a college field during warm-ups—he'll run routes, ask me to throw bombs to him, respectfully mingle with the players—that it's second nature to him. At Purdue one year, he had 15,000–20,000 students cheering for him as we played catch. We even tossed the ball back and forth with the students in the bleachers.

The curse is the isolation. Their circle of true friends is small. In the past, other kids have tried to be their friends for the wrong reasons. Adults have singled them out for criticism. As parents, we've become protective of them and have done our best to help them find a balance between a normal life and the realities of their last name.

Ohio State has as passionate a fan base as there is in all of sports. Their teams are almost always good, and those fans are almost always opinionated. I would put their energy level up against any fan base in the country, against any in the world. Ninety percent of them are wonderful people. They love their team, but they're also realistic. Their world doesn't end if the Buckeyes lose a game.

Then there are the 10 percent who are an absolute embarrassment to the other 90 percent, to the genuine Ohio State fans who love their program through thick and thin. The 10 percent think the head coach should be fired, the quarterback should be replaced, the defensive coordinator should be demoted, the refs should be investigated for taking bribes. It's ridiculous.

I see it at every major program. But when you're a former Ohio State quarterback and captain, and your dad was a captain, you wish the 90 percent was 100 percent. I'm more disappointed than I am upset with the OSU vocal minority. When did we become this? When did we get these kinds of fans?

Ohio State went more than thirty years between the time Woody won his last national championship in 1968 and Jim Tressel won one in 2002. During that gap, if you beat Michigan and made it to the Rose Bowl, you were forever hailed as a hero.

When Tressel won in 2002, the expectations and demands changed. It only got worse after Meyer later won a national title in 2014. The 10 percent said, "You better win a national championship or someone's ass is going to get it." It was never, "We lost to a better Michigan team today. We'll bounce back next year. Appreciate the effort this season, fellas."

I got paid to talk about college football. I learned to deal with the blowback from something I said on ESPN and ABC, and on WBNS Radio. But I wasn't going to let my family be subjected to the 10 percent. And honestly, I was tired of it, too.

I love Ohio State. Always have, always will. But I wasn't willing to trade my credibility and integrity in an effort to make the 10 percent happy. My job was to analyze what I saw, and comment in a fair and objective way—regardless of uniform color. The vocal minority thought it was a betrayal to speak the truth. They thought—and still do—that it was wrong to give Michigan credit for a well-earned win. I got crushed for it, to the point that my dad, in an interview with a local publication, tried to stick up for me.

"And some Buckeye fans think he doesn't love Ohio State?" my dad said. "That boy bled scarlet and gray."

The tipping point came when the *Dispatch* printed our address on the front page of the newspaper after we were involved in an IRS dispute. It was the first time Alli was afraid for our safety. That's when I said, "Let's jump. I'm ready to go somewhere else."

After looking in Austin and Fort Worth, we decided to visit Nashville on the recommendation of friends. We found a great school for the kids and that's what clinched it. We moved to Nashville in spring of 2011.

I miss Columbus. If I had to do it all over again, I don't know if I would have moved. Nashville is a wonderful city and we love it there, but Columbus and Ohio are still home in many ways.

Not long after moving to Nashville, I was asked to be part of a national ad campaign for Dove Men+Care. I had done some local endorsements in Columbus (a shoe store, a car dealership, that sort of thing), but this was my first real national spot. The campaign was centered on real-life experiences involving me, my career, and my family.

One of the ad agency directors or producers of the commercial—I can't remember which one—asked me, "Is there somebody you know who you'd feel comfortable talking to about these experiences in your career?"

Actually, I did. I picked up my cell and called someone who had held my hand during my early days of live television, who had helped me when I was on the set sweating through my dress shirt, who attended my wedding, and who has been a friend for years.

I called Jay Crawford.

Jay was on vacation with his family at Martha's Vineyard, but he didn't hesitate to help me once again. He flew immediately to Nashville, sat across from me as the interviewer during the all-day shoot, and then flew back to Boston and rejoined his family. He says he was honored and humbled to be asked to be part of the commercial, but it's really the other way around. I've been honored by his help and friendship through the years. Asking him to do the commercial was just a tiny gesture of thanks.

In the commercial—and there was nothing scripted about it—I talked about how my kids didn't look at me as a broadcaster, but as Dad, as the sheriff of the family. Alli is co-sheriff. Alli and I weren't raised in affluent families. During the most chaotic times in my own childhood, money and food were tight. We definitely weren't spoiled kids.

As our kids got a little older and I was becoming more visible because of my career, we pounded into their heads the importance of humility and perspective. We wanted them to understand that they weren't better than anyone else because of their last name. They weren't more special because they lived in this house, or in that neighborhood, or sat in the backseat of that car. None of that makes them—or their parents—superior to others.

We never wanted them to become sassy, punky, their-shit-doesn't-stink kind of kids. We reinforced that every day, perhaps to the point that they became too deferential, too humble. But we'd rather err on that side than the other.

We also tried to explain that our last name made them targets. There were going to be some kids who would try to take them down in a social setting, in a school setting, and in a sports setting. That was our boys' reality and they had to accept that as a challenge. Those were the rules of engagement, so now go out and compete in all of it. For the most part, they've done a great job of dealing with that dynamic.

In the twins' case, I didn't want Jake and Tye's smaller size as kids to be used as an excuse. Once they were about five years old, and the doctors assured us that they were getting stronger and bigger (just at a slower pace), we didn't impose any restrictions on them. My buddy Craig Schmidt called them "raptors," because of their aggressiveness. When we had a trampoline, they would jump out of it. When they would play football in the basement, you would have thought the winner was going to get $10,000. They did live tackling drills in the living room. They were ultracompetitive, but in a good way.

I didn't want them to feel they were at a disadvantage because of their size. I purposely tried to treat them tough. Again, not in a harsh way, but I wasn't a helicopter dad if they took a spill, or took a good, clean hit in Pop Warner ball. I never ran onto the field and said, "Are you okay? Are you all right?" I wanted them to figure it out on their own. If they needed help, I was there for them.

As I was asking them to be great kids, I was constantly evaluating the job I was doing as a parent and husband. I did it on a daily basis. I think it's just the way I am. Obviously, I was motivated by my past. All I knew for sure is that I didn't want to screw them up.

Besides the move to Nashville, there were other changes on the way. In 2014, Fowler replaced Musburger in the booth for the weekly Saturday night game. By then, the professional relationship between Musburger and me had been strained to its breaking point.

During our early years together, I was in awe of working with Brent. But by years seven and eight I was miserable. It had gotten to the point that I never knew which version of Brent I'd get: Happy Brent, the one who playfully called me "Herb-ola" when I arrived, or Territorial Brent, the one who made me feel like a visitor. There were times during those last two years when I would arrive at the booth, look at Deron (who was my spotter for the games), take a deep breath, and then turn the door handle and hope for the best.

I never said a word to Brent about how I felt. As a midwestern blue-collar kid who was the son of a coach, I had always been taught to respect your elders. I did that with my dad and mom, my uncles and aunts, my own coaches such as Coach Gregg, Coach Engleka, Coach Cooper, and Coach Corso. And I did it with Brent. From a broadcasting standpoint, he was a father figure in a way. I kept telling myself—and this was the coach's son in me—"Shut up and deal with it. You're working with Brent Musburger!"

I kept it all inside, which probably wasn't very healthy. I wanted him to think everything was great. I would walk into the booth and do the same fake laugh I had done years earlier with my step-dad and stepmom. *"Hey, how you doing?"* Meanwhile, every Sunday morning during those 2012 and 2013 seasons, I would talk to Alli about the situation and call Brian Chorpenning and my broadcast agent and close friend Nick Khan and say, "Man, they should take me off this game. This just isn't working. I'll just do *GameDay*." Then I would hope the next week would be better.

Sometimes it was, sometimes it wasn't. I don't know if I handled it the right way, but that's how I chose to deal with it.

What should have been one of the best experiences of my professional life had become the exact opposite. I wasn't having fun, and the toll it was taking on me personally was significant. I was so unhappy that I was willing to give up that seat. Who in their right mind would be willing to give up that seat and that prime-time television real estate? That just tells you where I was at the time.

Some of the disconnect between us wasn't anyone's fault. If *GameDay* and the Saturday night game were at the same campus that week, I would fly into town on Thursday, go to dinner with the *GameDay* gang, attend the Friday morning production meeting, meet with the coaches that afternoon, and then skip the weekly Friday night *GameDay* gathering so I could go to dinner with Brent and the rest of the Saturday night crew. I tried to do that as often as I could. It obviously was impossible when *GameDay* and the Saturday night game were in different places, or if I flew back to watch my boys play high school football.

That said, I'm proud of the work we did together, and I hope Brent is, too. Within the industry, within our company, and within the college football world, the on-air product was well received. However challenging I felt the situation was between Brent and me, it never compromised the quality of the games we called together and it never lessened the enjoyment I got from being part of those games. We had a lot of great seasons, but every so often Brent might slam down the TALK BACK button on our control panel in the booth and start yelling at the producer. I would get real quiet on the air, because I thought he was mad. It happened just enough to make it uncomfortable.

I want Brent to know that I have nothing but respect for him and his career. I learned by watching and listening to him. And I'll never forget how kind he was to my dad. We shared a booth for eight years, but I'm not sure we shared a friendship. That's okay, you don't have to be good friends to call a good game—though I wish we would have been better friends. For whatever reason, we didn't click personally.

Fowler's arrival changed all that. He didn't have the game-calling experience that Musburger had (nobody did; Brent is one of the all-time best), but Chris and I had spent eighteen seasons together on the *GameDay* set. I trusted him, he trusted me. We weren't competitors, but partners.

Brent and I did have some signature moments. One of them had nothing to do with the game itself.

You remember the famous September 7, 2013, appearance by Eminem/Marshall Mathers in our booth in Ann Arbor for the Notre Dame/Michigan game, right? We were going to use Eminem's "Berzerk" as the featured song in our Saturday night show opening, and for other college football series throughout the season. At halftime, the plan was to show a sneak peek of his new music video from the album.

The coordinating producer of our Saturday night game package is Bill Bonnell. He had friends in the music industry who helped arrange the visit. We were in Ann Arbor, Eminem had strong ties to Detroit, he had a new album coming out, we used some of his music, he could promote it—it was a win/win for everyone.

Eminem came into the booth during a commercial break at halftime. He couldn't have been nicer: "Nice to meet you, Brent. Been watching you since I was a little kid. What an honor." . . . "Kirk, nice to meet you. Appreciate the job you do."

Then he said, "Hey, man, I get really nervous on live TV. Where's the camera?"

I pointed at the Coke-can-sized camera in the booth.

"We'll have fun," I said. "You're going to call it, talk about your new album."

Three, two, one . . . we were back live.

Brent introduced Eminem and the world premiere video. But during the entire fifteen-second intro, Eminem did a zombie, *Night of the Living Dead* thing. He was in some sort of self-induced trance. I didn't know what was going on. Was he in his "Berzerk" character? Was he screwing around? Was he really scared stiff?

Thirty seconds earlier, we had been chatting like three guys talking about what kind of snowblowers we use on our driveways. Now he was swiveling slowly to the right and left, his eyes staring straight ahead.

After the video preview aired, Brent asked him a question about the producer of the album. Eminem was still in zombie mode and then, suddenly, he snapped out of it.

"Yeah, sorry, live TV," he said. "Live TV freaks me out a little bit."

Had you searched the entire earth, you couldn't have found two people less equipped than Brent and me to make small talk with a rap star about his new album. I mostly stared at a pen I was holding and let Brent ask all of the questions.

Bonnell was in my ear during the interview.

"What's happening? Talk, Herbie! Say something!"

I was back in Ms. Neidhard's English class, just happy to stay out of it: *Nah, I'm good.* I had nothing for him.

But Bonnell wouldn't give up. "Ask him what he's most excited about with the album release."

So I said, "What are you most excited about with the album release?"

"Uh, nothing," said Eminem.

Brent called him by his last name. I had a nervous smile on my face. It was a fabulous TV train wreck.

The interview, if you can call it that, went viral. It was awkward. It was uncomfortable. But it was genius on his part. He orchestrated something to create a buzz for his new album release, and Brent and me were characters in his halftime show.

I'll give Eminem credit for this: the man knew his Mount Rushmore of football announcers. Near the end of his visit, he named Pat Summerall, John Madden, Al Michaels, and Musburger as his dream team of announcers. Hard to beat that list, though I'd add two more: Keith Jackson and Dick Enberg.

———

Musburger became the lead announcer for ESPN's SEC Network game package, which made its debut in August 2014. Fowler, who had signed a new long-term deal with ESPN, would do *GameDay* in the morning and then we'd do the game at night. He had made no secret of his desire to grow as a broadcaster—and that meant doing live events at the highest level, including the newly established College Football Playoff.

Chris and I have distinctly different personalities, but when it came to *GameDay* and the Saturday night game, we wanted the same things: to be a team, and to deliver the best show and game broadcasts possible. It was that simple.

This time our roles were reversed. I was the more established broadcaster in the game booth because of my number of reps and overall experience. I did everything I could to make Chris feel comfortable when he joined our Saturday night team, just as he had done for me when I walked onto the *GameDay* set in 1996.

We were both lucky to be able to work with Bill Bonnell. I didn't know him when I made the jump from the Thursday night games to the Saturday night prime-time telecast. Not only did he become my No. 1 advocate at ESPN, but he became a good friend and an important part of my journey.

Sunday through Friday, Bill is laid-back, easygoing. But when the light goes on for the Saturday night game, so does Bill. He is intense and a perfectionist. He is hard on himself because he judges each game telecast by the standard of perfection. He relies on an excellent crew, but at the end of the day, he knows he is the one who oversees the show.

As much as I had my challenges with Brent during those years, so did Bill. A producer and play-by-play announcer work closely together during a game. When it works the right way, it's like a head coach in sync with his offensive coordinator. Too often, Brent wasn't on the same page as his head coach.

I've been so fortunate to work with the likes of Bill, Tim Corrigan, Steve Vecchione, Lee Fitting, Jim Gaiero, Lisa Kraus, and directors Derek Mobley, Tom Lucas, and Rodney Perez, among others. We've been through a lot and seen a lot during those many Thursdays and Saturdays. I'm fortunate to have been part of their crews.

––––––––

That 2014 season is responsible for one of my favorite college football moments, and one of my favorite teams. I'm a sucker for teams that overcome obstacles.

Ohio State lost its starting quarterback, Braxton Miller, to a shoulder injury in fall camp, and replaced him with a redshirt freshman, J. T. Barrett. It lost at home against unranked Virginia Tech in the Buckeyes' second game of the season and dropped as low as No. 23 in the rankings.

But Ohio State won its next nine games in a row before facing Michigan. The Buckeyes beat Michigan, but lost Barrett for the postseason because of a broken ankle. Third-stringer Cardale Jones came in after Barrett's injury early in the fourth quarter. Far worse was the tragic news that arrived the next day: backup defensive lineman Kosta Karageorge, who had been missing for several days, had been found dead of a self-inflicted gunshot wound.

The team mourned for its troubled teammate, and then returned to the field a week later with heavy hearts. They played Wisconsin in the Big Ten Championship with decals commemorating Kosta on their helmets, won 59–0, and the third-stringer Jones was named the game's MVP in his first-ever start. Entering the game, Ohio State was No. 5 in the CFP rankings, TCU No. 3 and Baylor No. 6. All three teams won their final games impressively.

I had said on the air that Ohio State should be the fourth team selected for the inaugural CFP, but that would require the selection committee to jump the Buckeyes over a TCU team that was two spots higher and that had won its final regular season game. But that's what happened: Ohio State moved to No. 4, Baylor to No. 5, and TCU to No. 6. Then, against all odds, the Buckeyes and Jones upset No. 1 Alabama in the semifinal.

Fowler and I had called Oregon's semifinal rout of Florida State in the Rose Bowl, and then returned to our Pasadena hotel to watch the Bama–Ohio State game with the entire crew.

On January 12, we were in Arlington, Texas, for the national championship game. A Buckeyes team that had gone through its quarterback depth chart, who had lost to an unranked team early in the season, who had lost one of its teammates to tragedy, who had to sweat out its place in the CFP, beat Oregon, 42–20.

During the broadcast, I treated Ohio State like any other team. But as the final seconds wound down, and the confetti began falling from the sky, and the Ohio State band began playing "Hang on Sloopy," and I saw Jones and Ezekiel Elliott (who had rushed for 246 yards) celebrating, and I soaked in the accomplishments of this team—of everything that it had overcome—I decided it was okay to be a Buckeye alum.

With the game and the broadcast complete, I dropped to my right knee in the booth and had tears of joy coming down my face. I was happy and proud for that team and the incredible journey it had taken. Deron and I were both overcome with emotion. I just loved their story.

Meyer has said it himself and I agree: you will likely never see another third-string quarterback lead a team to a national championship. In this age of transfer portals, third-stringers usually don't stick around three seasons as Jones had. As the years pass, that team and that national title will only become more legendary.

It's challenging to do both *GameDay* and the Saturday night game. For example, I spend Mondays, Tuesdays, and Wednesdays talking constantly with producers, coordinating producers, players, offensive and defensive coordinators, and head coaches. On Thursdays I fly to the *GameDay* site, all the time working on my game board for the Saturday night broadcast. On Fridays I have our *GameDay* production meeting, as well as meetings with the home team head coach and interviews with the local media. That afternoon I fly home to Nashville to see one of the boys play football that night, and then fly back to the *GameDay* site. On Saturdays, if it's an East Coast campus, I get up at 6 a.m., do *GameDay*, finish the show at noon, and then often get on a flight for the Saturday night game site in Austin, Happy Valley, Eugene, Columbus . . . wherever we need to be. When the game is done around midnight, I fly back home to Nashville.

I've got no complaints. I love it all.

At the end of the 2014 season, Fowler had to make a decision: *GameDay* or play-by-play. He chose the games.

I understood why. He loved calling the big events: the tennis majors, the national championships, the big games. He wanted to be the voice associated with those moments. But to do so, he had to leave the show he had helped raise from infancy.

It was really hard for Chris to leave *GameDay*. He drove that bus for twenty-five years. The show was a direct reflection of him, and he took so much pride in what it had become.

I'm sure it was a surreal moment for Chris to see Rece Davis in that *GameDay* anchor chair when we opened the season back in Arlington for a Bama-Wisconsin match-up. If I left the show after all those years and saw someone else in my place, I know I would struggle with that. It would be like seeing your son with a stepdad.

Chris actually appeared on that September 5, 2015, show as a guest of sorts. The *GameDay* crowd at the set gave him a big ovation. We all did. He had earned it.

Rece is a gifted broadcaster, one of the best in our business. We're lucky to have him. He had subbed for Chris on *GameDay* in 2006 when Fowler did the Breeders Cup. We also had worked together on various college-related shows in the past, had spent time at a function in Pasadena in 2014, had gone to an NBA playoff game together, and we share the same agent.

There was a time, though, when we were competitors at the same network. I was on *GameDay*, and Rece was the anchor of the Saturday highlight show featuring Trev Albert and Mark May, which later became May and Lou Holtz. It got a little feisty between our two shows in those early years. There was a competitive energy between the two crews and casts. There was enough friction between the shows that Mark Shapiro, the then–ESPN executive vice president of program and production, ordered the key players to Orlando to make the peace.

When Rece was chosen to replace Chris, I wanted to be among the first to congratulate him. "We're gonna kill it," I told him. "Keep doing your thing. I know you love the sport and it's going to be great."

Still, it was different. Anyone could have taken Fowler's place and it would have been weird for me. It took a little while to get used to looking across the desk and not seeing Chris in his customary Saturday morning spot.

We have a few traditions at *GameDay*, including a pre-show holding of hands on the set. I don't know how it started—I think Coach and I grabbed each other's hands one time, and then Coach grabbed Fowler's—but it has become our version of breaking the huddle. Minutes before Rece's first show began, we all held hands and did the "1-2-3 . . . win!" cheer. I don't think Rece was expecting that. I gave him a wink, a smile, and a fist bump.

It's not like Rece was a television rookie—he had been doing TV for twenty years—but it's a big deal to be the anchor of *GameDay*. I don't know how fast his heart was thumping as he opened the show, but I wanted to make him feel welcome, make him feel part of the family. It's not easy to parachute into a tight-knit group such as *GameDay*. I even told his family, who was there in Fort Worth for the show, that he was going to crush it. And he has—every week. And he's done so on his terms and in his own style. Just as I had my own voice after taking Craig James's spot, Rece had his own voice after replacing Chris.

It's hard to believe this will be his seventh year anchoring the show. I appreciate his partnership, his friendship, and I love how he's always committed to trying to raise the bar each week. His leadership, in his own way, has been instrumental in the direction of the show.

Rece and I have a few things in common: we both tend to be pleasers and it legitimately bothers us if somebody is mad at us. Generally speaking, we want to make it right with those folks. We have a similar background in faith, in putting family first and, of course, in our love for college football. Rece also played some high school option quarterback back in the day.

What makes *GameDay* special is its family atmosphere. We care about one another. Everybody, including on-air talent, crew, staff, production, reporters, researchers, security, etc., takes pride of ownership. Nobody is bigger than the show itself. We lose great and talented people on the show and staff every year, but we try to replace them with equally great and talented people.

For nearly five months a year, we are a traveling road show. If not for that idea of family, and if not for those fans who have spent their Saturday mornings with us at our campus sets or have watched from home all these years, *GameDay* wouldn't be *GameDay*.

———

The weekly *GameDay* location is usually decided at some point on Sunday, sometimes Monday. In late October, we were thinking about taking the show to Philadelphia for the October 31 Notre Dame–Temple game. Temple was unbeaten and was ranked No. 21, while Notre Dame was 7-1 and ranked No. 9.

I had mixed feelings about it. Philly is a pro town. Would people there even know about college football? It was one thing to do the game there that night, but were we making a mistake by bringing *GameDay* to Philly too?

Man, was I wrong.

By then, I was flying back to Nashville late Friday afternoons to watch the twins play high school ball, and then flying back to our show locations late Friday nights or in the wee hours of Saturdays. I got back to Philly, got a handful of hours of sleep, and then reported to Independence Hall, where our *GameDay* set was located. It was a ridiculous scene. The fans were fired up and it was a great show. We had the Phillie Phanatic as the guest picker, the Temple Owl mascot was on the set, the home crowd was going crazy . . . and Coach took Notre Dame.

That night at halftime of the game, I grabbed a quick bite to eat, ducked into the bathroom for a minute, checked with Fowler about a replay call, caught my breath, put my headphones on, and then waited for the countdown to start the second half. Temple was giving Notre Dame everything it wanted and I was looking forward to the third quarter to begin.

"Two minutes," said our producer, Bill Bonnell.

Usually we get a countdown to air, but this time Fowler started doing our second-half setup without me hearing a cue. We were full screen as he mentioned Temple's inability to rush the ball, yet the Owls only trailed 14–10.

As I started to respond, I noticed some sort of movement out of the corner of my eye. It was a little person darting toward our on-air shot. I gave a tiny wave of the hand, because I thought it might be my spotter and longtime friend, Deron Brown, crouched down walking into the shot. I sort of gave it a "We're live! What are you doing?" sort of gesture.

Then I saw this freaking troll creature leaping from the darkness at me. It was wearing some sort of prison outfit and had part of its skull missing at the top. There was another creature with it. I admit it: I shrieked in fear, and then tried to knock the creature off the set with one of those P90X workout kicks. My heart rate must have been off the charts.

Fowler doubled over in laughter. I thought it was an off-air gag, that we would get the scary people out of the booth and then we'd start the second half setup for real. But no, it was live. America saw and heard me shriek like I was a teenage girl in a chain saw horror movie.

Fowler and some members of the crew had visited Eastern State Penitentiary in Philly the night before. It was an infamous prison that had once held the gangster Al Capone, but had long since closed.

During Halloween, they converted parts of it to a haunted-house type of thing.

I don't do haunted houses. I don't do scary movies. I don't do scary stories. I didn't even realize it was Halloween until I caught my breath after the little monsters freaked me out.

Fowler and Bonnell had recruited the little creatures (they were actually two Temple University students) to stop by the booth. They had ducked behind the green screen and jumped out just in time to scare the heck out of me.

A few months later, I got my revenge on Fowler during an appearance on *The Jimmy Kimmel Show*. They arranged for someone dressed as a zombie to hide in the green room. When Fowler walked by the closet, the guy jumped out and Chris recoiled and let out a little terrified expletive. I got him, but not as good as he had gotten me on Halloween.

We have been blessed to call a lot of memorable, even historic, games together. The list is long and distinguished. But every so often, you get Ohio State at Rutgers in 2017.

Regardless of the score, Chris and I pride ourselves about staying connected to the game, out of respect for the players and coaches. But on that late October night, as Ohio State's second-half lead grew from 21–0, to 42–0 at the end of the third quarter, to 49–0 in the fourth, we ran out of things to say. We were literally left rooting for Rutgers to score so four older men dressed in Revolutionary War outfits, complete with three-corner hats and puffy sleeve shirts, could finally shoot off their cannon near the end zone. These poor guys had spent the entire night waiting and waiting and waiting for Rutgers to score, but every time, the Scarlet Knights missed their chance. Our camera crew had spotted them earlier, and it became a running theme: would the cannon crew gets its chance or not? It became the only drama left in the game.

Then, with just thirteen seconds remaining, Rutgers threw a touchdown pass.

"Get that cannon crew ready!" bellowed Fowler. "Rutgers finally on the board."

Derek Mobley, our director, had his cameras already zeroed in on the cannon crew, which by this time was hardly paying attention to the game. As they sprang to life and fired the cannon, I lost it. Feel free to YouTube it.

"Oh, *please* stop!" I somehow said through my uncontrollable laughter.

I had the church giggles and was completely useless. It was a combination of a seventeen-hour day, a lack of sleep, Fowler hitting his mute button at times so we wouldn't hear him laughing (which made me laugh even more), the Ohio State blowout, and finally, the cannon blast. Waiting for that game to end was like going to a horse race and watching seventeen horses cross the line, but there's still one horse left, and it's just now rounding the final turn. To this day, if Fowler casually says to me, "Fire up that cannon crew," I'll break into laughter.

For me to lose it like that was unusual, but not unprecedented. But for Fowler to get the church giggles on the air, that *was* a first. The man came out of the womb intense.

I've worked with Chris for twenty-five years and counting. In 2019, after we did the Rose Bowl broadcast, I, Chris, Deron, and producer Jonathan Whyley decided to pile into a Lincoln Navigator and drive up the California coast to the Bay Area, where the CFP Championship was to be played. I had never made that drive. Usually we'd get on a plane and head to the national title site.

Deron drove. Fowler rode shotgun and was in charge of music and discussion topics. I was in the backseat with Whyley. It was a flashback road trip: one hundred dollars spent on snack foods—pork rinds, candy, chips, my beloved sparkling water.

We stopped in Malibu to see tennis great Brad Gilbert, who is friend of Fowler's from ESPN's coverage of the Grand Slam events. We ended up in Santa Barbara, and moved up the coast to Big Sur, where we stayed at a place on the water. We drank wine. Lots of wine. We even rewrote the intro to the national championship game while sitting in a hot tub (me and Fowler on speakerphone with Bonnell).

We stopped at the Hearst Castle. We went down to the water to see the seals. We gave each other a hard time. We talked about our families. I also slept a lot in that car. It was the first time I had truly relaxed in months. And I'm not sure I had ever seen Fowler enjoying himself as much as he did on that trip.

Fowler is wired in a way that when he's working, when he's prepping for an assignment, he's a perfectionist. He is locked in. I get it. Doing live TV and calling big games can be stressful. But it was fun to see him—to see all of us—just relaxing, just hanging out. We didn't spend any real time talking football or about the upcoming Clemson-Alabama championship game. Instead, we turned off our football brains and just found a way to be friends.

Chapter 17

"He's Gone"

’ve always been able to memorize numbers: my wedding anniversary, the dates of my four boys' birthdays, Davey Concepcion's career batting average. I can recite national championship scores, Ohio State scores, jersey numbers from a lifetime of watching game film. I can even remember the exact snap counts from my mop-up duty in a Buckeyes blowout loss at USC in 1989.

But the number sequence I'll never forget is also the most painful: 3-17-2016.

That was the day my dad died.

Teri called with the news that morning. I was on the phone when she called, so I let it go to voice mail. But then she immediately called Alli's phone and said, "I need to talk to Kirk right now." Alli handed me her cell and told me it was Teri. By the look on Alli's face, I instantly knew something terrible had happened to either my mom or my dad.

Teri was sobbing.

"Kirk, I have some very bad news," she said. "Dad died of a brain aneurysm. He's gone."

The boys were getting ready for school. The dogs were running around. I walked outside and tried to process the news.

"Are you kidding me?" I kept repeating. "What happened?"

Teri explained that my dad woke up that morning in his care facility in Cleveland and told an attending nurse, "My head's kind of hurting." The nurse sat down next to him, and in that moment, as the brain aneurysm ruptured, my seventy-seven-year-old dad slumped sideways and fell dead into her arms.

His mental and physical condition had been slowly deteriorating since his Alzheimer's diagnosis in 2009. He hadn't been able to drive a car for several years. It had become harder for his wife to get him to take his medicine. He had mood swings, bouts of confusion. He was slipping.

Teri had brought him to her house and told him that his wife was going to put him in a facility, "and I'm not going to be able to get you out." Teri and Bryan wanted my dad to live with them.

Eventually, my dad's wife did place him in a facility. She couldn't care for him any longer.

It was not a great place. When Teri first visited the facility, she noticed an old man walking toward her. He had wild-looking, un-combed hair. He had a scraggly beard. It took her several moments to realize it was our dad. She literally hadn't recognized him.

I had talked to my dad on a semiregular basis when he lived at his own house. He could communicate fairly well. He knew who I was. We could talk. I would tell him that I loved him, and he would say it back.

It wasn't that way when I saw him in February 2016. I was so upset when I saw the conditions inside the facility. They were awful, worse than any of us realized. I learned later that because of the effects of Alzheimer's, my dad's temper and frustration level had become an occasional issue. When I visited him, he had been given so many meds that I couldn't tell what part of him was affected by Alzheimer's and what part of him was a result of the prescription drugs. This was a guy who didn't like taking an Advil, but now he was pumped full of who knows how many meds. He had a glazed look on his face, like Jack Nicholson's character, R. P. McMurphy, in *One Flew Over the Cuckoo's Nest*. It was heartbreaking to see.

Despite the meds haze, he still remembered who I was. He had remembered Teri when she had visited. And when my mom came to check up on him, he was able to reminisce with her about the 1950s and their early years together. It was emotional for my mom.

As soon as I saw the conditions at that place, I thought to myself, "I'm going to get you out of here, Dad." We did, too. We got Dad cleaned up, moved him to a much nicer facility that specialized in Alzheimer's care. In just a couple of days he had made friends with a few of the other residents. He died a week to the day of his arrival.

When Teri called with the news, I went into "Operation What Do We Need to Do" mode. Teri was incredible, too. She made the funeral arrangements and kept us updated on the daily details.

I had kept it together until I called Coach Corso. I got three words out—"My dad died"—before I started crying uncontrollably.

"I'm so sorry," said Coach. "That disease is so tough, but, hey, hey, *congratulations!*"

I was still sobbing, but suddenly I was like, "What did he say? Congratulations?"

"That's a bad disease," Coach said. "I'm older. I've seen my friends deal with it. God took him early and didn't make him suffer with the aneurysm. Congratulations."

That's Lee Corso in a nutshell. But Coach was right.

The night before the funeral, we all met at one of my dad's favorite restaurants in Chagrin Falls, which is the Cleveland suburb where my dad lived before the facilities. It's a beautiful, quaint little town. Everybody was there: family, friends, colleagues, out-of-towners who had come in for the funeral. Some of my dad's buddies did imitations of him: "*Don't get cocky and careless.*" I must have heard that phrase a thousand times growing up. We told stories. We laughed. We tried to make it a celebration of who he was. My dad would have loved it.

It wasn't until the next morning, when I saw him in the casket—when I touched his hand and felt its coldness—that the full weight of his death hit me. He was gone. He was really gone.

My mom brought my dad's Woody Hayes cap and placed it on the casket. She was crying harder than my dad's wife.

Teri and I noticed a man in his late sixties, early seventies at the service. We didn't know him, but assumed it was a friend of my dad's.

"Excuse me, sir," Teri said to the man. "How did you know my dad?"

"Your dad made sure I was a team captain at Akron," he said. "I deserved to be named a captain, but your dad made it happen."

His name was Nate Hagins, and at the time, he was only the second black team captain in the history of the University of Akron football. The first had been in 1956.

No matter how conflicted Teri and I felt about our dad over the years, we were never prouder of him than at that exact moment. Mr. Hagins said he had seen the obituary in the local paper and had wanted to pay his respects. He said that when a CEO dies, he leaves money behind. But when a coach dies, he leaves pieces of his own life behind in the form of his players.

I was so moved by his words. It meant a lot to me and Teri. In the past, I always thought that if a friend of mine lost a parent that I shouldn't bother him, that he had too much on his mind. Boy, was I wrong. When my dad died, it was so uplifting to get a phone call, a text, or a card from a friend. It was so uplifting to meet one of Dad's former Akron players, or any of his other former players and teammates. It was so comforting to see so many friends, colleagues, and familiar faces.

I couldn't speak at the funeral service. I just couldn't do it. Teri read a poem and spoke for our family. Because I'm an emotional guy, I just chose to deal with his loss in my own private way. Later, in a rare light moment that day, Teri looked at me and in her best Coach Corso imitation, said, "Congratulations."

I had so many mixed emotions during the funeral service. Grief. Loss. Sadness. Fondness. Happy memories mixed with bittersweet ones.

One of my dad's stepsons, who was a priest, conducted the service. Uncle Rick spoke, too. He took off his jacket and spoke from the heart about growing up with my dad.

I've always been able to talk to Uncle Rick about my relationship with my dad. He was about seven years younger than my dad and he readily admits that their own relationship wasn't very strong. Within their family, they would half-joke about my dad being self-centered, incapable of listening to others.

It wasn't until 1992, when I became a starter at Ohio State, that my dad and Uncle Rick started spending quality time together. They came to almost every game I played that season. They shared car rides and became closer than they'd ever been. They reconciled some of their own long-standing differences. According to Uncle Rick, he never had a better four months than the fall he spent with my dad watching me play my final season at Ohio State.

My dad had a hard time expressing his feelings. He told Uncle Rick that he knew he had screwed things up with us. He couldn't articulate those feelings, but they were there. Uncle Rick said he saw my dad beam with pride when Tovar and I had led the team onto the field at Syracuse and upset the Orangemen. He said he and my dad both teared up when I played Michigan for a final time. He said my dad was proud of my success, and proud of Alli and our four boys.

Uncle Rick also will tell you that because of my dad, I have those athletic genes, but also a few demons flying around. He says that I always wanted my dad to be something that he couldn't be. "Jim was so much into Jim," is how he puts it.

Uncle Rick talked to my dad about the inability to build relationships with me, Teri, and John. According to my uncle, my dad didn't recognize what we needed until it was too late. By then, we had our own families and new priorities. My dad couldn't make up for that lost time.

It's true. I had poured all my energies into my marriage, my kids, my career. I still talked to Dad, but it was often just small talk. Then he had Alzheimer's. Then he died. Then he was in a casket. We never had that chance to reconcile like he and Uncle Rick had done.

Teri will tell you that I was cheated, that I didn't get the full version of my dad, that he changed as the years passed. He was so proud of me, she will tell you, but he also was insecure. Her theory is that if I told my dad a story about a coach or player I met, a game I saw, a television moment I experienced, an audition I had, a radio guest I interviewed, a scheme or play that I admired . . . whatever it might be—he felt a need to compete, to make himself relevant in the conversation. He didn't understand that I just wanted to *share* something with him. I was looking for a way to connect.

He died on St. Patrick's Day. He died among strangers. He died after three marriages and is survived by three children, three stepchildren, and twelve grandchildren. The obituary mentioned that he enjoyed playing tennis, working in his garden, cooking in the kitchen. There were his beloved dogs and cats. And few things made him happier than navigating the back roads of Ohio with a full tank of gas and his trusty maps.

Throughout it all, we were always tethered by football. That was our link to one other. That's what kept us together even when we were apart. That was the one thing we always had in common, despite the separations, the divorces, the remarriages, the stepfamilies, the countless moves, the chorus line of new schools, the fragile peace, the fractured times, the Alzheimer's.

Even today, when I return to the Columbus campus for *GameDay* or to call a game, I often find myself at the St. John Arena, which opened in 1956, the year before my dad arrived at OSU. On the walls in the concourse are dozens, maybe hundreds of framed photos of different Buckeye sports teams, players, and coaches from the past. I can't tell you how many times I've stood in front of the photos of my dad's teams, which are just down the hallway from the OSU teams I played on. Am I proud of that? You're damn right I am.

He was a good, decent, and kind man, but for large parts of my life, a disconnected father. He cared, but not always enough. He loved, but not always when we needed it the most. He heard, but he rarely listened.

If there is a string that runs through the length of my life it is family, faith, and, of course, football. Life is a mystery, isn't it? Everything, in its own way, eventually comes full circle. My dad passed football along to me, and I passed it along to my own sons.

He left a bruise mark on my heart in life and in death. I miss him. And I miss what might have been. I didn't want to disappoint him, even though he disappointed me at times. Our relationship should have been more than it was, but I'll take what I got and make the best of it.

There is residual pain, but there isn't anger. I try to concentrate on the positives of the man: the undersized and determined Ohio

State freshman who became a senior team captain . . . the guy who got a diploma and then got hired immediately as a full-time assistant by the great Woody Hayes . . . the guy who loved to coach . . . the husband who endured difficult times . . . the dad who would stay up for hours on Christmas Eve to painstakingly paint those plastic electric football players for his youngest son . . . the dad who would move in with us during my high schools years, cook for my buddies, draw plays on napkins and chalkboards, spend those Friday nights on the sideline watching me play for Centerville, convince me to stay at Ohio State, travel the country watching me play for the Buckeyes, be there for the birth of the twins, be part of Alli and my four sons' lives and, as best as he could, be part of my life.

He had such a peaceful soul and spirit, and such good intentions. I'd like to think that some of those qualities rubbed off on me. He didn't always read the vibe of the room, but despite his flaws, he was liked and loved by those who knew him.

When he was buried, it was like a piece of me had been buried, too. There was a kind of numbness that came with it. His death left a hole in my life. It's a missing part and that feeling doesn't really go away.

I try to honor his legacy by learning from the best of him, and learning from the mistakes made by him. He hurt me—perhaps not intentionally—but I can't pretend I didn't feel the hurt. What I've tried to do is not make those same mistakes with my family. My own experiences have taught me the importance of listening to my kids, of not only telling them that I love them, but showing them, too, with honesty, empathy, and openness. My family has helped me heal.

I've reached a truce with my past. I've always prided being there for my mom and helping her in any way I can. I've embraced the memories of my dad. I try to live in the present. It's easier that way.

Chapter 18

Bill Murray, Katy Perry, and Dark, Cold Buses

If you had told me in August 1993, when I made my very first appearance in the WBNS Radio studio as a newly hired, $12,000-a-year/no-benefits sports talk cohost, that in 2021 I would have the career that I have, I would have said you were crazy.

But I would have hoped you were right.

I can't fully explain how it happened. I was lucky. I was persistent. I worked hard. I took nothing for granted. I was helped by others. I was in the right place, at the right time, with the right people. I stayed true to myself. I stayed true to the sport I love. I never became a cynic.

Whatever you want to say about me as a broadcaster, you can't say that I'm jaded. I think every game has a chance to be a classic. I think every *GameDay* has a chance to be memorable. I think every CFP selection show, or Heisman Trophy presentation, or preseason show has a chance to be one of a kind. Otherwise, what's the point?

I never take sports for granted. I might think I know how a game is going to play out, but then comes the martini mix of players, coaches, plays, schemes, weather, pressure, the crowd, the unpredictable bounce of an oblong ball, and, of course, luck. And when that happens, you get Appalachian State beating Michigan in 2007, the Vince Young Rose Bowl in January 2006, Tua Tagovailoa coming off the bench to throw the national-championship-winning touchdown in overtime against Georgia in January 2018, the Kick Six in 2013, a third-string quarterback leading Ohio State to a national title in 2014, the "Bush Push" in 2005, Boise State's Statue of Liberty play against Oklahoma in January 2007, Watson-to-Renfrow in January 2017, Wide Rights and Wide Lefts, a fumbled punt snap by Michigan in 2015, and the birth of Surrender Cobra . . .

When I walk into the Rose Bowl, I still get goose bumps. I'm still that little kid from Ohio who thinks that that stadium is a football shrine and that game is the greatest of all time. Never in my life would I take that experience for granted. I've called the Rose Bowl for thirteen years and counting (the most of any analyst), and after every game I look at that field and I think, "Those players are so lucky." Every year I take a photo of the stadium and field. Every year before the game starts, I tell the players and coaches, "Make sure you take it in. Don't take this for granted—this isn't a normal bowl game in a normal stadium. Soak in the atmosphere and setting; it's the best in sports."

When I see Coach for the first time each season, I break into an involuntary smile. I never take him and that relationship for granted.

I don't take *GameDay* for granted. How could I? I've been married to it longer than I have to my own wife. I've spent more years on that studio set than I have with my own kids. In fact, when Sam Ponder was a reporter on *GameDay* and a sideline reporter on our game crew, I used to hold her infant daughter, Scout, so she could get some work done at our production meetings, or go do an appearance on the set. Sam was a working mom and brought Scout on the road every week during the 2014 season. I wanted to help and support Sam any way I could as she did the mom/ESPN double duty. Alli and I knew what it was like to bring your kids with you.

Because of *GameDay* and college football, I've been from Seattle to Coral Gables, a Navy ship in San Diego to an Army chopper at West Point, the tranquility of the Par 3 course at Augusta to the deafening noise of Bristol, Tennessee. I've seen entire city blocks shut down for our show, from Fargo, North Dakota, to Memphis. I've watched the Oregon Duck fluster Fowler, the man who never flusters. I've witnessed Katy Perry give one of, if not *the* greatest *GameDay* guest picker performance in the show's history. I've cowered whenever Coach is reunited with shotguns or rifles—even when they're loaded with blanks. I've been covered in snow in Kalamazoo, and become a sweat puddle on South Beach. I've been lucky enough to bring my dad, my mom, my boys, my relatives, and my friends to the show. I've had my vocabulary improved by Tom Rinaldi. I've received an invitation to the White House, where in February 2003, President George W. Bush acknowledged me in a crowd of visitors during a ceremony in the East Room honoring a handful of national championship teams and said, "There you are. You look just like yourself." I loved that. (And just to keep me humble, the initial transcript released by the Office of the Press Secretary referred to me as "Kurt.")

And because of *GameDay* and the Saturday night game—and the friendships and relationships we make—I've been honored to witness the legacy of people such as Tyler Trent.

Tyler, a student at Purdue, was the subject of a deeply moving feature done by Tom during the 2018 season. Tyler loved Boilermaker football, and that Boilermaker team loved him back. He was battling a rare bone cancer called osteosarcoma, and through his courage, strength, and constant optimism, his story touched a nation.

In late October of that year, he summoned the strength to attend the Purdue game against second-ranked and highly favored Ohio State. Don't tell me one person can't make a difference, or that his strength of spirit didn't inspire that team—Purdue upset the Buckeyes that night, 49–20.

He died on January 1, 2019, at the tender age of twenty. A memorial service was scheduled in Carmel, Indiana, just outside Indianapolis, for Tuesday, January 8, the night after the national championship. Rinaldi planned to attend the ceremony.

I had never met Tyler. But his story, his struggle, his love of his school, the relationship between him and his family, the relationship between Tyler and that team . . . they all resonated with me. That could have been one of my sons. It could have been anybody's son.

We did the call of Clemson's win against Alabama on Monday evening in Santa Clara, California, and then the next morning I asked Rinaldi if Tyler's family would mind if I also attended the memorial service. I didn't want to be a distraction. I just wanted to pay my respects to a young man for the imprint he had made on the sport and on fans across the country. Tyler's story moved me like it moved many others.

Scott Van Pelt was there. Adrian Wojnarowski was there. The College Park Church was filled with Tyler's friends, family, and admirers. He had touched our lives, and now we wanted to honor his.

Tony and Kelly Trent, Tyler's parents, were kind enough to talk to me for a few minutes. We were all connected by the spirit and soul of their son. I was so grateful that they allowed me to attend.

Tyler never played a down of college football, but it didn't matter. He was connected to the game, and through that connection, we learned of his story and his courage. I think often of the Trent family. I think of many of the families that have opened their hearts and homes to *GameDay* and have let us tell their stories.

GameDay isn't a studio show. It's sort of the People's Show. Whenever I do interviews with local media from a *GameDay* site,

I'm usually asked about the show's success. I tell them the same thing: it isn't because of us, it's because of the people watching us, the people who come to the show at the crack of dawn (and even earlier) with those homemade signs.

In 2018, after years of trying to get there, we finally took the show to Washington State in Pullman. Their Ol' Crimson flag had flown at our shows for decades, so it was great to complete the circle and make the trip there.

On the night before the show, an older gentleman approached Rinaldi at a restaurant not far from campus. The man wore a Washington State ball cap and politely introduced himself to Tom. Then, with tears in his eyes, he thanked Tom and the show for coming to Pullman.

"You don't know what this means to this town," he said.

But that's the thing, we do. And we don't take that for granted, either. The next morning, in the darkness and late October cold of the Palouse, about 20,000 people (more than the entire undergraduate enrollment of the school) were there at the opening of the show. That night, the Cougars beat Oregon.

Washington State was an all-timer. So was James Madison, Times Square (Coach dressed up like the Statue of Liberty), Ole Miss, Harvard, Clemson in the mud, Virginia Tech, Penn State . . . the list goes on and on. In fact, Penn State and a white-out game is my favorite regular season spectacle.

All-time guest pickers? There's Perry, of course. She was doing a concert in Memphis and her manager was an Ole Miss alum. She didn't know a thing about football, but she knew how to put on a show.

She had a list of props that she requested from Patrick Abrahams: corn dogs, a giant pencil (thank you, Ole Miss woodshop facility), a Trevor Knight cutout stick, a cutout stick of me when

I was at Ohio State, a tray of hot toddies. She had been coached up, too, on all things Ole Miss.

Bill Murray showed up just in time for his Clemson appearance. When a slightly stressed Patrick tried to get him off the *GameDay* bus to make his way to the set—we were up against the clock—Murray put his finger over Abrahams's mouth and said, "Relaxxxx." Then he massaged Patrick's temples and shoulders.

"You've got too much tension," he said soothingly. "Too much tension. You need to relax."

Later, he was on the demo set next to the main set and started hitting real golf balls into the crowd. He body-slammed Coach, threw the FSU spear toward the cheerleaders, and afterward, took the suite tickets we had arranged for him and gave them to four strangers across the street.

"Patrick, I'm going to need four more," he said.

Then he asked another one of our ops specialists, Fu Takumi, to drive him to a nearby state park, where he ended up crashing some sort of religious function. Fu took a photo of Murray posing with the religious group near the welcome center of the park. Then Fu drove him back to Clemson, where he watched fifteen minutes of the game and then wanted to fly home.

You can't make this up.

Will Ferrell is a keeper. Charles Barkley is always good—and he's the only one who never needs notes. He knows the game. Eric Church is another guy who follows the game closely. He's like an analyst. Kenny Chesney is another huge college football fan who does a great job.

The Oregon Duck can't talk and he/she still was a fantastic guest picker. Craig T. Nelson was strong. Ventriloquist Jeff Dunham and his puppet Walter were hilarious—they crushed Coach. But it's interesting to watch some of these big stars come on the show and get really nervous. They're out of their lane, out of their comfort zone.

My guest picker wish list includes Peyton Manning, The Rock, and Kevin Hart. I want Kevin Hart to be on the whole show.

Animals? Keep that South Carolina gamecock away from me. I fear the talons. But anything involving a dog—Smokey, Reveille, Dubs, UGA, Handsome Dan—I'm all in, though a few of them have tinkled on us out of nervousness.

If *GameDay* is at the same place as our Saturday night game, then the post-show routine goes like this: pose for photos on the set with our sponsors and guests, and then make the move to the Allstate bus, which is our comfort headquarters for the Saturday night game.

The Allstate bus is our refuge from 12:20 p.m. Eastern to early evening, when we head to the field for our pregame work, and then our go-to spot after the game, too. It is also our refrigerator on wheels. As soon as I walk in, I make sure the temperature and the lights are turned down as low as possible. It's freezer-section cold and movie-theater dark in there.

Everyone has their assigned seating. I've got the second chair to the right. Bear has front left. Deron or one of the boys has front right. Fowler has the second seat to the left, but he doesn't arrive until later. Whyley is in there someplace, too.

Kickoff begins at noon for the early games. We've got darkness, privacy, cold, food, and football. There's nothing better.

There are five TV monitors (one large one, four smaller ones) at the back of the bus. Bear is the only guy I let use the clicker. We put audio on the best game, but keep a close eye on the other four games in that time slot.

Later in the afternoon, often without warning, the front lower left monitor will switch from, say, the Purdue–Penn State game to the second race at Del Mar. That's Bear.

Bear never tells us what's coming. He'll never say, "All right, here we go, second race at Del Mar. I've got the five horse, Mr. Fabulous." Bear doesn't work that way.

Instead, you'll see him talk in hushed tones to someone on his cell phone. Then the race starts, and he'll start talking to the horse: "C'mon, get this five up. C'mon!" To the jockey: "C'mon, Edgar. You can do this, Edgar." His voice becomes tighter, more intense. He has transported himself to the Del Mar grounds.

As they round the final turn, Bear will start hitting his right thigh, like he's riding the damn horse. "C'mon, five! C'mon, Edgar!"

If the five horse wins, Bear will stand up and simply say, "I told you so."

But if the five horse loses, he'll go into a funk. Don't even try to talk to him. He's mad at the horse. He's mad at Edgar. And whatever you do, 100 percent do not get near Bear's seat. He'll kill you. I'm convinced he would snap your neck off in anger.

At three thirty, the commissioner of collegiate athletics—Fowler (we call him "the Commish")—enters the bus and whoever is sitting in his seat darts to another spot. In deference to him, we turn the lights up a little bit, raise the AC from 64 to maybe 67.

If we're doing the Saturday night game somewhere else, we lower the temp on the plane to a nice, comfy low-sixties number. Maria Taylor, who also does the sideline reporting for those games, is in full sweats and maybe pulls out a blanket. She says it's cold enough for ice caps in there. Sounds good to me.

I love working on the plane. I pull out my game board and work on my notes, review the names, talk to my man, Bear, about some games, maybe call up a game on TV. I can't get enough of it.

This is my football Saturday, and it's the best job in the world. I have my *GameDay* family. I have my Saturday night game family. I get to go home to my real family, and then do it all over again the following week.

I never get tired of it. No game is ever the same. No show is ever the same. I still feel like the nobody who sat in that radio studio chair decades earlier, the guy who had the big smile on his face, the guy who kept saying to himself, "I can't believe they're paying me to talk football."

And I definitely don't take that for granted.

Chapter 19

The Herbstreit Method

In the Herbstreit house, the two events that matter most are The Game and the Rose Bowl. But in the Non–College Football/Non-Work category, one event towers above all others: the Kentucky Derby.

When I was growing up, I watched the Derby every now and then, but it wasn't like I knew anything about horse racing. If a horse was going for the Triple Crown—and if I remembered it was race day—I'd turn on the TV. Even though Columbus was only about three hours from Louisville, I had never thought of going to Churchill Downs.

My dad wasn't much of a horse racing guy, either, but his brother Rick made up for both of them. Uncle Rick knew everything about horse racing.

He and his son Brian have my sports DNA. We can sit and watch games all day. We can watch a Reds game and not say a word for two hours, but we're having a great time. We just love watching ball. The same thing goes for horse races.

When I was at Ohio State, Uncle Rick, who lived in Louisville, had a small ownership interest in several Thoroughbreds. He had an owner's badge, which gave him access to the barns and the back-stretch area at Churchill Downs. In 2000, he secured some Derby passes and invited me and Alli to the races.

Half the fun was the spectacle of it all. I got dressed up in a suit. Alli wore a dress and a big hat. We sat in the grandstands from morning to late afternoon, read the Daily Racing Form (or tried to), bet on a few races, drank a couple of mint juleps, BS'ed with people, maybe cashed a ticket or two for a few bucks. I loved the betting, but I didn't understand any of the terminology. I was a ten-dollars-to-win kind of guy.

Uncle Rick was our horse racing instructor. He had the Racing Form in his back pocket and handed out pens to everyone. Then he conducted a class in Betting 101.

Allison became the best Form reader in the family. It just made sense to her. She could look at all the numbers, all the history, all the times, all the tracks, the track conditions, the speed ratings, and decipher it for us. It was like a scene from *A Beautiful Mind*.

We returned to the Derby in 2002, thanks to a friend who had connections at the track. He could always dig up some tickets for us. Hotel rooms were impossible to find, so we crashed at Uncle Rick's.

Each year, our party grew larger, from four, to six, to eight, and then twelve. Someone offered me a chance to sit in the Millionaire's Row suites on the sixth floor of the clubhouse. No, no, no—I wanted to be on the third-floor area and mingle with folks. I wanted to feel it.

We'd get to town on Thursday night, have a big dinner, and then return to Uncle Rick's. Alli and I slept on an air mattress in a walk-in closet. Jorge the Dentist slept on a couch with his wife, Cyndi. My buddy Jared and his wife, Tamara, also slept on an air mattress. Teri and her husband shared a room. Uncle Rick's son Brian crashed on a floor. Bear started showing up on some of the trips. It was like a forty-eight-hour frat house, all thanks to the hospitality of Uncle Rick and his wife, Judy.

On Fridays we went to the Kentucky Oaks. On Saturdays, we went to the Derby. It didn't matter how hard I studied the *Daily Racing Form* with Alli. It didn't matter if Bear was there as one of my horse racing coaches, teaching me the ways of Pick-4s, -5s, and -6s (four, five, six winners in a row), exactas (the top two finishers, in order) and trifectas (the top three finishers, in order), and superfectas (the top four finishers, in order). It didn't matter if I listened to the expert handicappers on the racetrack TV feed. It didn't matter if I took a flyer pick from my dad, who joined our traveling party for the 2008 Derby.

It didn't matter because I lost year after year after year. You would think I would cash a decent ticket now and then just by accident. Nope. Me losing money became a Derby tradition, like the playing of "My Old Kentucky Home."

I had a system, though, and I stuck with it. I bet the odds.

I wasn't interested in the horses that were 2/1 odds. That didn't pay much. That was like picking Alabama to beat Vanderbilt. I wanted some value in my bets.

I looked at it like a football game. I wanted a horse that was the equivalent of Arkansas hosting a night game against Bama, or Purdue taking on Ohio State the week before the Buckeyes played Michigan. If I caught the right circumstances, then, boom, my horse would pull off the big upset at nice odds and make my betting ticket sing. I wasn't looking for super long shots, but something in the 8/1, 10/1, 15/1 range.

The Herbstreit System worked so well that I rarely cashed enough tickets to offset my losses. I lost a lot because I risked it on the underdogs. I always bet the underdogs, and the underdogs rarely come home.

What actually happens in the Herbstreit System is that the long shots tease you, torture you, give you hope, and then crush you. *My horse is winning, he's winning, he's winning . . . now he's fading, he's fading . . . wait, he's going to hold on for the last twenty yards, he's holding on! . . . oh, crap, he's neck-and-neck . . . sigh, he just lost by a nose. Why do I do this to myself?*

Why? Because the Derby is the highlight weekend of my year, which is saying a lot, considering the games I get a chance to call each season. But that's work. It's a lot of fun, but it's still work.

The Derby is my chance to be a fan. To escape. To hang out. To be with family and friends. To meet new people. To blend in. To lose.

Once in a while, I get it right. In 2006, Rece subbed for Fowler on our Nov. 4 *GameDay* show at Texas A&M. Fowler had to be at Churchill Downs that day to host the network's coverage of the Breeders' Cup.

When it came time for the game picks that day, Bear and I dressed up like jockeys and also picked the Breeders' Classic. With an assist from Bear, I picked Invasor at 7/1 to win, and race favorite Bernardini at 11/10 to finish second for the exacta. And that's exactly what happened later that day.

During our Saturday night broadcast, Musburger, who is a huge gambling expert, mentioned the race on the air.

"Ah, I was watching *GameDay* this morning, and not only did you make the pick for the winner, but also the exacta," Musburger said. "How'd you make that one, laddie?"

I didn't brag. Instead, I did the Coach thing: *When you lose, say little. When you win, say less.*

Uncle Rick moved to Texas about five years ago, so I started renting a house each Derby weekend. No more air mattresses in walk-in closets.

In 2019, our group included me, Chorpenning, Fallica, quarterback coach and former *GameDay* contributor George Whitfield, Uncle Rick, Deron, Jorge, Brian, and a half-dozen others. Anyone who watches *GameDay* knows that the Bear loves the ponies. He doesn't go anywhere without printouts of races at tracks across the country. He can fall out of bed in the morning and pick an exacta. If there were a race between his love of college football and the Kentucky Derby, it would be a photo finish.

We went to the Oaks on a rainy Friday and it was disastrous. The Herbstreit System was its usual failure, but Bear had one of the worst days of his betting career. I don't think he cashed a ticket in any of the races. He was beat up, distraught. He is so competitive when it comes to picking the ponies that it really bothered him to have such an awful performance. After all, this is a guy who has qualified multiple times for the world's most prestigious Thorough-bred handicapping championship.

He called his wife, Molly, and told her he was coming home. He wasn't even going to stick around for the Derby, which to Bear is like the pope passing up Easter mass at the Vatican.

"Stay," she told him. "Have some fun."

He stayed, but he was a broken man on Friday.

On Saturday, we got suited and hatted up and headed back to the track. Bear had a new attitude. He also had to deal with lots of calls and texts from people he rarely heard from during the year. They all wanted to know the same thing: *Who do you like today?*

I don't make any final decisions about my bets until I talk to Bear. We had discussed some possibilities on Friday night, but it wasn't until Saturday that I locked in on the choices.

What I've learned through the years is that it's a long day at the Derby. If you're going to have a julep or two, it's probably best not to wait until 5 p.m. to make your bets. Plus, the longer you wait, the longer the lines are at the betting windows. I like to make my bets early and all at once, so I don't hold up the people waiting behind me.

I looked at my *Daily Racing Form*, consulted with Bear, jotted down my bets, stood up, and said what I always say before I head to the betting windows: "I'm going in."

I bet and boxed just about everything that day: exactas, trifectas, superfectas, Pick-everythings, long shots—especially the long shots. I wanted the bums that no one was talking about. Sure, they weren't going to win, but if they hit the board in the top four, then they'd pay big. That's something I learned from Bear: don't be afraid to take a moon shot.

I even split a crazy trifecta bet with Chorpenning and another buddy, neither of whom had ever been to the Derby. They knew virtually nothing about Thoroughbred racing. I split up a lot of the bets with the group. It was a way to make the most of our betting pool.

Every year I always go to the same betting window and ticket agent. When I'm at the window, it's a business trip to me. I don't want to be interrupted by anyone.

The ticket agent has been so kind to me over the years, mostly because I always lose. She sees me when I place the bets, but rarely sees me after the races. As she handed me my tickets, she told me what she tells me every Derby weekend: "Maybe this will be your year!"

I made about fifteen bets for the Derby and stuffed the tickets into my pants pocket. Then I visited the paddock, talked to some trainers, walked around with my buddies, made bets during the whole day on the other races had a julep, saw several racing writers (Pat Forde, who lives in Louisville and has covered horse racing and college football for years, was there), and eventually circled back to our seats in time for the big race at 6:50 p.m. It was raining, but nobody cared.

One of my main big-money bets was a five-horse exacta box, which means I had bet all the combinations of those five horses to finish in the top two. Bear had recommended it.

There was one constant in all fifteen of my Derby bets: I didn't take the favorite, Maximum Security. First of all, the Herbstreit System likes the long shots, not the 9/2 favorites like Maximum Security. Second, Bear hadn't told me to bet him.

Instead, Bear had mentioned a 65/1 long shot named Country House. Forde wasn't impressed.

"Nobody in their right mind would have bet that horse," he later told one of my friends.

What the hell, I bet it. Arkansas over Bama, right? Or in this case, even more of a long shot: Vandy over Bama.

Our seats were near the finish line. The nineteen horses in the field marched by. They were popping—high asses, thin ankles, light on the dirt, spatted up. They were magnificent.

A few minutes later, as they were loaded into the gates, you could feel the energy building. And then . . . they were off! They thundered by to begin the best two minutes in sports.

As the race began, I glanced down at my tickets and tried to keep track of the leaders. *Okay, I got that one, that one, but I don't have that one. Wait, I've got that one on this ticket.*

As they came around the final turn and down the stretch on the sloppy track, the whole place rose as one. The roar was what LSU's Death Valley sounds like, times five, when the Tigers win a game on the last play.

My horses were positioned perfectly. But there was a problem.

Maximum Security.

I yelled. I pleaded. Maybe I prayed to the Thoroughbred gods. It made no difference. Maximum Security crossed the finish line first by a length and a half.

I turned to Bear and shot him a death stare. I was furious. Why didn't he tell me to bet Maximum Security? How could he do this to me? To all of us?

Wait! Maybe I had made a mistake. Maybe I had Maximum Security, after all. I went through every ticket. No Maximum Security.

All around us, people were celebrating. They were waving *their* winning Maximum Security tickets.

I wanted to cry. I crumpled up my fifteen tickets and threw them to the ground, which by then was covered with mint julep spills, peanut shells, half-eaten pretzel twists, hot dog wrappers, empty mustard packets, countless other losing tickets, and who knows what else—and it was all mixed with the afternoon rain.

Bear cursed under his breath.

"This is why I should have gone home," he said.

Poor Bear. He felt terrible. He had done his best to help us and now this had happened. When he lost, we all lost. But we were at a stage of grieving where we blamed him, not us. It was incredibly unfair to him, but that didn't stop us from doing it. He became our post-race piñata.

"Let's go," I said, disgusted with yet another year of losing all my betting money.

Then I noticed that Bear had pulled out his phone. A post on Twitter had caught his attention. He read the post to us: "*I hope there's no inquiry.*"

I snapped my head in Bear's direction. An inquiry? What does that mean? Is that good?

Bear shook his head.

"Never in the 145-year history of the Derby have they disqualified the winner the day of the race," he said.

He explained that the Derby had the biggest field in horse racing, that there was a lot of congestion and traffic early in the race, that there always was bumping and jostling. It happened.

Then a light started blinking on the results board. The inquiry was officially under way by the race stewards.

Bear texted some of his contacts in the horse racing business.

"*Is this legit?*" he wrote to his friends.

They said there had been an issue about three-fourths of a mile into the race. Maximum Security had veered out from the rail, possibly causing other horses to check up. Now they had to decide if it was enough of a foul to change the outcome of the race. Of course, the only way I could win any of my bets was if Maximum Security was disqualified, not just dropped to second place. Talk about a long shot.

Five minutes turned into ten. Ten turned into fifteen. Fifteen turned into twenty-two minutes. And then . . .

The light quit flashing on the board, and Maximum Security was taken down and replaced at the top by our 65/1 long-shot Country House. The payoff amounts were updated, too.

A $2 bet on Country House to win paid $132.50. A $2 exacta paid $3,009.60. A $2 trifecta bet paid $22,950.60. A $1 superfecta paid $51,400.10. A $2 Pick 3 paid $2,555.20, and the Pick 4 paid $45,302.

I looked at Bear. He looked at me. We hugged. We jumped up and down. We screamed with joy. We sang. We damn near cried. In fact, I think I saw tears in the Bear's eyes.

That's when it hit me.

My tickets! What have I done with my fifteen winning tickets?!

They were strewn somewhere on the cement floor, which was now sopping wet from the rain. I was wearing a nice navy blue blazer, a pink shirt and tie, and a pair of slacks, but I immediately dropped to my hands and knees and sifted through the mustard packets, the mint julep cups, the hot dog wrappers, the discarded *Daily Racing Forms* and tickets. It was like going through the bottom of a dumpster.

I didn't care. I needed those tickets.

Somehow—and it was a miracle—I found a small clump of them and carefully peeled them apart like an archaeologist examining the

Dead Sea Scrolls. Then one by one, I found a ticket here, a ticket there until I had all fifteen. Half of them were wet and ripped. It was like trying to pick up waterlogged butterfly wings.

I put them all in the palms of my hands and walked them up to my favorite window agent. She could see the panic in my face.

She tried to insert a few of the less-wet tickets into the machine, but it kept spitting them back out. Bless her heart, she pieced each ticket together on the counter and inputted the ticket numbers by hand. It worked!

The crazy trifecta with my buddies? It hit. The exacta that Bear recommended? It hit. The Pick 3 and Pick 4? They hit. The superfecta? It hit. You should have seen the eyes of the ticket agent as the payouts popped on the screen. You should have seen my eyes. I gave her a nice tip and floated away.

It wasn't all mine; a lot of the bets were split between me and our group, but who cared? It was the most I'd ever won at a track. I've never been happier to ruin a suit.

Better yet, I still had one ticket remaining: a Pick 5, and I had won the first three races.

Only the true degenerates stay for the last two races. Everybody else leaves after the 12th race, the Derby. But there was Bear and me, hoping to have the winner in the 13th and 14th races of the day. By then it was dark and hardly anyone was left in the stands.

Compared to the Derby, the field in the 13th race was small. I had bet on three of the horses in the race. Didn't matter which of the three won, just as long as one of them finished first.

One of my horses was up by three lengths coming down the stretch. My other two were out of it. Then another horse made a charge. Back and forth they went as they came to the wire. It was a photo finish . . . and my horse lost on a nose bob at the end.

Of course, one of my horses won the final race of the day, which would have completed the Pick 5 for me and my buddies. A $2 payout for the Pick 5 was worth $173,047.20.

It was hard to be disappointed, especially after our Country House miracle. We all piled into our limo shuttle, returned to the rental house, spread the money on the floor, and divided up the winnings. Chorpenning, a Run for the Roses rookie, said, "This Derby thing is pretty easy."

For the record, I haven't won a bet since. It's like the betting gods have decided, "All right, big boy, bring it on back."

Over the years, I've become friends with Hall of Fame trainers Bob Baffert and D. Wayne Lukas. Baffert, an Arizona alum, has been a *GameDay* guest picker. Thanks to both of them, I've become involved in racing as a part-owner of several Thoroughbreds.

Through it all, I've learned one important lesson: never throw out your tickets.

Chapter 20

Perspective

March 26, 2020, was supposed to be Opening Day for Major League Baseball. I had a reserved seat on my basement couch for the season opener between the St. Louis Cardinals and my Cincinnati Reds. On my annual sports calendar, few things are more important to me than Opening Day.

Instead, there was no baseball. Spring training games had been canceled two weeks earlier because of COVID-19 concerns. Then, MLB announced that the regular season would be delayed.

Meanwhile, the NBA had already suspended its season. The NCAA had canceled its spring and winter championships, including the Final Four and the College World Series. College football programs were canceling their spring games. The Masters had been postponed.

Sports, as well as every other facet of our lives, had no choice but to bend to the will of a global pandemic. We were in the early stages of the virus in the United States, but there was no question that its effects were going to change everything.

Earlier in the day, I had been asked if I would appear on the *Freddie & Fitzsimmons* ESPN radio show. Ian Fitzsimmons was my buddy and former Columbus radio sports talk cohost. I knew

Freddie Coleman from previous appearances. The planned topics: Reds baseball, my favorite Opening Day memories, the upcoming MLB season, whenever that might be.

The late Thursday night interview lasted just eleven minutes and thirty-six seconds, long enough for me to unintentionally turn the world of college football upside down—and my world with it.

The question posed by Coleman early in the interview had something to do with how MLB could figure out a way to begin playing again. I talked about the void of sports in our lives, but also about the seriousness of the virus and its unprecedented impact. Then, at the 3:18 mark of the interview, I said:

"When you think about sports, you think about stadiums and you think about locker rooms, how realistic is that right now? In my opinion, until we have a vaccine where we can really just, 'OK now we've got some control over this' . . . I'll be shocked, honestly—I haven't talked with anybody—I'll be shocked if we have NFL football this fall, if we have college football—I'll be so surprised if that happens.

"Just because from everything I understand, people that I listen to, you're twelve to eighteen months away from a vaccine. Until you have a vaccine, I don't know how you can let these guys go into locker rooms, and let stadiums be filled up, and how you can play ball. I just don't know how you can do it with the optics of it.

"If I'm a commissioner, if I'm in charge, if I'm the NCAA, I just don't know how you can do that. The next thing you know you've got a locker room full of guys who are sick, and that's on your watch. I wouldn't want to have that. So as much as I hate to say it, I think we're scratching the surface of where this thing's going to go."

There was silence for a few moments and then Fitzsimmons said, "Okay, right now, Herbie, I hate you . . . You drop that on us. *Damn*, dude."

"I mean, am I wrong?" I said. "Tell me I'm wrong. I just don't see it."

My comments began to trend on social media. Headlines in newspapers and websites began popping up everywhere.

"Kirk Herbstreit Casts Serious Doubt on 2020 College Football Season"—*SI.com*.

"Kirk Herbstreit anticipating no college football, NFL in 2020"—*USAToday.com*.

"ESPN's Kirk Herbstreit Is Telling Fans Hard Truth: Coronavirus Could Cancel Football Season"—*Forbes.com*.

"Kirk Herbstreit fears coronavirus doomsday scenario for NFL, college football"—*New York Post*.

On and on it went. You couldn't swing a chin strap without hitting a headline of me predicting doom and gloom for college football. Then came the reactions. Notre Dame coach Brian Kelly told WSBT Radio in South Bend that I didn't know what I was talking about. "He's not a scientist," said Kelly. "He's a college football analyst." Missouri coach Eli Drinkwitz said on a Zoom press conference that picking a game on *GameDay* "is a lot different than getting the world in a panic about whether or not we're going to play a college football season."

The reaction was incredible and over the top.

I never claimed to be a scientist. I wasn't trying to create a panic. I hadn't testified before Congress, or stood on a mountaintop with stone tablets in my hand and said, "THOU SHALT NOT PLAY FOOTBALL THIS FALL!"

Instead, while talking to a longtime friend on an evening radio show, I had expressed my personal concerns about the scope and seriousness of COVID-19, questioned the ability of college football and the NFL to be played without an available vaccine, and said we were only beginning to face the challenges of the pandemic. And when I was done, I had said, "Tell me I'm wrong."

I wanted to be wrong. I wanted college football to be played. Are you kidding me? That's the game I love. That's my livelihood. Nobody was rooting harder for a 2020 college football season than I.

But how could you see the rising numbers (by April 1, Johns Hopkins University School of Medicine reported more than 215,000 cases of COVID-19 in the United States, and more than 5,000 COVID-related deaths) and not wonder how college football—or any sport, for that matter—was going to play a season in 2020? How could you not be worried about the well-being of the players, the coaches, and the fans? How you could not be shocked if we somehow started and finished a season?

I wasn't being a pessimist. I was being a realist. In March 2020 I had said we were only scratching the surface of COVID-19's emergence. As I sit here in mid May 2021, there have been more than 33 million confirmed cases of COVID-19 in the United States—and I was one of them. There have been more than 586,000 COVID-19-related deaths in this country.

We did play college football (and the NFL) in 2020, and I'm still shocked that it started and finished. It was miracle. A miracle of ingenuity, sacrifice, and commitment. I'm in awe of the people who made it happen.

I don't regret saying what I said to Fitzsimmons and Coleman. I gave my perspective of the situation during a fluid, uncertain time. If that annoyed certain coaches, then so be it. (Drinkwitz later apologized for his comments.) But the reality was that COVID-19 was mushrooming in this country, that social distancing and mask wearing wasn't universally accepted or practiced, and even within the college football community there was disagreement on when, where, and how to play games, or even if games should be played at all.

The Big Ten and Pac-12 conferences, as well as the Mid-American and Mountain West conferences, were out, then in. The SEC,

ACC, and Big 12 waited patiently before making a final decision and ultimately were able to play a majority of their games. Other conferences had much-reduced schedules.

In all, about 80 percent of the FBS games were played in 2020. It wasn't pretty, and it definitely wasn't normal, but FBS college football somehow made it from September to January. There were conference champions, a Heisman winner (Alabama wide receiver DeVonta Smith), a playoff (Notre Dame, Clemson, Ohio State, Alabama), and a familiar national champion (Saban and the Tide).

It was the twenty-fifth season that Fowler and I had spent together covering college football, including *GameDay*, the Thursday night games, the Saturday night games, the postseason games (and even a couple of *Monday Night Football* games). I'm not sure a pair of national college broadcasters has ever been together longer. And I'm not sure there's ever been a stranger season.

There were cardboard cutouts, mostly empty stadiums, Notre Dame in the ACC, player opt-outs, last-minute match-ups (BYU at Coastal Carolina), COVID-depleted rosters, and controversy surrounding Ohio State's five-win "regular" season. According to SI.com, 16 bowls were canceled and 21 schools publicly opted out of bowls. Assorted star players opted out of bowls. For all intents and purposes, the FSC didn't play in 2020. The same goes for Division II and III, as well as the junior colleges.

The sacrifices by those players, those coaches, and those staffs is what I'll always remember about college football in 2020. They weren't sitting around complaining about their situation, doing the "woe is me" thing. Instead they improvised, adjusted, and overcame.

I don't know if the average fan has a full appreciation of what these players went through to play one game, five games, thirteen games. I'm not sure fans understand the mental and physical wear and tear they experienced. From a football standpoint, it was heroic. They sacrificed, they endured isolation, played in empty or near-empty stadiums, went months and months without seeing their families. Some players contracted COVID-19 and had to deal with the virus and its effects. Some players made the difficult decision to opt out.

When you're a 17-, 18-, 19-, 20-, or 21-year-old college kid, this isn't how it's supposed to be. College is supposed to be the best time of your life, not the most stressful. They didn't get to experience that in 2020.

On the day before the national championship, I was part of a Zoom call with Ohio State center and team captain Josh Myers. When we asked him about the toll the season had taken on him and his team, he hesitated at first, but then told us what I'm sure was a sentiment shared by players everywhere: he just wanted it done and finished.

He did the interview from his apartment, with its mostly bare, white walls that reminded you of a prison. In a way, that's what he was in. The apartment or the football facility—those were his two COVID-safe choices.

He told us he had been in the same room since March and hadn't seen his family since July. He was proud of what he and his team had accomplished, but he was counting the moments until the CFP championship on January 11, 2021.

I could relate to some of what Josh was saying. I wasn't a player, but I'd be lying if I said the season didn't take a toll on me, too. (And just to be clear, this is from a college football perspective—nobody is comparing what they did, or what I do, to what a frontline health care worker does.) I entered the season looking at it as a challenge of perseverance. I wanted to be realistic, but also optimistic and upbeat—not only in my job, but with my own family. Once it became obvious that we were going to try to start and finish a season, I was all in.

As the weeks and months passed, it became harder to be the glass-half-full, Mr. Positive guy. I felt terrible for the players, the players' families, the fans, the bands, the people whose livelihoods depended on working at those games. I missed the tailgates, the traditions, the noise, the energy of a game-day Saturday. I don't know how those players played without the energy created by a full house. By the time we got to the finish line, I was ready for it to be done and hope for the best in 2021.

My own frustrations with where we were at that point in the season contributed to a poor choice of words during a CFP rankings show. I made the mistake of suggesting Michigan "waves the white flag" and would opt out of its rivalry game against Ohio State.

I was wrong, and said so publicly, and also said so privately in apologies to Big Ten commissioner Kevin Warren, Michigan athletic director Warde Manuel, and Michigan coach Jim Harbaugh. I have so much respect for the Michigan program.

Meanwhile, the players not only dealt with the weight of COVID-19, but they also carried the weight of a national movement battling social injustices in our country. Stick to sports? No. In 2020, they stood up, spoke up, and spoke out. They had a voice and they used it. They used it responsibly and effectively. It was amazing to watch.

The deaths of Ahmaud Arbery in Brunswick, Georgia, of Breonna Taylor in Louisville, of George Floyd in Minneapolis, forced America to confront its past, its present, and its future relative to racial injustices and systemic racism. I know it forced me to do so.

In early July 2020, there was an ESPN conference call with all of the company's college football on-air, production, management, and staff members. It was a forum for everyone to speak freely about their own experiences with racism. During that call, I listened as colleagues bared their hearts and souls with powerful and personal examples of having dealt with racism.

As a player, I didn't look at color. I wanted to know only one thing, Could you play or not? Were you a great teammate or a selfish one? Could I depend on you as a friend and could you depend on me? The football doesn't care what color the hands are that throw it, catch it, kick it, or tackle it.

But life isn't color blind. I knew that, but I didn't live in that world. If you had asked me in 2019 if racism existed in this country, I would have said it did, but it existed in the inner cities and in the most rural parts of our country. It was at KKK rallies, but it wasn't prevalent in mainstream America.

Then, on our September 5 *GameDay* show, I watched a nine-minute piece—one of the longest features we've ever done on our show—that Maria Taylor did with a handful of college football players. They discussed racism in this country in a way that cut right to my heart.

I had been told about the powerful nature of the conversations Maria had had with the players. I had been told to watch the piece before it aired, but I didn't. I wanted to watch and react to it in real time. In fact, I wasn't sure I wanted to react to it all.

I'm not a political person. I'm a Christian, but I don't wear it on my sleeve. I care about people and I care about what's right. But in sports television, we've been trained to nod your head and move on when the topics of religion, race, and politics are raised.

The day before the show, Alli and I went for a four-mile walk through the hills near our house and discussed how to approach Maria's roundtable. I bounced my opinions off her and as always, she was a voice of reason.

Maybe it was best that the white guy just kept quiet. Maybe it was better to say nothing than to pretend to have an answer. Was I really qualified to speak about systemic racism?

I pride myself on the willingness to do my own research, to make my own calls, to talk to those who know best. I called Stanford coach David Shaw and then–Vanderbilt coach Derek Mason. Yes, they are black coaches, but more important, they are men who have lived through these times, who have a perspective that I wanted and needed to hear. They are wise and compassionate men.

During my conversation with David, he told me about a quote from Benjamin Franklin: "Justice will not be served until those unaffected are as outraged as those who are." Those words resonated with me. I even wrote them down. I found so much comfort in talking to Derek and David.

That night, I couldn't sleep. I tossed and turned until 5 a.m., all the time thinking about Maria's segment. When I got up and began getting ready for the show, I had made up my mind: I was going to take the safe road. I was going to say something generic after the piece ran and just get the show back in Rece's hands again. I would defer to others. Then we'd move on to Serious Football Talk.

But as I listened to the conversation, as I heard those players talk about their experiences with racial profiling, with racism on a near-daily basis, I became frustrated, embarrassed, almost mad at America. These were some of the best and brightest players in the game. They were cheered on Saturdays, but subjected to racism the rest of the week? One player told Maria that he wore Texas Longhorn gear as a way to identify him to police, so they wouldn't pull him over.

The longer I listened, the more upset I became. I couldn't believe—or, at least, I didn't want to believe—that these young men could give so much to a school, to a football program and to a community, and be treated like this.

Was I naïve? Had my own skin color shielded me from this type of treatment? Of course it had.

As the piece came to a close, my chest was pounding—and I'm someone who doesn't get nervous on TV. I was so moved by those players. They convinced me to not play it safe. They hadn't.

When it was my turn to speak (Des, David Pollack, Coach Corso, Maria were doing the show remotely while Rece was in the ESPN studio) it was almost like a voice in my head said, "Go for it. Just let it go."

In my hand, I had a piece of paper with the Benjamin Franklin quote that Coach Shaw had recited to me. I read it and then said, "The black community is hurting. If you've listened—the word 'empathy' and 'compassion' over these last four months—how do you listen to these stories and not feel pain and not want to help, you know what I mean?"

And then my emotions took over. My voice broke. I could fear the tears well up. I was angry and sad and in disbelief all at the same time.

"It's like, wearing a hoodie and, uh, putting your hands at ten and two—'Oh, God, I better look out because I'm wearing Nike gear.' Like, what? What are we talking about? And so you can't relate to that if you're white, but you can listen and you can try to help because this is not okay. It's just not.

"And, uh, we've got to do better, man. We've got to, like, lock arm in arm and be together. In a football locker room, that stuff is gone. Those barriers are gone. We got to do better."

Rece took us to break. I sat in my basement studio and tried to compose myself after the segment. Maria had done such a wonderful job moderating the players' discussion. Through her work with her own charitable foundation, and with her TV and social media platform, Maria had become a voice to be heard and respected on the subject of social and racial injustice. Des also offered a powerful voice and perspective.

Afterward, I wasn't even sure what I had said. I had spoken from the heart and the words had tumbled out. I didn't have an agenda. I wasn't condemning anyone. I didn't want to create divisiveness—we have enough of that in our country. I was speaking for myself, speaking to my own awareness, or lack of it. I didn't say it for effect. I said it because I needed to say it for myself. I needed to acknowledge it. By doing so, maybe it helped others to acknowledge that we all can make a difference, that black lives don't just matter on Saturdays, but also on Sundays, Mondays, Tuesdays, Wednesdays, Thursdays, and Fridays.

According to the NCAA database demographics from 2019, about 46 percent of the players in Power Five conferences are black, while about 52 percent of the players in non–Power Five conferences are black. These are young people who, along with their teammates, are marching, are promoting dialogue, are trying to make a difference. In my own small way, I wanted to support them that day, and I hope in the days and years to follow.

———

It was a bizarre, trying, sometimes uplifting, sometimes comical, always-evolving season. From a television standpoint, we had to do what the players, coaches, and staffs did: improvise, adjust, overcome.

Travel restrictions reduced the size of our *GameDay* cast and remarkable crew. There were no fans at our set. At times, it was like doing the show in a vacuum.

Coach Corso spent the entire season doing his *GameDay* appearances from his back and front yards at his house in suburban Orlando. Patrick Abrahams was his on-site producer, and he helped create a football theme park. During the course of the season, you saw Coach sitting on top of a seventeen-foot-high fake elephant. You saw him in a winter wonderland of snow. You saw him in a canoe with the Minnesota mascot. You saw him walking on water as he stood on coastal Carolina blue artificial turf placed over his pool. You saw him with a make-believe Toomer's Corner tree in the background. You saw him wearing the makeup applied by his wife of sixty-four years, Betsy. You saw a then-eighty-five-year-old entertainer extraordinaire.

I missed having him on the *GameDay* set, missed turning to my immediate right and seeing that familiar smile, seeing that familiar B-2 stealth bomber lapel pin given to him during a trip to the Air Force Academy. It wasn't the same without him. Nothing was really the same that season. We had a one-second delay because of the signal pinging off satellites or whatever, and there wasn't any spontaneity between us.

Early in the season, I had to do a show remotely from my house because of COVID-19 contact tracing protocols. Des contracted the virus and had to do a show from his Miami-area home. Maria tested positive for COVID-19, and in late December, I also tested positive and couldn't travel to New Orleans for our January 1 *GameDay* show and that night's CFP semifinal between Clemson and Ohio State. I was heartbroken not to be able to go. Not only would I miss the game in person, but I would miss seeing the twins in person. Once again, they would dress for a national playoff game.

In order for me to call the Sugar Bowl game with Fowler, ESPN sent a tech team to install five different state-of-the-art monitors in my basement. Studio-quality lighting was set up. There was a control laptop and monitor, as well as a sound box that connected me with the booth and the production truck. The setup by our remote ops and production team was incredible.

With about twelve minutes remaining in our New Year's Day *GameDay* show—just as we were going to start the most-watched segment of the program, the game picks—my home fire alarm system activated itself. I nearly jumped out of my skin as the alarm echoed through our house and the entire neighborhood. A computer-generated voice added to the mayhem: "Fire! Get out! . . . Fire! Get out!"

Alli scrambled to the key code box to turn off the alarm, but the system kept running on its own. She called the home builder's office for help, but it was closed for the holidays. She checked the information screen and it read "Basement Door 22." Who knew what that meant? She ran around the house making sure there wasn't an actual fire. She called the home builder himself, who actually drove to the house and tried to unplug the entire system.

Meanwhile, the alarm was wailing and the voice kept telling us, "Fire! Get out!" And I had a show to do.

The production crew back in Bristol had no choice but to cut my live feed to the show. Our producer, Jim Gaiero, said, "Don't worry about it, the show's almost over."

I looked at my show clock and there were only a few minutes remaining. And then, miraculously, the alarm stopped. Rece somehow saw me on the monitor, realized that the alarm was off, and decided to come to me.

"Hey, Herbie, who do you got in this one?" he said.

You want to talk about the madness of live TV? This was it. I didn't know where we were on the rundown, didn't know which bowl game he was referring to, didn't know anything. I just started talking. I told everyone about the fire alarm. I tried to have fun with the situation.

We got through it (thanks, RD), but to this day we're not sure why the alarm decided to give us tiny heart attacks.

But the day wasn't done.

If you watched that Sugar Bowl game that night, you saw me and Fowler call the Buckeyes' win over the Tigers. What you didn't see was the exact moment that all—and I mean all—of my state-of-the-art monitors went dark during the third quarter of the game. It was like flying a 747 in clear skies and then suddenly you're in thick fog and can't see a thing. That was me. I was flying blind.

I had no idea what happened, and I didn't have to time to care. Whatever it was, I needed it fixed, and quick.

In the meantime, I freaked out. There was a remote camera positioned in front of me and I began waving my arms to let the producer and director know there was a major problem. I could hear the broadcast, but I couldn't see it. What the heck was I supposed to do?

My phone rang. It was Bear. He wanted to FaceTime. What? I didn't have time to do that! I hit the Decline icon. He called again requesting a FaceTime. I hit Decline again.

A moment or two later, I heard my cell buzz with a text.

"Answer Bear's FaceTime!" it read.

Bear called again and I hit Accept. When it connected, I saw the most beautiful sight: not Bear, but Bear holding his phone in front of the TV program monitor in the production truck. I could see what the viewer was seeing at home. I could do the broadcast again.

For about fifteen minutes, as the engineers reconnected my studio feed, I managed my way through the call on the game, all thanks to Bear pointing his phone at the program monitor. I think I aged five years that day because of the fire alarm and the technical difficulties.

After I recovered from COVID-19 (my condition was relatively mild, mostly like a head cold) I was cleared to travel for the CFP National Championship at the Orange Bowl in Miami Gardens. I felt fine, except I had no sense of taste or smell. I could bite into a raw lemon and taste nothing. A freshly baked chocolate chip cookie could be placed under my nose and I wouldn't smell a thing. And at times, I had a little trouble remembering names or coming up with the right word. It was a form of COVID brain fog.

I don't make *GameDay* picks on games I'm calling, but it wasn't a surprise that Alabama beat Ohio State in the national championship, which gave Saban his sixth national title at Bama and his seventh overall—the most by any major college coach in the AP poll era. He has won AP/Coaches poll national championships in three different decades, the first coach ever to do so.

I've called all of his national championship games, beginning in 2003 when he won the BCS Championship at LSU, the six title wins at Bama (2009, 2011, 2012, 2015, 2017, 2020), and his two losses in the championship (both to Clemson, 2016 and 2018). Saban has had more talented teams than the one he had in 2020, but he hasn't had a more unified and determined team.

DeVonta Smith won a Heisman, and then went back to work. His attitude was, "I'll just put this trophy away for now, and concentrate on winning." Running back Najee Harris was the same way. So was quarterback Mac Jones, who was an afterthought for years at Bama—stuck first behind Tua Tagovailoa and Jalen Hurts, and then projected to be stuck behind big-time recruit Bryce Young in 2020. Instead of giving up, he worked harder. He finished third in the Heisman voting and helped lead Bama to an undefeated season and that 52–24 win against the Buckeyes.

That whole team was about winning, and it began at the top with Saban, and worked its way throughout the entire program. You would have never known Steve Sarkisian was the new head coach at Texas. Instead, he was arm in arm with Bama as its offensive coordinator until the final second ticked off the clock. Offensive tackle Alex Leatherwood and center Landon Dickerson were the heart and soul of that team. Dickerson, who had knee surgery in December, still dressed for the game and convinced Saban to let him take the final few snaps when Bama went into the Victory formation. The reaction of Dickerson's teammates—there were hugs, they told each other how much they loved one another—was all you needed to know about the togetherness of that Bama team.

Ten, twenty years from now, when we remember the 2020 season, we're going to remember that team for what it did under the most extreme circumstances. We're going to remember the talent and unselfishness of Smith. For me, that 2020 Tide team will go down as one of the great teams I'll ever cover.

By the time I got back to the hotel after the game, it was about two o'clock in the morning. I know Nick doesn't like to text, so I called him. He was still up.

"Coach," I said, "I don't want to wait to tell you this. I don't want time to pass and I never get a chance to say how much I appreciate you. It is an honor to cover the best who has ever coached the college game. Your teams just play. They get in the huddle and they play the game. So I just wanted to thank you."

I meant every word of it.

I've always admired the way he coaches. I love his style. He has a simple philosophy: "It's my team and my rules. If you don't want to follow those rules, you won't play." I think too many coaches are so desperate to have difference-makers on their teams that they cut corners; they don't want to risk losing a player because of a rule that matters. They don't do their players any favors by cutting those corners.

It's been fun to watch his career develop as a head coach, from Toledo, to Michigan State, to LSU, to the Miami Dolphins and to Bama. He and I have always had a good working relationship. The outside world sees his press conferences, when he can run a bit hot, or his sideline reactions, when he can run really hot. People think that's who he is.

I've seen the other side. Yes, he is a no-nonsense coach. He's hyperfocused on his job and the details of that job. But I see a very different guy, a guy who can't intimidate his wife, Miss Terry, a guy who can give *and* take a little ball-busting, a guy who has the respect of every player on his roster, a guy whom I would have loved to have played for.

I've been in those team meeting rooms when he walked down the ramp to the podium. The room grows instantly quiet. He commands the room. And if he is such a bad guy, such a tyrant, then why the heck do so many great high school players want to play for him?

Players—the smart ones—want to be coached hard. They're not afraid to learn, to be challenged. Saban is sixty-nine years old, but he has adjusted to the times, to the changing schemes, to the importance of the passing game, to the players themselves. Coach Saban, at the end of the day, wants his players to earn a diploma and grow as people. He doesn't cut corners, and he won't allow his players to do it, cither. It doesn't matter if you're a Heisman winner or the third-team tight end.

On the first day of practice each year, he lays down the law. One of the laws is that Bama players don't talk to the other team. He won't allow the Bama offensive players to chirp to the Bama defensive players in scrimmages, and vice versa. If you do, you get kicked out of practice.

I think he's great for the game. The people who don't like him are simply jealous of his success. He is the greatest college coach in the history of the game. Everyone else is on the next tier below him. He is right up there with Belichick as the greatest coach in the history of football.

Meanwhile, people ask me if Alabama's domination is "good" for the game, if the SEC's eleven national championships since 2006 are "good" for the game. I don't know how to answer that. I admire excellence and achievement, so I respect what Alabama and the SEC have done. To do what Saban has done is remarkable, and should be celebrated. I also know that when you beat a Saban-coached team, that needs to be celebrated, too.

I'm more worried about the soul of the sport than I am about Alabama and the SEC's success. We have reached a tipping point in college football, a place in its history where either the sport evolves and grows stronger, or it collapses because of its failure to remember what made it successful in the first place.

I'm terrified that college football is headed the wrong way. It is being attacked on so many different levels. There is so much money at stake that decisions are being made that aren't always in the best interests of the game and the players.

First, we need to fix the postseason. We've created the equivalent of a four-team December/January Madness and a perception that everyone else is playing in the NIT. I used to brag to the NFL people I know that college football didn't need a playoff. "The whole season is a playoff," I'd tell them. "Every game matters."

But after living seven years of the CFP system, nobody is saying the playoff system is great for the game, or that it's close to perfection. Instead, its critics want the CFP expanded to six teams, eight teams, even twelve teams.

I always thought four teams would be plenty, that the regular season wouldn't be compromised. Now I don't know if we should expand to twelve or return to the original two of the BCS era. I know this: when we had No. 1 versus No. 2, the regular season and the other bowl games mattered.

Players are being raised on a playoff-or-bust mentality and now think the non-CFP bowls aren't worth the effort. They're being told, "Why are you playing in the Citrus Bowl, or the Alamo Bowl, or whatever bowl that isn't a semifinal or championship game? It's an exhibition game. You'll get nothing out of it."

When I hear people say that, I want to scream, "What the hell are you talking about?"

What do you get? You get to wear the jersey one more time. You get to compete with your boys one more time, the guys you've spent days, months, years with in the weight room, in the meeting rooms, in conditioning drills, on the practice fields, in scrimmages, on the road, at home. You've sweated with them, hurt with them, become lifelong friends with them.

Players should think of playing college football as a privilege, not a right. It's an honor to play college football. It's an honor to receive a full scholarship. I've seen too many players act as if they're doing the school a favor by signing with it.

Sure, if you have a legitimate NFL future and you decide to opt out of a bowl game because you don't want to risk injury, then more power to you. I wasn't one of those guys. I never had an NFL future.

But even if I had been one of those guys, I would have suited up for whatever bowl game was available. I have never understood the pit-stop players, the players who look at college ball as nothing more than an inconvenience on their way to the NFL. They want to do their three years, get out, and get paid. They're not invested in their program, in their school, in the traditions, in the fans, in establishing roots. Instead, everything is, "I'm going to the League. I'm going to get my money." The minute they step on campus they start staring at their three-year clock.

Huh? I don't get it.

I don't know if it's a reflection of the system, or a reflection of this generation of players, but college sports—and college football, in particular—has to be more than a waiting room for someone who wants to play pro sports. It has to be more than a minor league for the NFL.

I wish I could help those players understand that while it's great to have the goal of reaching the NFL, the numbers are against you. I wish I could tell them that I've never met an NFL player—and I've met and known a lot of them—who has said, "I couldn't stand the college game. I'll never go back to campus again." Instead, I hear, "I'd give anything to go back and play one more college game."

I wish they saw the same NCAA research numbers I've seen: that of the 73,712 participants on all levels of NCAA football, 16,380 were draft eligible, and only 254 of them were drafted— a 1.6 percent probability rate of going from college to the pros. That same data says that an NCAA Division I athlete has an 86 percent likelihood of earning a college degree.

Right now, if the system remains the same, I can tell you that Alabama, Clemson, and Ohio State are likely to be in the playoff in 2021, 2022, 2023, and beyond. It's just a matter of who the fourth team is going to be. That's the reality of college football right now. If you recruit the best players and have the best coaching—as those three teams have—then you have the best chance to reach the CFP.

There is an inequality in the sport when it comes to financial resources. People say we need parity in the game. No, we need parity in the resources. It is virtually impossible for a program with half the budget, staff, and facilities to compete with the elite teams. It has become a Have versus Have-Nots, and the gap grows wider each year.

If we don't fix that, then the same teams are going to continue to dominate the sport. For the health of the game, more teams need to have a chance at a national championship run. We need Texas, Tennessee, Michigan, Florida State, Miami, USC, Penn State—the traditional powers—to become relevant again. We miss those teams in the mix. We need to give less traditional programs some real hope. Do you do that by expanded revenue sharing, by some form of a coaching salary cap? Do you expand the CFP to give a non–Power 5 team a chance if it has a magical season? Do the Power 5 conferences form their own league?

Everything should be on the table.

I think it's inevitable that the Power 5 will have its own separate national championship. But I'm not the Commissioner of College Football—though, I think we should have one of those, too.

A CFB commissioner isn't a new idea, but if ever there was a time for one, this is it. (The legendary Mike Krzyzewski of Duke has suggested college basketball have its own commissioner.) If we learned anything about college football in 2020, we learned that the conferences have their own best interests in mind. The SEC is about the SEC, the Big Ten about the Big Ten, and so on. Otherwise, there would have been a unified decision on how best to approach football in the COVID-19 era.

Right now, the leadership in college football is too fragmented and regionalized. The commissioners work out of their own silos, concerned mostly about their own presidents, chancellors, athletic directors, fans, television rights, players, coaches, media sites, schedules. Everything is about "How does it affect us?" instead of "How does it affect the sport?" Nobody is looking at the health of the game through a national lens.

Look at the Pac-12. It is one of the great historic conferences in college football. But it is losing its fan base. It has made strategic miscalculations. It is a forgotten conference. If you're a fifteen-year-old high school freshman, you've never seen a Pac-12 team win a national championship. You've seen only one Pac-12 team play in a national title game.

We need to look at our sport from coast to coast, not state to state, region to region. We need someone with college football's best interests in mind, someone who has actual decision-making power. The conferences would have input and a voice but would abide by the national commissioner's decision.

College football faces all sorts of big issues: transfer portals, Name/Image/Likeness policy, the direction of the CFP, the future of bowls, the role of the NCAA and the rewriting of its antiquated rules, etc.

I'm accused sometimes of being antiquated in the way I think. I'm told I'm out of touch for believing in traditions, in the value of a scholarship, in the purpose of going to college. The truth is, I'm the furthest thing from a guy who is out of touch. I played the game, I broadcast the game, I'm the father of three kids who play the college game, I'm immersed in the game on a daily basis, I constantly talk to the fans, players, coaches and decision makers in the game. I'm in the front row of the game.

Out of touch? Because I want players to respect the game and their opponents? Because I don't like players taunting each other? Because I don't think college football should be the NFL Jr.? Because I worry about the effects of the transfer portal? Because I'm concerned that this generation of kids doesn't care who Herschel Walker or Eddie George are, doesn't care about the history of the game?

I don't want to be hypocritical about it. Had I played in this era of the transfer portal, I probably would have bolted from Ohio State. But I'm glad I stayed put. It was a tough life lesson, but those are lessons I think some of these players are missing. If you give up, it takes away from what makes the game—and you—special: the ability to persevere.

Maybe that's why I love walk-ons. They ask for nothing but a chance. They appreciate every moment. They want to be part of a team. They love the game.

My three sons began their college careers as preferred walk-ons. (A preferred walk-on doesn't receive a scholarship for at least his first season, but is guaranteed a place on the roster and will usually get first crack at an opening on the depth chart.) Zak, a tight end, is the latest. I wish you could have been there that night when Alli and I heard him tell someone on speakerphone, "They're right here, Coach. I'll get them."

Then Zak called us into the room and Ohio State's Ryan Day was on the other line.

"We talked to Zak tonight," Ryan said. "We've been following him all season as you know, and we want to offer him the opportunity to join the team as a preferred walk-on."

Oh, my gosh, to see the look on Zak's face made us so happy. Ohio State was his dream school. Those are the small moments that make college football so special. We need to protect those moments, both big and small.

I can't pretend college football is without problems. There is so much good about the game, but little by little, we're losing what makes college football so special. Our priorities are confused, our long-term, comprehensive plan nonexistent—or at least, it seems that way.

College football is still the best sport, but it can only withstand so much. There are some cracks in the foundation, and they're growing wider. It's now or never for the game.

Chapter 21

A Proud Father

When it comes to being Handyman Dad, I'm useless. I can't do anything when it comes to stuff around the house. My dad moved out when I was a kid. He never taught me how to change the oil in the car, or swap out the plugs, or assemble a bike. He never said, "C'mon, son, I'll show you how to build a pressure-treated cedar deck." That didn't happen in my life.

We didn't have a garage, or even a toolshed. And even if we had, I would have wanted to play outside. All I cared about was sports.

I did used to mow the grass, but that was about sports, too. I loved trying to make the lines perfectly straight, as if I were mowing the outfield grass at Wrigley Field. In the winter, I would ask the grandmas in the neighborhood if they wanted me to shovel their driveways for a few bucks. That was the extent of my household abilities.

I can't fix a thing. Allison handles that in our house. In fact, during a visit to our house one time, Bear helped Alli put together the beds for the boys, and also helped assemble a barbecue for me. I'm not even sure if we own a toolbox.

I do know football, though. Because of football, I know the importance of hard work, of dedication, of discipline, of patience, of competition, of respect of tradition. I can't teach my sons how to operate a miter saw, but I can teach them football and all that it entails.

My boys have grown up around football. Just as my dad passed the game along to me, I've tried to pass it along to them. And just as my dad never forced me to play, I've never forced my boys to play. They gravitated toward the game on their own.

Sure, they were influenced by their grandfather's legacy at Ohio State, as well as my career there. They've grown up on *GameDay* and being around iconic stadiums, big games, great coaches, and All-America players. They were born in a college football town and have a former Ohio State cheerleader as a mom.

But I would have supported them had they wanted to pursue soccer, swimming, dance, chemistry, classical piano, or car repair. It has never been about what they do, but how they do it.

They played different sports as kids, which I think is important. I would encourage every kid to play multiple sports. I think parents do a disservice to their kids by concentrating on one sport at an early age. You can't walk past our front door without tripping over a baseball bat, a golf bag, or pairs of cleats.

Eventually, the twins zeroed in on football—all the boys have. We're an Ohio State family, but when Dabo Swinney and his staff offered Jake and Tye the chance to come to Clemson in 2019 as preferred walk-ons, they couldn't turn it down.

Alli and I will never forget the summer day in 2018 that my cell phone rang while we were having lunch in the cliffside village of Positano on southern Italy's Amalfi Coast. We were there celebrating our twentieth wedding anniversary. Chase was staying with friends, and Zak and the twins were at Clemson's football camp for high schoolers.

It was Coach Swinney.

"I know you're over there in Italy, but I've got to tell you about your boys," he said. "They're having a great time."

Dabo was fired up. He told us how Tye and his team had advanced to the finals of the camp competition and had caught the coaches' attention. He said that Jake had impressed them with his toughness. At the end of one of the final practices, Jake had taken off his cleats, and the team trainer noticed that Jake's socks were soaked in blood. Apparently his new cleats had caused clusters of blisters over the course of the camp, but Jake had never said a word. Instead, he just kept playing. Dabo loved that.

Their attitude and work ethic contributed to Coach Swinney's decision to consider the twins as FBS prospects, and to later offer them preferred walk-on status. Jake and Tye had been to Clemson's camp twice, and also to Alabama and Ohio State's camps. USC's Clay Helton had talked to them about becoming preferred walk-ons. They also visited TCU.

In the end, I did with them as my own dad had done with me: I let them make the decision. They chose Clemson.

Just by chance, Clemson opened its 2019 season at home on a Thursday night against Georgia Tech—and *GameDay* was there. It was a perfect storm: Clemson was the defending national champion and the ACC Network was broadcasting its first-ever game. Otherwise, I'm not sure *GameDay* would have been there.

As our show got under way, Clemson's players came out for their pregame warm-ups. I was trying to concentrate on what Rece was saying from across the desk, but every time I had a chance, I'd take a glance behind me and try to find Nos. 86 (Tye) and 37 (Jake) on the field.

I turned back to reengage with the show and saw one of the monitors on the set. Our cameras had zeroed in on Tye just after he had a caught a pass and returned to the wide receivers' line.

I don't try to hide my emotions. I'll cry watching *American Idol*, so you can imagine what was swirling in my head as I saw my twins in uniform at Death Valley.

I tried to play it cool on the air, but a thousand thoughts were going through my mind: pride, love, happiness. It was such a surreal moment that I couldn't help but get misty eyed. I wondered out loud what they were thinking at that exact moment.

When they were newborns, I could slide my wedding band up and down their tiny legs. But here they were, having overcome more obstacles than I ever had.

I stayed for most of the first half, but then had to catch a flight to Dallas–Fort Worth. We had meetings on Friday and then *GameDay* on Saturday in Fort Worth. I tried watching on the drive to the airport and also when I got on the plane, but the Wi-Fi kept freezing up.

Alli had stayed for the game and was sitting next to the mother of another Clemson walk-on.

"You think they'll get in?" the mom said to Alli.

"This is their first college game," Alli said. "There's no way they're getting in."

That's what I thought, too. Then I got a text. It was Alli.

"Tye just got in! Oh, my god!"

Then . . .

"Oh, my gosh—he blocked a guy! He blocked a guy!"

I wish I would have seen it, but I could imagine it. I've always remembered my first college snap. They'll always remember theirs.

I talked to both of the boys not long after the game. As the season progressed, they each got onto the field for four games and then were designated for redshirt seasons. As football fate would have it, Clemson and Ohio State both finished their regular seasons undefeated and were matched against each other in the CFP semifinal at the Fiesta Bowl.

Jake and Tye were brainwashed Ohio State fans. My dad, mom, Teri, John, and Alli and I had never hidden our love of the Buckeyes, and that scarlet-and-gray love rubbed off on all the boys. Having gone to high school in SEC country, the twins were never shy about standing up for Ohio State and the Big Ten.

But now they were part of Clemson's program. They had invested blood and sweat into that team. They had made friends, bonded with teammates, worked to earn the respect of the coaches. They will always have a soft spot for Ohio State, but they wanted to beat the Buckeyes and advance to the national championship.

A few nights before the game, we went to dinner together in the Scottsdale area. Zak and Chase are incredibly passionate Ohio State fans and during the course of dinner, they started zinging the twins with predictions of what quarterback Justin Fields was going to do to the Tigers. It began in a kidding manner, but then escalated to the point where I had to step in and turn down the intensity.

The Herbstreit family was all over the place on game night: me, the former Ohio State player, in the booth calling the game with Fowler . . . Alli, the former OSU cheerleader, decked out in Clemson orange and purple and sitting in the Clemson section . . . Zak and Chase decked out in Ohio State gear from head to toe—and refusing to sit in the Clemson section (we found them seats in the Buckeyes section) . . . the twins in uniform and down on the field.

I was on the field an hour or so before the game. Jake and the defensive backs were warming up on the other side of the field, but Tye was close enough that I could talk to him for a moment.

"Dad, how cool is it that we're playing Ohio State in the semis?" he said.

I told him I loved him, and just before I headed up to the booth, I turned around and saw Jake and Tye looking back at me through their face masks. The "babies," as Alli calls the twins, had grown up.

There had been several newspaper and website stories about our "divided" football family. I had tried to downplay it. But it was Fowler who gently reminded me that it was okay to appreciate this intersection of family, football, and fate.

"You're doing a great job," he said, "but don't forget to take this in. Don't forget to be in the present and understand how rare and special this is. You couldn't have scripted this. Savor it."

It was so cool of Chris to say that. But for the game itself, I did what I always do: I became Switzerland; I was neutral.

There were some controversial plays in the game, the most glaring being a scoop-and-score by Ohio State that was overturned by the review booth. I thought it was a touchdown, and would have said so had it been Clemson that had picked up the loose ball and scored.

Clemson overcame a 16–0 first-half deficit, lost the lead early in the fourth quarter, regained it on a 94-yard drive with less than two minutes remaining, and then held on as the Tigers intercepted Fields in the end zone with just thirty-seven seconds left. It was a classic.

As I always try to do after a playoff game, I went down to the locker rooms to pay my respects and thank the coaches and players for their time during the week and season. I first went to see the Buckeyes.

There is no quieter place than a locker room after a season-ending loss. I popped in quickly to tell Ryan Day what an unbelievable job he had done in his first year as a head coach at Ohio State. He was gracious, but still upset about several replay calls that had gone against his team.

Buckeyes running back J. K. Dobbins, who had rushed for 174 yards and had played on a bad left ankle, sat silently in front of his locker, his jersey off, his grass-stained game pants still on, his ankles still taped. He stared at the carpet floor.

I knew that feeling. I knew what it was like to have played your final college game. The reality is crushing. Dobbins had done everything that he could. I loved watching that kid play.

Chase was with me, and as we started to walk out of the locker room, he began bawling, just like I would have bawled as a kid who worshipped the Buckeyes. He had come to know some of these players in the past few years and was devastated by the loss. Nobody roots harder for Ohio State than Chase.

Defensive tackle Robert Landers saw Chase crying and came over and gave him a hug. Fields saw the tears running down his face and dapped him up. Dobbins even came over to hug him. Those players, man. They'd just lost a national semifinal game, but they took the time to give comfort to a little kid. That says a lot about who they are as people.

Seeing Chase cry—and seeing how those players treated my son—I began to tear up, too. I was touched by the entire scene.

Chase and I composed ourselves and walked down the concourse to the Clemson side, where the Tiger parents, including Alli, were cheering as the players made their way to the team bus. To see the twins' faces was to see the definition of joy.

"First year!" I said to Jake and Tye. "Dudes, your first year and you're going to the national championship!"

"Can you believe this, Dad?" said Jake. "We're going to the national championship!"

We took a family team photo. Chase's eyes were still red from crying. The twins got on the bus and later flew back to Clemson. The rest of us went back to the hotel.

In 2020, Ohio State beat Clemson in the national semifinals, and then Bama beat the Buckeyes in the championship game.

For the twins, Clemson has been a perfect fit for them. In two seasons, they've earned two ACC Championship rings, a Fiesta Bowl ring, and been part of three playoff appearances, including one national championship game. I never won a conference championship. I never reached a national championship.

Anyway, not bad for two kids who the doctor said would never play contact sports. In fact—and I don't mean this in a spiteful way—I hope that doctor saw them in uniform. Perhaps in the future he'll be more aware of the human spirit and what people can achieve. I hope other parents who wonder if their kids can overcome physical challenges—as Alli and I wondered about our twins—will see Jake and Tye's story as small inspiration.

I'm proud of the twins for reaching those games, but I'm prouder of what Dabo once said of them. He told me they didn't want anything handed to them, that the staff and teammates respect them because of their work ethic. Hearing that is better than any catch or tackle they'll ever make.

I am a lucky man. I have Alli, the boys, and our three dogs. I have my mom, who is in her early eighties and has been through thick and thin. I have my sister and brother, close relatives and close friends. I have a career built on hard work and built with the help of others. I have gifted colleagues. I have my faith. I have my second dad in Coach.

I wish my own dad were still here to share in it all. He would have loved to have seen the twins on the field. He would have been among the first to congratulate Zak for signing with Ohio State. He would have consoled Chase after the Ohio State playoff losses.

I am a reflection of my dad, of my mom, of the complex and layered circumstances of my childhood. My friend Nick Khan says I'm tough, but with a sweet disposition, that I can't be pushed around. There's truth to that. My life could have gone in a dozen different directions. I could have let those circumstances dictate the arc of my life. I could have blamed others. I could have been a self-pity guy.

I chose resilience. I chose toughness. I chose compassion and a smile on my face.

I miss my dad. He made mistakes as a father—we all do—but I've tried to learn from his mistakes, and from my own. Alli says that you can't escape where you've come from, but that you can fight against what you've been taught. That's what I've tried to do when it comes to my dad. Deep down, he was a good man, but not the best father. I try to pull out the goodness of those memories, and everything else is a work in progress.

By the time this book is published, I'll have celebrated another wedding anniversary in June and another Father's Day. I'll have three boys in college and a fourth in high school. Maybe it's time to call Archie Manning again.

I want to set an example for my kids. What's that line: "To whom much is given, much is required." I have been given a chance to make a difference in the lives of others, so I'm going to do that.

I remember what it was like to see my own mom struggle to pay the bills and feed our family. So with the help of Patrick Abrahams and Ohio State's Diana Sabau, I've become involved in KIPP Columbus (Knowledge Is Power Program). In the COVID-19 era, when people are losing their jobs and are living week to week, day to day, we try to ease the financial burden on them. To hear their stories of struggle, to see their faces of relief when we're able to help is such a blessing for us.

We've supported 25 families and nearly 100 children, and paid nearly 300 monthly bills. Families were able to keep their houses. Parents were able to find other jobs. One mom was able to keep open her neighborhood salon.

My boys don't have those concerns. They don't have to worry about having a roof over their heads, or paying the monthly bills, or paying for college. But I want them to appreciate what it means to be able to attend school. I want them to know that much has been given to them, and now much will be required of them. I think they do.

They're good boys. They'll introduce themselves to you. They'll look you in the eye and shake your hand. They'll say hello and show respect. Alli has been such a good mom to them. They are a reflection of us, too, but especially of her. I hope I'm doing right by them.

I've evolved over the years, but my core values haven't changed. I value passion, friendship, empathy, sincerity, humility, and generosity. I try to eat healthy, but I have a weakness for Dairy Queen Blizzards. I eat frozen pizzas. I like a glass of wine every so often, but a friend had to explain what a decanter and sommelier was. I don't need either. I'll take a great mom-and-pop Italian restaurant over a place that has something fancy like quail eggs on the menu. If I get a Chipotle burrito bowl, it's always with double chicken. If I get a deli sandwich, it's always with double turkey. I have a closet full of suits, but I'd rather wear Nike shorts, a T-shirt, and a ball cap any day of the week. I'm like you—give me a couch, a roomful of close friends, a big game, and a TV remote with fresh batteries and I'm a happy man.

I'm anxious to see how the next chapter of our lives will unfold. I want to grow as a broadcaster, as a father, husband, son, brother, friend, colleague, and person. Life is too short to carry regret and resentment around like a cinder block chained to your ankle.

I'm ready for whatever is next. I've dealt with the past. It's time to move forward. Always forward.

Acknowledgments

My life is a bit of a contradiction. I make my living on television, but I'm not entirely comfortable talking about myself. Football, yes. Me, no.

I spent the last several years debating whether I wanted to write a book. If I did it, I wanted to tell my whole story, not just the successes, but the struggles, the obstacles, and my lifelong pursuit of trying to prove myself. I decided to share my journey because I thought it might help other parents and kids who are facing similar struggles. Maybe there was part of my story that is also part of their story. Maybe they could relate to what I've been through as a kid, as an athlete, as a son, as a husband, and as a father. Especially as a father.

I don't pretend to have the answers. But I have the experiences. If those experiences resonate with others, then this book has been a success.

There was a TV sitcom in the 1980s and early '90s called *Cheers*. It took place in a Boston pub owned by a former Red Sox pitcher, and one of the barflies was a character named Norm Peterson.

Whenever he walked into the bar, everyone yelled, "Norm!" He was a regular, and a regular guy, too. He just liked to talk sports, watch the world go by, and get along with everyone.

I can identify with Norm. I like to think of myself as that guy you can sit next to at the bar and just shoot the bull. I like listening to stories, meeting people, and being one of the regulars. I'm not special; I'm just on TV.

In a lot of cases, I've been through what you've been through. And in some cases, I hope you never go through what I've gone through. But that's life, and that's why I ultimately decided to write this book.

I couldn't have done it without my wife, Allison, and our four boys. Thank goodness she picked up the phone and called me in 1993. Better yet, I'm glad I answered.

My boys—Tye, Jake, Zak, and Chase—make me proud to be their father every day. And if you count our goldens—Ben, Theo, and Mitch—we've got seven kids. My family, especially Alli, has done a remarkable job rolling with the demands of my profession. They are my partners.

My journey began in Ohio. It began with my parents, Jim and Judy, and with my sister, Teri, and brother, John. It continues with them, or, in my dad's case, with my memories of him. Mom calls our boys her "treasures." We feel the same about her.

I am fortunate to still be connected to so many friends, former teammates, coaches, and teachers from my high school and Ohio State days. When it comes to friends such as Deron Brown, Brian Chorpenning, Craig Schmidt, Joey Galloway, George Tzagournis, and Jared Zwick, it reminds me of a line I heard used by a famous New York newspaper columnist, the late Jimmy Breslin. When he referred to a longtime buddy, he said, "He was a friend behind your back."

There are so many others who have meant so much to me, friends such as Troy Hutto, David Rosenbaum, Steve Milano, and Josh Johnston. And mentors and coaches during my high school years, such as Bob Gregg, Ron Ullery, and Tim Engleka.

There are friends' parents who have had a positive impact on me, including Bob and Maureen Rosenbaum, Dale and Connie Trent, Steve and Barb Milano, Jim and Barb Enis, and Darwin and Hildy Brown.

I also want to acknowledge some former Ohio State teammates: Paul Sherrick, Derrick (Big D) Foster, Brian Stablein, Chris Sanders, Jeff Cothran, Eddic George, Butler B'ynote', Raymont Harris, Steve Tovar, Jack Thrush, Korey Stringer, Len Hartman, and Cedric Saunders, as well as former Ohio State coaches and staff, such as John Cooper, Dave (Coach K) Kennedy, Dave (Coach L) Langworthy, Larry Romanoff, and Dr. Budd Ferrante.

From my days in Columbus radio and TV, thank you to Terry Smith, Tony Pollina, Ian Fitzsimmons, Ted Holbrook, Paul (Moose) Spohn, Jay Crawford, Dave VanStone, Dom Tiberi, Mick Lewis, and Michael Fiorile, as well as Tim May and Bruce Hooley.

To ESPN management, past and present: Bob Iger, Bob Chapek, Jimmy Pitaro, Stephanie Druley, Norby Williamson, John Skipper, Howard Katz, Mark Shapiro, Al Jaffe, John Wildhack, and Connor Schell. And to Mo Davenport, I'll never forget the opportunity that you gave me.

To the *College GameDay* production team, past and present: Mark Gross, Michael Fountain, Steve Vecchione, Lisa Kraus, Stu Barbara, Tom Lucas, Lorenzo Lamadrid, Scott Favalora, Ben (Boonie) Webber, Jonathan Whyley, Joe (Fudd) Disney, Rick (Stripes) Thomas, Rodney Perez, Brian Albon, Drew Gallagher, Jim Gaiero, Tom (Beethoven) Engle, Steve Turnberger, Trish

Ferguson, Aaron Katzman, Scott Clarke, and Phil Ellsworth and Geoff Brown.

To the *GameDay* production support crew: Patrick Abrahams, Lindsey Lloyd, and her great team, (including Stephen Rebout, Parker Daigle and Stephen Hensler). A special thank-you to Ryan Miller and Fu Takumi for going above and beyond every single day.

The "offensive line" of our *GameDay* team is Tommy Marshall and his Roadkill crew, as well as the gifted and hardworking members of our camera, audio, and ops crew: Bobby Stephens, Mike Ruhlman, Judi Weiss, Jayne Bonn, Luther Fisher, Dean Ellington, Ben Branch, Jake Daigle, Eric Kimmel, Chris Boler, Jason Levin, Bama Dave Smith, David Barnes, Joe (Tree) Andreasen, Mike Pacheco, Eddie Stachulski, Brie Michaels, Cameron Sheckels, Jay Clarke, Chad Hanna, Duncan Morgan, Scott Mulvihill, Mike Martin, Dave McDonald, Josh Bero, Tony Johnson, Justin Endres, Gerry Glass, Bill Verberkmoes, Michael Jefferson, Logan Whitford-Endres, John Stull, Pat Hally, Mike Hally, Josh Bender, Danny Reifert, Jeremy Wright, and Carl Heinemann.

Many thanks to our ESPN Security team, including Paul Daly, Amedeo Carta, and my right-hand man, Kinely Williams.

Thank you to Dawn Wind for keeping me organized during all these seasons. I'd be lost without you. Also thanks to the ESPN PR team, including Derek Volner, Anna Negron, Bill Hofheimer, and Keri Potts.

To my teammates on *GameDay*, past and present: Desmond Howard, David Pollack, Maria Taylor, Gene Wojciechowski, Tom Rinaldi, Sam Ponder, Jen Lada, Pat McAfee, George Whitfield, Sandy Rosenbush, Michael Allan, Marisa Dowling, Reva Labbe, Adam Bauer, and Derek Chang.

To my Thursday night crew: Tim Corrigan, Mike Tirico, Tom Archer, Mike Schwab, Greg Swartz. You guys were invaluable to me, especially early in my ESPN career.

I also would like to thank the crew of *ABC Saturday Night Football*, many of whom I've been with for more than fifteen years: Bill Bonnell and Derek Mobley. Nobody cuts a game like D-Mob. And Billy, I can't tell you how much I've appreciated your partnership and support over the years. You guys are the best game producer/director combo in television. Also, I'm appreciative of the leadership of Steve Ackels and Ed Placey. Thanks also to Brian Fahey, Steven Kim, Kyle Brown, Matt Brooks, Rob Adamski, Bob Salmi, Adam Daly, Courtni Regan, Mike Black, Darren Gaul, Gary DeMarco, John Beil, Jack Coffey, Harris Feibischoff, Scott Johnson, T. J. Tart, and Curtis Wilson.

To my *Saturday Night* on-air teammates past and present: Brent Musburger, Lisa Salters, Erin Andrews, Heather Cox, Maria Taylor, Dave Cutaia, Bill LeMonnier, and Bob Davie.

I owe a special gratitude to Lee Corso and Chris Fowler, who were there for me in my early days at ESPN—and ever since. Lee Fitting has been both a friend and a reliable sounding board. Rece Davis, who has become a terrific teammate and good friend. And a special mention to that big, lovable Bear, Chris Fallica.

I also want to thank Nick Khan for his dependable advice and even more dependable friendship. The same goes for the legendary late, great Barry Frank.

And a special thank-you to Kenny Dichter for all that you've done for me and my family.

And a heartfelt thank-you and much appreciation to "Team Herbstreit": Team captain Brian Chorpenning, Nick Khan, Whitney Logan, Jarrod Grubb, Glenn Harper, and Peter Webb.

Thanks, too, to David Black and Amar Deol.

Thank you to the college coaches, players, conference commissioners, athletic directors, CFP committee members, and sports media relations officials who have helped me over the years. I appreciate your trust and your knowledge. Thanks also to the campus police and law enforcement officials who have helped us during and after our broadcasts. And finally, thank you to the college football fans who make the sport so special.

Kirk Herbstreit

May 2021

It is no small thing to open up your heart, your soul, and your past for all to see. Many thanks to Kirk Herbstreit for doing exactly that, and for doing it with honesty, with patience, and with genuineness. These pages are the result of his authenticity, and of a family—Allison, Tye, Jake, Zak, and Chase—that supports each other in ways that are a joy to witness.

My thanks also to those who agreed to background interviews: family members, relatives, boyhood friends, teammates, coaches, colleagues past and present, associates and friends made on campuses throughout the country. Their insights, anecdotes, and reflections provided essential context to this project. Special appreciation goes to Judy and Teri Herbstreit, Craig Schmidt, and Chris Fallica for their considerable help.

Also deserving of mention are Ohio State's Jerry Emig, Kyle McKee, and Michelle Drobik, ESPN's Scott Clarke and Phil Ellsworth, Joe Wojciechowski, Tom Young, Jon Fish, and Marisa Dowling, and the University of Akron's Sean Palchick and Ken MacDonald.

As always, countless thanks to T. L. Mann for his constant presence, and much appreciation to literary agent David Black and editor Amar Deol of Atria Books.

Indiana Jones once said, "It's not the years, honey, it's the mileage." To my wife, Cheryl, thank you for being there with me every mile of the way.

Gene Wojciechowski

May 2021

Notes

Supplementary background interviews, sometimes multiple in nature, were conducted by the coauthor with Teri Herbstreit, Judy Herbstreit, Rick Herbstreit, Allison Herbstreit, Desmond Howard, Sam Ponder, Paul Spohn, Deron Brown, Eddie George, Joey Galloway, Butler B'ynote', Craig Schmidt, Jay Crawford, Jonathan Whyley, Kinely Williams, Paul Daly, Urban Meyer, Ian Fitzsimmons, Tim Corrigan, Brian Chorpenning, John Cooper, Tim May, Patrick Abrahams, Chris Fowler, Rece Davis, David Pollack, Maria Taylor, Tom Rinaldi, Lee Corso, Jim Gaiero, Aaron Katzman, Drew Gallagher, Chris Fallica, Tricia Ferguson, Tim Engleka, Howard Katz, Mike Ruhlman, Mike Tirico, Marty Smith, Terry Smith, Pat Forde, Bob Gregg, Sandy Rosenbush, Mo Davenport, Nick Khan, and George Whitfield.

In some cases, quotes not attributed to a specific publication, television station, or website were the result of the quote being said in a group setting interview or press conference.

In addition, some material in this book was the result of the coauthor's firsthand coverage and/or access to past games, events, press conferences and assorted ESPN shows, including *College GameDay*.

Facts, figures, and statistics were the result of the coauthor's own research or were found in or provided by athletic department websites, media guides, record books, and databases, as well as ESPN. Specific research resources are listed below.

Supplementary background material was used from ESPN.com, ESPN Statistics and Information Group, Associated Press, *Dayton Daily News, Columbus Dispatch, The Athletic, New York Times, Cincinnati Enquirer, Los Angeles Times, Chicago Tribune, Cleveland Plain Dealer, Times Picayune, Denver Post, USA Today, Nashville Tennessean, Milwaukee Journal/Sentinel, Chattanooga Free Press, St. Petersburg Times,* United Press International, *Orlando Sentinel, Sports Illustrated, Iowa Gazette,* Awful Announcing, *Washington Post,* SI.com, NBCNews.com, CBSNews.com, *The Missourian, The Oklahoman,* Yahoo.com, WSBT.com, *Columbus Monthly, KREM.com, Indianapolis Star, Orlando Magazine, Dallas Morning News,* Outkick The Coverage, *Adweek,* the *Official Ohio State Football Program,* University of Wisconsin Collection, NCAA.com, White House.archives.gov, Ohio State Athletic Communications Media Guides—1960, 1961, 1962, 1987, 1988, 1989, 1990, 1991, 1992, 1993, 2019, 2020, *Those Guys Have All the Fun,* by Tom Shales and James Miller, *ESPN College Football Encyclopedia, The Heisman Trophy—The Story of an American Icon and Its Winners,* by Cory McCartney, *War As They Knew It: Woody Hayes, Bo Schembechler and America in a Time of Unrest,* by Michael Rosenberg, *This Is B1G—How the Big Ten Set the Standard in College Sports,* by Ed Sherman, the Johns Hopkins University Coronavirus Research Center, and transcripts from the 2017 Sports Video Group Sports Summit.

Credits

1 Courtesy of Judy Herbstreit
2 Courtesy of Ohio State Department of Athletics
3 Courtesy of The Ohio State University Archives
4 Courtesy of Judy Herbstreit
5 Courtesy of the Herbstreit Family
6 Courtesy of the Herbstreit Family
7 Courtesy of Ohio State Department of Athletics
8 Courtesy of Brockway Collection at The Ohio State University Archives
9 Courtesy of the Herbstreit Family
10 Courtesy of the Herbstreit Family
11 Courtesy of the Herbstreit Family
12 Courtesy of Joe Faroni, ESPN Images
13 Courtesy of Scott Clarke, ESPN Images
14 Courtesy of Phil Ellsworth, ESPN Images
15 Courtesy of Judy Herbstreit
16 Courtesy of the Herbstreit Family

About the Author

Kirk Herbstreit joined ESPN in 1995, establishing himself as the face and voice of college football, both as a member of the critically acclaimed *College GameDay* show, as well as the lead analyst for ESPN and ABC Sports prime-time game broadcasts. He is the most honored ESPN commentator in the network's history, having won multiple Sports Emmys as an event analyst and also as a studio analyst. Herbstreit graduated from The Ohio State University, where he was the Buckeyes' starting quarterback and team co-captain as a senior. You can follow him on Twitter @KirkHerbstreit.

Gene Wojciechowski is a *New York Times* bestselling author whose titles include *The Last Great Game: Duke vs. Kentucky and the 2.1 Seconds That Changed Basketball*. He joined ESPN in 1998 and has won a Sports Emmy and Edward R. Murrow award during his nine seasons as a features reporter on *College GameDay*. Wojciechowski also serves on ESPN's coverage of the Masters, the PGA Championship, and assorted *SportsCenter* projects. You can follow him on Twitter @GenoEspn.